W. H. AUDEN

Modern Critical Views

Henry Adams
Edward Albee
A. R. Ammons
Matthew Arnold
John Ashbery
W. H. Auden
Jane Austen
James Baldwin
Charles Baudelaire
Samuel Beckett
Saul Bellow
The Bible
Elizabeth Bishop
William Blake
Jorge Luis Borges
Elizabeth Bowen
Bertolt Brecht
The Brontës
Robert Browning
Anthony Burgess
George Gordon, Lord
  Byron
Thomas Carlyle
Lewis Carroll
Willa Cather
Cervantes
Geoffrey Chaucer
Kate Chopin
Samuel Taylor Coleridge
Joseph Conrad
Contemporary Poets
Hart Crane
Stephen Crane
Dante
Charles Dickens
Emily Dickinson
John Donne & the Seven-
  teenth Century Meta-
  physical Poets
Elizabethan Dramatists
Theodore Dreiser
John Dryden
George Eliot
T. S. Eliot
Ralph Ellison
Ralph Waldo Emerson
William Faulkner
Henry Fielding
F. Scott Fitzgerald
Gustave Flaubert
E. M. Forster
Sigmund Freud
Robert Frost

Robert Graves
Graham Greene
Thomas Hardy
Nathaniel Hawthorne
William Hazlitt
Seamus Heaney
Ernest Hemingway
Geoffrey Hill
Friedrich Hölderlin
Homer
Gerard Manley Hopkins
William Dean Howells
Zora Neale Hurston
Henry James
Samuel Johnson and
  James Boswell
Ben Jonson
James Joyce
Franz Kafka
John Keats
Rudyard Kipling
D. H. Lawrence
John Le Carré
Ursula K. Le Guin
Doris Lessing
Sinclair Lewis
Robert Lowell
Norman Mailer
Bernard Malamud
Thomas Mann
Christopher Marlowe
Carson McCullers
Herman Melville
James Merrill
Arthur Miller
John Milton
Eugenio Montale
Marianne Moore
Iris Murdoch
Vladimir Nabokov
Joyce Carol Oates
Sean O'Casey
Flannery O'Connor
Eugene O'Neill
George Orwell
Cynthia Ozick
Walter Pater
Walker Percy
Harold Pinter
Plato
Edgar Allan Poe
Poets of Sensibility & the
  Sublime

Alexander Pope
Katherine Ann Porter
Ezra Pound
Pre-Raphaelite Poets
Marcel Proust
Thomas Pynchon
Arthur Rimbaud
Theodore Roethke
Philip Roth
John Ruskin
J. D. Salinger
Gershom Scholem
William Shakespeare
  (3 vols.)
  Histories & Poems
  Comedies
  Tragedies
George Bernard Shaw
Mary Wollstonecraft
  Shelley
Percy Bysshe Shelley
Edmund Spenser
Gertrude Stein
John Steinbeck
Laurence Sterne
Wallace Stevens
Tom Stoppard
Jonathan Swift
Alfred, Lord Tennyson
William Makepeace
  Thackeray
Henry David Thoreau
Leo Tolstoi
Anthony Trollope
Mark Twain
John Updike
Gore Vidal
Virgil
Robert Penn Warren
Evelyn Waugh
Eudora Welty
Nathanael West
Edith Wharton
Walt Whitman
Oscar Wilde
Tennessee Williams
William Carlos Williams
Thomas Wolfe
Virginia Woolf
William Wordsworth
Richard Wright
William Butler Yeats

These and other titles in preparation

Modern Critical Views

W. H. AUDEN

Edited and with an introduction by
Harold Bloom
Sterling Professor of the Humanities
Yale University

CHELSEA HOUSE PUBLISHERS ◊ 1986
New York ◊ New Haven ◊ Philadelphia

Library of Congress Cataloging-in-Publication Data
Main entry under title:

W. H. Auden.

    (Modern critical views)
    Bibliography: p.
    Includes index.
    1. Auden, W. H. (Wystan Hugh), 1907–1973 –
Criticism and interpretation – Addresses, essays,
lectures.   I. Bloom, Harold.   II. Series.
PR6001.U4Z88   1986   811'.52   85-29090
ISBN 0-87754-640-1

Contents

Editor's Note

This volume offers a representative selection of the best criticism published upon the work of W. H. Auden. The editor is grateful to Wendell Piez for his erudition and judgment in helping to locate and choose the essays that make up this book.

The introduction dates back to 1968, when Auden was alive and in his poetic prime. Dealing as it does with *Secondary Worlds*, Auden's weakest book, it is reprinted here to represent what William Blake called "the Devil's party," since I am of a very different critical tradition than the one which exalted Auden during his lifetime. But I am the only dissenting voice in this volume, and the varied strength of the other critics reprinted here is, in my judgment, only enhanced by an initial appearance of the Romantic sensibility's case against Auden.

Christopher Isherwood's personal reflections upon the early poetry fittingly commence the chronological sequence. Writing in 1937, Isherwood conveys something of the vital aura of the Auden circle. Celebrating Auden's sixtieth birthday in 1967, the poet John Hollander charmingly studies the nostalgias and accurately characterizes Auden, despite his piety, as the laureate of our age's secular humanism.

In an intricate study of Auden's personae, Justin Replogle traces a dialectical pattern in which the roles of Poet and Antipoet continuously alternate. Frederick Buell's analysis of Auden's poetic voice in the Forties pursues a related topos, and leads naturally to Wendell Stacy Johnson's meditation upon the stance and tone of "reticence" that Auden shares with one of his precursors, Gerard Manley Hopkins. Reflecting upon the lack of serious playfulness in many of Auden's critics, John Bayley usefully arrives at a view that balances Auden's naturalism and personalism with his cognitive symbolism.

Four of the remaining essays center upon Auden's achievement in more extended texts. The McDiarmids study *The Sea and the Mirror*, finding in it both an inward movement towards a willing subjectivity, and an outward drive towards a more dispassionate sense of freedom. David Bromwich, in an overview of "the Auden canon as planned by Auden," allows himself to speculate usefully upon the subtle and artful pattern of Auden's interplay between being a moralist and accepting "his own all-too-human nature." Akin to Bromwich's speculation is Willard Spiegelman's study of the Stravinsky–Auden–Kallman opera, *The Rake's Progress*, which sees Auden's pastoral myth as being at once serious and comic moralizing. Auden's biographer and learned editor, Edward Mendelson, arguing that the poet was the most authentic revisionist of literary modernism, can be said to provide this volume's most pungent answer to my Romantic polemic against Auden in the introduction.

Two advanced studies by John R. Boly, of *The Orators* and *The Age of Anxiety*, may be said to provide a more balanced answer, since Boly argues for Auden's central place in the Romantic tradition. A rather different emphasis is highlighted in Edward Callan's analysis of Auden's disenchantment with Yeats, the major High Romantic poet of our century. These clashing perspectives remind us that Auden's achievement is still vital and controversial, and that much remains to be seen and judged in it.

Introduction

*Attacking bad books is not only a waste
of time but also bad for the character.*
                                      —AUDEN

*While an author is yet living we estimate his powers by his worst
performance, and when he is dead we rate them by his best.*
                                      —JOHNSON

S*econdary Worlds* is a bad book, and Auden's worst performance. These four
lectures in memory of T. S. Eliot deal in turn with *Thomas Cranmer*, a pious
verse drama by Charles Williams; Icelandic sagas; the three opera libretti by
Auden and Chester Kallman; the relation between Christian belief and the
writing of poetry. Since the title, *Secondary Worlds*, refers to works of art as
against "the primary world of our everyday social experience," the rationale
for printing these four talks as a book must be their linked relevance to what
has long been Auden's overt polemic against the Romantic view of poetry.
Coleridge's ill-chosen terms, Primary and Secondary Imagination, are here sub-
verted by Auden's wit, since by secondary Auden, unlike Coleridge, does mean
"inferior."

Of all Auden's writings, *Secondary Worlds* comes most directly out of the
neo-Christian matrix of modern Anglo-Catholic letters: Eliot, Williams, C. S.
Lewis, Tolkien. I search in vain only for references to Dorothy Sayers. Auden
compensates with a quotation from *The Future of Belief*, by Leslie Dewart, a
book one might not otherwise know:

> The Christian God is not *both* transcendent and immanent. He is
> a reality other than being Who is present to being, by which presence
> He makes being to be.

1

"To believe this," Auden modestly says, "is to call into question the art of poetry and all the arts." In *The Dyer's Hand*, an admirable performance, Auden remarked that "the imagination is a natural human faculty and therefore retains the same character whatever a man believes." In his new book, the imagination of a humane man-of-letters and talented comic poet appears to be hardening, which would be a loss.

Johnson definitively stated the difficulties of devotional verse when he observed that the good and evil of Eternity were too ponderous for the wings of wit. The mind sinks under them, and must be content with calm belief and humble adoration, attitudes admirable in themselves but perhaps not conducive to the writing of poems. One of Auden's many virtues is that, unlike Eliot and other literary Christians, he has spared us, and mostly refrained from devotional verse. *For the Time Being*, a work dear to many churchwardenly critics, is a long and unhappy exception, but even it, unlike much Eliot, does not offer us the disciplined humility of the poet as our aesthetic experience.

It is of course one thing to deprecate the possibility of Christian poetry, or of poetry being Christian, and quite another to deprecate poetry itself, all poetry. In Auden's criticism, and particularly *Secondary Worlds*, the two are not always kept apart. When this happens, I find it is bad for my character. On a higher level the experience of reading Auden then becomes rather like reading Kilmer's *Trees*. "Poems are made by fools like me," yes, and by Dante, Milton, Blake, and Homer, but only God makes primary worlds. Or, as Auden says:

> it is possible that artists may become both more modest and more
> self-assured, that they may develop both a sense of humour about
> their vocation and a respect for that most admirable of Roman
> deities, the god *Terminus*. No poet will then produce the kind of
> work which demands that a reader spend his whole life reading
> it and nothing else. The claim to be a "genius" will become as strange
> as it would have seemed to the Middle Ages.

It is possible that other artists may become more like Auden. It is likelier that other critics may become more like him for, with Arnold and Eliot, he is a poet-critic who appeals greatly to critics, little as the splendor of becoming a "poet of professors" appeals to him. Books about Auden all tend to be fairly good, just as books about, say Wallace Stevens, tend to be quite bad. This is probably not because admirers of Stevens love him less well than the lovers of Auden, but because more genuinely difficult poets do not reduce to structures of ideas and images so readily as Auden does.

Auden's poetry now maintains a general esteem among academic critics. If one's judgment of Auden's poetry is more eccentric, one needs to take up the sad burden of literary dissent. Auden has been accepted as not only a great poet but also a Christian humanist sage not because of any conspiracy among moralizing neo-Christian academicians, but because the age requires such a figure. Eliot is gone, and Auden now occupies his place, though with a difference. The difference is refreshing; Auden is wittier, gentler, much less dogmatic, and does not feel compelled to demonstrate the authenticity of his Christian humanism by a judicious anti-Semitism. He has more wisdom and more humor than Eliot, and his talent is nowhere near so sparse, as the enormous range of his lyrics shows. I think it unfortunate that he should find himself in apostolic succession to Eliot, but *Secondary Worlds* seems to indicate that the succession is not unwelcome to him.

Much of *The Dyer's Hand*, despite its generosity as criticism, is darkened by Auden's obsessive doubts about the value of art in the context of Christianity. Similar doubts have maimed many writers, Tolstoi and Hopkins in particular. Insofar as Auden's uneasiness has prevented him from devotional poetry, he has gained by it, but unfortunately the effect upon him has been larger, and has resulted in a trivialization of his art. As a songwriter he remains supreme, being certainly the best in English in the century, but as a reflective poet he suffers from the continual evanescence of his subject matter. As a satirist, he may have been aided, yet the staple of his poetry is neither song nor satire but rumination on the good life, and his notion of the relation between Christianity and art has troubled that rumination. Auden is one of the massive modern sufferers from the malady of Poetic Influence, a variety of melancholy or anxiety-principle that our studies have evaded. Poetic Influence, in this sense, has little to do with the transmission of ideas and images from an earlier poet to a later one. Rather, it concerns the poet's sense of his precursors, and of his own achievement in relation to theirs. Have they left him room enough, or has their priority cost him his art? More crucially, where did they go wrong, so as to make it possible for him to go right? In this revisionary sense, in which the poet creates his own precursors by necessarily misinterpreting them, Poetic Influence forms and malforms new poets, and aids their art at the cost of increasing, finally, their already acute sense of isolation. Auden, like Byron, gives the continual impression of personal sincerity in his poetry, but again like Byron this sincerity is the consequence of a revisionary swerve away from the sincerity of the precursor. In Byron's case of Poetic Influence the great precursor was Pope, with his highly dialectical sincerity; with Auden the prime precursor is Hardy, and the poetic son's sincerity is considerably more dialectical than the father's.

Auden, in his very fine *New Year Letter* (1 January 1940, at the height of his poetic power), wrote an important poem about Poetic Influence. His precursors are invoked there as a summary tribunal sitting in perpetual session:

> Though
> Considerate and mild and low
> The voices of the questioners,
> Although they delegate to us
> Both prosecution and defence,
> Accept our rules of evidence
> And pass no sentence but our own,
> Yet, as he faces them alone,
> O who can show convincing proof
> That he is worthy of their love?

He names these fathers and judges: Dante, Blake, Rimbaud, Dryden, Catullus, Tennyson, Baudelaire, Hardy, and Rilke, connecting this somewhat miscellaneous ninefold (except for Dryden, there for his mastery of the middle style) by their common sense of isolation, fit companions "to one unsocial English boy." Of all these, Auden's most characteristic poetry is closest to Hardy's, not merely in its beginnings, and like Hardy Auden remains most convincing as a ruminator upon human incongruities, upon everything valuable that somehow will not fit together. Auden's best poems, such as the justly esteemed *In Praise of Limestone*, brood upon incongruities, swerving from Hardy's kind of poem into a more double-natured sense of ruinous circumstance and thwarted love, yet retaining their family resemblance to Hardy. But where Hardy's strenuous unbelief led him to no worse redundancies than an occasional sharp striving after too palpable an irony, Auden's self-conscious belief and attendant doubt of poetry mar even *In Praise of Limestone* with the redundancy of uneasy and misplaced wit:

> But if
> Sins can be forgiven, if bodies rise from the dead,
>   These modifications of matter into
> Innocent athletes and gesticulating fountains,
>   Made solely for pleasure, make a further point;
> The blessed will not care what angle they are regarded from,
>   Having nothing to hide.

The blessed, as Auden says so often in prose, need neither to read nor to write poems, and poems do not describe their sanctity with much success, as Auden also sadly notes, contemplating the verse of Charles Williams. Close thy Auden, open thy Stevens, and read:

> If, then, when we speak of liberation, we mean an exodus; if when
> we speak of justification, we mean a kind of justice of which we

had not known and on which we had not counted; if when we experience a sense of purification, we can think of the establishing of a self, it is certain that the experience of the poet is of no less a degree than the experience of the mystic and we may be certain that in the case of poets, the peers of saints, those experiences are of no less a degree than the experiences of the saints themselves. It is a question of the nature of the experience. It is not a question of identifying or relating dissimilar figures; that is to say, it is not a question of making saints out of poets or poets out of saints.

CHRISTOPHER ISHERWOOD

Some Notes on the Early Poetry

If I were told to introduce a reader to the poetry of W. H. Auden, I should begin by asking him to remember three things.

First, that Auden is essentially a scientist: perhaps I should add, "a schoolboy scientist." He has, that is to say, the scientific training and the scientific interests of a very intelligent schoolboy. He has covered the groundwork, but doesn't propose to go any further: he has no intention of specializing. Nevertheless, he has acquired the scientific outlook and technique of approach; and this is really all he needs for his writing.

Second, that Auden is a musician and a ritualist. As a child, he enjoyed a high Anglican upbringing, coupled with a sound musical education. The Anglicanism has evaporated, leaving only the height: he is still much preoccupied with ritual, in all its forms. When we collaborate, I have to keep a sharp eye on him—or down flop the characters on their knees (see *F6 passim*): another constant danger is that of choral interruptions by angel-voices. If Auden had his way, he would turn every play into a cross between grand opera and high mass.

Third, that Auden is a Scandinavian. The Auden family came originally from Iceland. Auden himself was brought up on the sagas, and their influence upon his work has been profound.

Auden began writing poetry comparatively late, when he had already been several terms at his public school. At our prep school, he showed no literary interests whatever: his ambition was to become a mining-engineer. His first poems, unlike Stephen Spender's, were competent but entirely imitative: Hardy, Thomas, and Frost were his models:

The Carter's Funeral

Sixty odd years of poaching and drink
and rain-sodden waggons with scarcely a friend,

Chained to this life; rust fractures a link,
    So the end.

Sexton at last has pressed down the loam,
He blows on his fingers and prays for the sun,
Parson unvests and turns to his home,
    Duty done.

Little enough stays musing upon
The passing of one of the masters of things,
Only a bird looks peak-faced on,
    Looks and sings.

Allendale

The smelting-mill stack is crumbling, no smoke is alive there,
Down in the valley the furnace no lead-ore of worth burns;
Now tombs of decaying industries, not to strive there
    Many more earth-turns.

The chimney still stands at the top of the hill like a finger
Skywardly pointing as if it were asking: 'What lies there?'
And thither we stray to dream of those things as we linger,
    Nature denies here.

Dark looming around the fell-folds stretch desolate, crag-scarred,
Seeming to murmur: 'Why beat you the bars of your prison?'
What matter? To us the world-face is glowing and flag-starred,
    Lit by a vision.

So under it stand we, all swept by the rain and the wind there,
Muttering: 'What look you for, creatures that die in a season?'
We care not, but turn to our dreams and the comfort we find there,
    Asking no reason.

The saga-world is a schoolboy world, with its feuds, its practical jokes, its dark threats conveyed in puns and riddles and understatements: "I think this day will end unluckily for some; but chiefly for those who least expect harm." I once remarked to Auden that the atmosphere of *Gisli the Outlaw* very much reminded me of our school-days. He was pleased with the idea: and, soon after this, he produced his first play: *Paid on Both Sides*, in which the two worlds are so inextricably confused that it is impossible to say whether the characters are really epic heroes or only members of a school OTC.

Auden is, and always has been, a most prolific writer. Problems of form and technique seem to bother him very little. You could say to him: "Please write me a double ballade on the virtues of a certain brand of toothpaste, which also contains at least ten anagrams on the names of well-known politicians, and of which the refrain is as follows. . . ." Within twenty-four hours, your ballade would be ready—and it would be good.

When Auden was younger, he was very lazy. He hated polishing and making corrections. If I didn't like a poem, he threw it away and wrote another. If I liked one line, he would keep it and work it into a new poem. In this way, whole poems were constructed which were simply anthologies of my favourite lines, entirely regardless of grammar or sense. This is the simple explanation of much of Auden's celebrated obscurity.

While Auden was up at Oxford, he read T. S. Eliot. The discovery of *The Waste Land* marked a turning-point in his work—for the better, certainly; though the earliest symptoms of Eliot-influence were most alarming. Like a patient who has received an over-powerful inoculation, Auden developed a severe attack of allusions, jargonitis, and private jokes. He began to write lines like: "Inexorable Rembrandt rays that stab. . ." or "Love mutual has reached its first eutectic. . . ." Nearly all the poems of that early Eliot period are now scrapped.

In 1928, Spender, who had a private press, printed a little orange paper volume of Auden's poems. (This booklet, limited to "about forty-five copies," is now a bibliophile's prize: the misprints alone are worth about ten shillings each.) Most of the poems were reprinted two years later, when Faber and Faber published the first edition of their Auden volume: here is one of the few which were not:

> Consider if you will how lovers stand
> In brief adherence, straining to preserve
> Too long the suction of good-bye: others,
> Less clinically-minded, will admire
> An evening like a coloured photograph,
> A music stultified across the water.
> The desert opens here, and if, though we
> Have ligatured the ends of a farewell,
> Sporadic heartburn show in evidence
> Of love uneconomically slain,
> It is for the last time, the last look back,
> The heel upon the finishing blade of grass,
> To dazzling cities of the plain where lust
> Threatened a sinister rod, and we shall turn
> To our study of stones, to split Eve's apple,
> Absorbed, content if we can say 'because';

> Unanswerable like any other pedant,
> Like Solomon and Sheba, wrong for years.

I think this poem illustrates very clearly Auden's state of mind at that period: in this respect, its weakness is its virtue. Auden was very busy trying to regard things "clinically," as he called it. Poetry, he said, must concern itself with shapes and volumes. Colours and smells were condemned as romantic. Form alone was significant. Auden loathed (and still rather dislikes) the sea—for the sea, besides being deplorably wet and sloppy, is formless. (Note "ligatured"—a typical specimen of the "clinical" vocabulary.)

Another, and even more powerful influence upon Auden's early work was non-literary in its origin—in 1929, during a visit to Berlin, he came into contact with the doctrines of the American psychologist, Homer Lane. (Cf. Auden's own account of this, in his *Letter to Lord Byron*, Part Four.) Auden was particularly interested in Lane's theories of the psychological causes of disease—if you refuse to make use of your creative powers, you grow a cancer instead. References to these theories can be found in many of the early poems, and, more generally, in *The Orators*. Lane's teachings provide a key to most of the obscurities in the *Journal of an Airman* (Mr. John Layard, one of Lane's most brilliant followers, has pointed out the psychological relationship between epilepsy and the idea of flight).

The first collaboration between Auden and myself was in a play called *The Enemies of a Bishop*. The bishop is the hero of the play: he represents sanity, and is an idealized portrait of Lane himself. His enemies are the pseudo-healers, the wilfully ill and the mad. The final curtain goes down on his complete victory. The play was no more than a charade, very loosely put together and full of private jokes. We revised the best parts of it and used them again, five years later, in *The Dog Beneath the Skin*.

It is typical of Auden's astonishing adaptability that, after two or three months in Berlin, he began to write poems in German. Their style can be best imagined by supposing that a German writer should attempt a sonnet-sequence in a mixture of Cockney and Tennysonian English, without being able to command either idiom. A German critic of great sensibility to whom I afterwards showed these sonnets was much intrigued. He assured me that their writer was a poet of the first rank, despite his absurd grammatical howlers. The critic himself had never heard of Auden and was certainly quite unaware of his English reputation.

The scenery of Auden's early poetry is, almost invariably, mountainous. As a boy, he visited Westmorland, the Peak District of Derbyshire and Wales. For urban scenery he preferred the industrial Midlands; particularly in districts where an industry is decaying. His romantic travel-wish was always towards the north. He could never understand how anybody could long for the sun, the blue sky, the palm-trees of the south. His favourite weather was autumnal; high wind and driving rain. He loved industrial ruins, a disused factory or an abandoned mill: a ruined abbey would leave him quite cold. He has always had a special feeling for caves and mines. At school, one of his favourite books was Jules Verne's *Journey to the Centre of the Earth*.

A final word about influences—or perhaps I should say, crazes. For Auden is deeply rooted in the English tradition, and his debt to most of the great writers of the past is too obvious to need comment here. The crazes were all short-lived: they left plenty of temporary damage but few lasting traces. The earliest I remember was for Edwin Arlington Robinson. It found expression in about half a dozen poems (all scrapped) and notably in some lines about "a Shape" in an Irish mackintosh which malice urges but friendship forbids me to quote. Then came Emily Dickinson. You will find her footprints here and there among the earlier poems: for example,

> Nor sorrow take
> His endless look.

Then Bridges published *The Testament of Beauty*, and Auden wrote the poem beginning: "Which of you waking early and watching daybreak...." which appeared in the first Faber edition, but was removed from later impressions. Finally, there was Hopkins: but, by this time, Auden's literary digestive powers were stronger; he made a virtue of imitation, and produced the brilliant parody-ode to a rugger xv which appears at the end of *The Orators*.

JOHN HOLLANDER

Auden at Sixty

Since February, W. H. Auden has been sixty years old. It is hard to think of another writer in English the progress of whose *lustra* — those five-year periods by which the Romans marked out life's phases or stages — would seem to matter so much. It is not only that he is our foremost poet, but that his career has been full of the ambivalences and paradoxes that have marked the moral history of the past forty years. Certainly the most articulate and cosmopolitan of all English poets to be born in this century, he left his native England at the height of his promise and influence in 1939 and has lived here ever since.

A critic of pre-war Europe who composed witty dirges for its immanent sickness and imminent collapse, he regularly spends part of each year abroad. Once he breathed an intellectual element full of Marx, Freud, and Nietzsche; now he moves in an Anglican faith as orthodox, in the main, as its keeper is undogmatic. A pioneer, with Christopher Isherwood, in experimental English poetic drama (*The Dog Beneath the Skin* and *The Ascent of F6* are still unequaled and remain a kind of natural link to certain elements of Brechtian theater), he has become, in collaboration with Chester Kallman, the most distinguished librettist for grand opera since Hofmannsthal.

And yet all these transformations have occurred in the course of a consistent evolutionary growth: Auden's artistic career is only superficially one of those, like Picasso's or Stravinsky's, marked out by the dramatic shifts of phases, "periods," or stylistic moments. Some of his critics were bound to feel that Auden's work of the past quarter century had softened rather than ripened — in England, particularly, the transplanting in American soil was held to blame by audiences who still feel that the essential Auden was the young poet of crisis and commitment, neatly parodied by his contemporary William Empson

From *Atlantic Monthly* 220, no. 1 (July 1967). Copyright © 1967 by John Hollander.

as "waiting for the end, boys, waiting for the end." But for most of his readers, who and where that poet is today, and what he has been writing, seem as natural and inevitable as their own intellectual and moral histories. And a part of them as well.

Perhaps it is this quality of Auden's work that made his sixtieth birthday the sort of anniversary that creeps up on one to take him by a not wholly unpleasant surprise. Auden has given voice in the past to the intellectual conscience of the entire generation that was growing out of childhood between the two world wars. For that generation he seemed not only an English poet but a European one. Verse has always been a mode of public eloquence for him — as it was for a poet like Ben Jonson, for example — rather than a meditative instrument assisting the articulation of the Self. He has always written magnificent occasional poetry; an uncrowned laureate, he has spoken not for national affairs or victories, but on events and crises in the world of the moral imagination. What he said of Yeats once, that he transformed the occasional poem "from being either an official performance of impersonal virtuosity or a trivial *vers de société* into a serious reflective poem of at once personal and public interest," is even more true of himself.

For, whether writing memorial poems to Yeats, Freud, or the German socialist leader and writer Ernst Toller; whether meditating on Voltaire, Pascal, Melville, Rimbaud, Edward Lear, Montaigne, or at the grave of Henry James; whether catching up a historical moment of the life of the mind in a Phi Beta Kappa poem for the first post-war graduating class at Harvard in 1946, or celebrating (in "Goodbye to the Mezzogiorno") his own purchase of a house in Austria in 1957, when he stopped summering in Ischia; whether celebrating a Gaudy night at Christ Church, his old Oxford College, or less ceremonially chronicling his and his generation's continuing encounter with the cultivations of the mind and the savageries of the heart, he has led his best poems beyond the enclosures of the occasions for which they were offered, out into generality and truth.

It is a peculiarity of Auden's own kind of poetic modernity that he has never felt the concept to be the enemy of the image, or discourse to be destructive of poetry. Some of his poems have the structure and power of essays, just as his critical and speculative prose writings reflect concerns that appear in his poems. But he is even more unusual in feeling so close to the concerns of natural science. His poems abound in scientific allusions and technical terms. One cannot imagine any other poet of his age, save Empson perhaps, observing the workings of the goddess Mutabilitie in the fact that "Two of the Six/Noble Gases have, I hear,/Already been seduced" (indeed, how many laymen know that only within the last few years was argon, which chemistry textbooks main-

tained to be aloof from all other elements, first compounded?). He still likes
to remark that the only magazine he takes "is not literary, but the *Scientific
American*."

This attitude toward science stems from his childhood, when, as he says,
"there was no nonsense about two cultures—it never occurred to one that science
was not humane." His father was medical officer and professor of public health
at the university in Birmingham, where Auden grew up. At preparatory school
he first met Christopher Isherwood; at Gresham's School, Holt, he concentrated
in biology, and in 1924 published his first poem. He went up to Christ Church
in 1925; at Oxford he and Stephen Spender, Isherwood, C. Day Lewis, and
Louis MacNeice began to be known as a literary circle. A first collection of
poems was printed in a tiny edition at Oxford in 1928; in August of that same
year, he went with Isherwood to Berlin, arriving in time to catch the premiere
of the Brecht-Weill *Dreigroschenoper*. If Isherwood has permanently preserved
the *Geist* of the period in his *Berlin Stories*, that bleak, ironic moment of wit
and harshness and cabaret, hovering at the brink of the Nazi thirties, must
have become a time of self-discovery for Auden.

Not only his long and deep attachment to German literature dates from
then, but a sense of civilization as a beleaguered cosmopolitan City (and he
has since noted many times the resemblances between New York and pre-
Hitler Berlin) may have matured there as well. When he returned home and
in 1930 began five years of schoolmastering, he was ready to strike a note
for which his earlier poetry would be famous. His morally bogus headmaster
at the beginning of *The Orators* remarks, scarcely understanding his own irony,
"What do you think about England, this country of ours where nobody is
well?" The brilliant mixture of the wildly colloquial and the obscurely learned;
the interest in puzzles, riddles, games, and mock strategies; the devoted crafts-
man's attitude toward meter and verse form; the acute sense of stylistic openness
and of the need for a whole array of formal and rhetorical modes for different
themes and occasions that have become so familiar in his work all got their
start in these early years. And if by now his guise has become that of a wise
but unwearied schoolmaster or vicar instead of the conspiratorial public school
boy, he has constantly devoted his vision to the task of not breaking faith
with one's whole set of nesting childhoods. Here again, what he said of another
(in "In Memory of Sigmund Freud") is true in good part of his own work:

> he would unite
> The unequal moieties fractured
> By our own well-meaning sense of justice.
> Would restore to the larger the wit and will

> The smaller possesses but can only use
> For arid disputes, would give back to
> The son the mother's richness of feeling.

(One might notice how in this brief passage a disarmingly prosaic tone is deepened by a suddenly concrete verb like "fractured," how the seemingly careless use of "wit and will" unleashes the force of the Renaissance English meanings parallel to "instinct and reason," and most typical of all, the verse form: a strophe of cryptically syllabic lines of eleven, eleven, nine, and ten syllables, arranged without regard to stress, respectively, at the same time arrayed on the page to look like the sort of adaptations of classical alcaic stanzas made by German romantic poets like Hölderlin.)

Through his many volumes of verse, constantly revised for collected editions, his long poems like *The Sea and the Mirror*, *New Year Letter*, and *For the Time Being*, his essays, reviews, introductions, and his songs and opera libretti, Auden has striven constantly to put his virtuoso talents to the service of a seriousness which transcends mere solemnity, seeking to avoid that commonest of failings which leads us to "ruin a fine tenor voice/For effects that bring down the house." His concerns with science and with society on the one hand, and with the intensely personal on the other have bred a sense of the meaning of life in the conceptual metropolis in whose complex and polluted air modern human awareness lives and moves and has its being. The task of his poetry has been that which he has ascribed to fallen human existence: to redeem "the time being...from insignificance." He has, too, always spoken to the urban condition *in* as well as *of* man, and the image of the City—whether of the Augustinian contrast between the Heavenly and the fallen Earthly one, or the Utopian model of the Just one, or the historical city-states, or an actual London, Berlin, or New York.

It is no accident that this list should end with the American metropolis in which he has now been domiciled for almost half his life. In 1922, T. S. Eliot could tick off, toward the end of *The Wasteland*, the falling towers of the failed cities of the European past and present, perishing in a historical and visionary twilight: "Jerusalem Athens Alexandria/Vienna London/Unreal." New York was not part of the world of Western civilization for Eliot (consider its mythical importance in Whitman and Hart Crane, for example). Yet if New York is only one instance of Auden's mythological city, it has clearly become his hometown. "It's the only city in the world that isn't provincial," he said recently. "I don't feel like an American, but I am a New Yorker."

And so he is. Almost from the moment of his arrival in early 1939 (he became a U.S. citizen in 1946), a vision of New York began to unroll in many of his poems, as the American language began to enter his diction (he now rhymes "clerk" with "work," rather than with "dark" — surely an empirical test for American English). Thus, for so many Americans, the opening lines of "September 1, 1939" came to stand for the declarations of a civilized voice calling out from the explosion of Europe, and rebuking not just a nation, or, indeed, a self, but a whole state of being ("mature," shall we say, but not really grown-up) for its self-absorption:

> I sit in one of the dives
> On Fifty-second Street
> Uncertain and afraid
> As the clever hopes expire
> Of a low dishonest decade. . . .

College texts today must needs annotate this poem, which moves from the unstated news bulletins from Europe, meditating on Germany and Hitler, to a darkening of the "neutral air" and "blind skyscrapers" of New York, and ending not entirely hopelessly as "dotted everywhere,/Ironic points of light/Flash out wherever the Just/Exchange their messages" — ever since, a canonical vision of those same skyscrapers, now in another role, that wink and glitter in the seediest of thirties movies. But any New Yorker would know that, alas, those famous opening lines need additional annotation, as much as if they referred to eighteenth-century London. Gone are not only the pre-war "dives," but the famous clubs of the forties where Charlie Parker and Dizzy Gillespie were giving the concept of "Fifty-second Street" a new meaning.

To see Auden at home these days, in the light of some gray afternoon in his second-floor apartment, is to be struck by the way his face confounds one's memories of early photographs of him: the long, angular oval surmounted by a straight shock of hair has become squarer, wrinkled, and somehow more *present*. One might remember a friend's remark that "Wystan has been years building up that face," but there also comes to mind the dedicatory epigragh to *The Orators*, that glittering and perplexing book of prose, verse, schoolboy games, and private jokes written when he was twenty-five: "Private faces in public places/Are wiser and nicer/Than public faces in private places." For here is the undersong to all the variations of his career, whether earlier, as a political and spiritual radical, or now, as a Christian, returned through encounters with Kierkegaard and Charles Williams in the early forties. The hostilities of Authority, the possibilities for love in broken and demoralized communities, and the temptations that beset the most responsible intelligences in a fallen City that has not only undergone a failure of nerve but has compounded the felony by understanding what that failure means — these have always been his subjects.

But Auden's actual presence today — that famous face surrounded by books and recordings, that reassuring dry voice ranging from the rhetoric of the international literary man to the minute enthusiasms of some eccentric clergyman — reminds one of the way in which he has sought to avoid in his art the masks, the mythical externalizations of parts of the psyche that Yeats called *personae*, which so many twentieth-century poets have felt forced to wear for a world in which the bare visage of a poet has seemed more grotesque than any false face (try telling your neighbor on a transcontinental plane that you're a poet, when he asks what you do. Then watch how uncomfortable he gets).

His life in the city might, from certain points of view, be a rural one. For years he has been known in New York for going to bed early and getting up before most of the municipal day has begun — perhaps because the Imagination, like the morning star, fades in the major daylight. He is, as always, singularly loath to gossip about literary sociology and politics. If he has long outgrown the notion that a poet must move through the world like a kind of spy (*vide* Isherwood's early novel *All the Conspirators*, whose title must have been resonant for the whole circle of friends), his riper views about the relation of Art to Life have a similar effect in discouraging revelation: "Either the relation between them is so simple that nothing *need* be said, or so complicated that nothing *can* be said" is the way he usually puts an end on it.

He continues to feel, he says, "like an implacable Northern hater of the Roman Empire — a barbarian from outside the lines." His Northern ancestry has always meant a lot to Auden, both imaginatively and in a kind of literary-historical way. Some of his earliest formal poetic concerns were with alliterative poetry; J. R. R. Tolkien's reading of Old English poetry affected him strongly while at Oxford, and it is not surprising now to find him at work on translations, most recently, of "The Song of the Sybil," from the Icelandic *Edda*. (He is still drawn to Iceland, which he admires as "the only absolutely classless society.")

His more recent poetry has become, like his discourse, more personal, even to the point of homeliness, as exemplified by a suite of poems, each one devoted to establishing the myth of a different room in the modern dwelling, that gives its title to his last book, *About the House*. In this case, the house in question is in Austria, but there is something almost American in the appreciation of the concept of comfort that keeps appearing throughout the poems. Perhaps without being committed to thinking of him as either an English or an American poet, one might mark off Auden's past thirty years as a kind of swap for T. S. Eliot's rather Jamesian sort of expatriation. While the American from St. Louis had been able, in *The Wasteland*, to catch up the spirit of a war-torn London, emerging morally stillborn into the twentieth century, Eliot's later poetry led to an avowal of a quietistic insularity. After the horror of the London blitz, his spiritual voyage inward and backward led him, in *Little Gidding*, to a "quiet church at smokefall," where he could conclude that "history is now and England."

But with Auden there have always been the journeys that led outward: to Iceland, China, Spain, America, annual transatlantic ferryings. His voice continues to be directed *out* and *across* the space that separates a poet from his readers. And he remains a kind of familiar radio voice of our Western City, the city that has both blossomed and poisoned in its time and will continue to do so. And yet his debt to the older American poet, showing from time to time in the accents of his verse, was avowed in a short poem written in 1948, on Eliot's sixtieth birthday:

> When things begin to happen to our favourite spot,
> A key missing, a library bust defaced,
>   Then, on the tennis-court one morning,
>   Outrageous, the bloody corpse and always,
>
> Blank day after day, the unheard-of drought, it was you
> Who, not speechless from shock but finding the right
>   Language for thirst and fear, did much to
>   Prevent a panic. . . .

We are at a moment in history now when secular humanism and the kind of eloquence to which it has always been committed are under fire from their own progeny. A critic like George Steiner will claim that there are thirsts and fears for which there is no language, and has begun to question the very authenticity of disclosure as a model of developing human culture; and the logos has been marked for erasure by certain sorts of new American poetry and left politics alike. But that secular humanism for which Auden's voice has always spoken will probably remain the spirit of the age, despite the shocks of inhumanity in war and what has always passed for peace. To have seized words like "decency" and "love" from out of the mouths of their bawds has been the rhetorical triumph of his poetic career; to have mirrored some of the room still left on a sadly crowded planet in which human freedom might grow has been its imaginative task. And amid all the uncertainties about what our own age and our knowledge will, finally, have meant, Auden's work will always be seen to have sharpened the outlines of what Shelley called "the gigantic shadows which futurity casts upon the present." To have achieved one's literacy in his time is to be dated as much as by slang or hemlines. But it is a condition which one need never regard with the condescensions of nostalgia.

JUSTIN REPLOGLE

The Pattern of Personae

In "Nocturne I," an otherwise unassuming poem in *The Shield of Achilles* [*SA*], the speaker makes a most unusual public statement. He admits that he is pulled in different directions by highly contradictory impulses, and, dividing his personality in half, he gives separate beliefs and voices to each. While they squabble over apparent trivialities, these voices carry on a familiar debate that for nearly thirty years had smoldered beneath the surface of Auden's poetry. These are the voices of two opposing parts of Auden's temperament, and their opposition, more than anything else, has made his poetry the kind of thing it is. In "Nocturne I" the moon, that old poetic stage prop, makes them flare up once more. "'Adore Her, Mother, Virgin, Muse,'" begins one voice in full fustian, singing robes firmly in place, declaiming from some high podium. "'You will not tell me,'" responds the other, feet and style solidly on the ground, "'That bunch of barren craters care/Who sleeps with or who tortures whom'" (*SA*). Labeled "heart" and "mind" in the poem, these two "natures" (Auden's term) in reality are the voices of much larger and more complicated parts of Auden's poetic self. I propose to call them Poet and Antipoet.

Since by nature language is a lively thing, the mere repeated appearance of the terms Poet and Antipoet will soon tend to turn these abstractions into metaphor, metaphor into allegory; and before long Poet and Antipoet will seem to be living entities romping around in some physical organism called "Auden," moving his hand across this line, choosing that image for his pencil, directing his every breath like Groddeck's It. This can threaten to turn a critical tool into an imaginative drama with a will of its own. I will begin then with some definitions and disclaimers designed to make tools remain tools. By "Auden" I mean not the flesh and blood mortal, but the Grand Persona, the Maker

From *Auden's Poetry*. Copyright © 1969 by the University of Washington Press.

as he is fashioned by his own writing. While it is tempting to think this Grand Persona resembles the man (and some evidence suggests it does), to yield to this can invalidate every descriptive statement. Even the most confessional Romantic poet "makes" his poetry but not his life. And if Poet and Antipoet appear to be second and third parties living in a world called "Auden," this is critical allegory. The man in the Austrian house does not suffer from fugal personalities, as far as I know. My complete and only purpose, ultimately, is to *describe the poetry*, not the man behind it, and my critical terms are an apparatus to make this task easier. I want also to avoid building my description on some central "thesis" that, if shaky, may topple the whole descriptive structure. What I am setting up then is a model that is neither the "truth" nor complete. But it is useful; it works. And if incomplete, it is not false. If successful it will not be destroyed by, but incorporated into, later models that provide even more useful descriptive structures.

The things I want to attach to the words Poet and Antipoet vary a good deal — ideas, most obviously, beliefs and doctrines — but not just these. Ideas, beliefs, thoughts, philosophies, moods, feelings, experiences are all carried in a voice, and a voice is created by such things as syntactical habits, rhetorical patterns, levels of usage, favorite words, repeated figures, and dozens of such matters. Verbal behavior, rather than beliefs or ideas, often separates Poet from Antipoet. In short, they are more personalities than mere animated ideas, and like all personalities can be distinguished by a wide range of habits — regardless of what they believe or think they believe. For instance, though Auden's Antipoet is inclined to believe that Art is a small thing, to delight in mocking speech, low-brow diction, slangy abuse, jokes, and buffoonery, no one of these is essential to his existence. On special occasions he can praise Art or use the most elegant sort of diction and syntax. Some personality features remain to set him off from the Poet. What these are will emerge from the examples that follow.

Poet and Antipoet owe their existence in part to the difference between Art and Life, the cause of a moral dilemma Auden struggled with for much of his career. Reduced to its fundamental paradigm, the dilemma is that "Art is not life," and vice versa [*The Collected Poetry*; all further references to this text will be abbreviated as *CP*]. If both seem valuable, how can their dissimilar virtues be connected? How can one cross from the aesthetic world where "heroes roar and die" to the mortal world where ethical choices must be made, where "Shall-I" must become "I-Will" — or I won't (*CP*)? Wavering back and forth between the poles of this dilemma, never completely able to reconcile their opposing claims on him, Auden has at times favored Art, at times, Life. If the Poet preferred Art, the Antipoet felt "deep abhorrence" when he "caught anyone preferring Art/To Life and Love. . ." [*Letter to Lord Byron*; all further references to this text will be abbreviated as *LLB*.] If the Poet believed his craft to be "The greatest of vocations" (*CP*) and sang grandly at the top of his voice from Mount Parnassus ("O Love, the interest itself in thoughtless Heaven," *CP*), the Antipoet generally countered with some wry observation: "none are lost so soon as those/Who overlook their crooked nose" (*CP*). Pleasant though it may be, even "useful," the Antipoet remarks, Art is

> not be be confused
> > With anything really important
> Like feeding strays or looking pleased when caught
> > By a bore or a hideola. . . .
> > [*Nones*; all further references to this text will be abbreviated
> > as *N*.]

Compared to Life, the Antipoet nearly always reminds, Art is a puny, feeble, insignificant pastime that makes "nothing happen" (*CP*), a thing overlooked entirely by Gaea, Clio, and Dame Kind, those monumental makers and movers of Life. "I dare not ask you if you bless the poets," says the speaker ruefully to the muse of history in *Homage to Clio*, "For you do not look as if you ever read them/Nor can I see a reason why you should" [*Homage to Clio*; all further references to this text will be abbreviated as *HC*]. Poet and Antipoet owe their being and their temperaments, in part, to Auden's inability to conjure away his incompatible attractions to both Art and Life.

Whatever he believes about Art and Life, a poet's every poem will carry at least one inescapable message: poetry is worth while. A poem's very existence asserts this dogma. The poem's speaker, of course, may propose something quite different: I am unhappily in love, life is short, the world is evil, anything— even "Nothing is worthwhile." In such cases a work's total meaning, a composite of two messages, may be quite different from what the author intended. The type case is a poem whose speaker says, "Nothing is worthwhile." If all artifacts inevitably assert that "Art is worth while," no artist can convey the message "Nothing is worthwhile," or even a special case of this, "Art is not worth while." In serious jeopardy also, if not entirely ruled out, is "Art is less worth while than other things." What will happen if a poet puts such messages into his art? If he states in his poem that "Art has no value," or "I doubt whether Art has value," the message of his work will be: "The poet has mixed feelings," or "The speaker and the poet do not agree about Art's value." In either case personae begin to emerge from the split between what the poem *shows* and what it says. Obviously, the reader thinks, the speaker cannot be the creator—or at least not the *whole* creator—since what the speaker doubts or denies the creator asserts by making the poem. Poems of this sort suddenly become very complicated. Is the poet deliberately separating himself from the speaker, we wonder, and, if so, what further significance are we to draw from this separation? Or has he failed to recognize the distance between himself and his speaker? If the latter is true, we must watch the behavior of two personae within the poet, and just what his poems mean will not be easy to describe. The difficulty is in trying to resolve such contradictions into a single message. How does one weigh the meaning of what a speaker says against the meaning asserted by the artifact's existence? How does one reconcile *what* the speaker says with *how* he says it when the what and how conflict? If a speaker tells us nothing is worthwhile in an artful language overflowing with creative ebullience and delight, how do we describe what the poem means?

Only the most naïve artist, of course, will believe his speaker's message can remain unaffected by the material of its environment. Experienced artists have always known that a message antagonistic toward art must attack the medium itself. The total artifact, with its inescapable positive plea, must be destroyed. But since no one can totally destroy art by making artifacts, only more modest ambitions have any chance for success. If it cannot be annihilated, the medium can at least be maimed, cut up, spit on, or laughed at. Thus any artist with serious doubts about the value of his vocation will inevitably come to meddle, consciously or not, with the very bones, sinews, and tendons of the medium whose value he doubts. He must try to alter its built-in message. And, in trying, he will certainly produce an object that will appear odd, out-landish, or ugly to an audience nourished on artifacts made by men who never ceased to believe in the great worth of what they were doing. These elementary propositions will help the reader of Auden, in a variety of ways, to understand the kind of thing his poetry is.

Sometimes Auden translated his doubts about Art into philosophical and ideological doctrine—especially in his prose. Sometimes poetic speakers openly talked about these matters. But far more often his doubts caused him to bend, mutilate, twist, or in some way mock the very medium that insisted, by its implacable existence, that Art had great value. In the 1930's especially, the Antipoet in Auden believed Art might be an escape from Life, not a mirror held up to nature. He suspected that Art was magic, unreal. The Poet, on the other hand, preferred Art to anything else, and, if not held rigorously in check, moved further and further from Life. Peering down from on high with the eye of a detached authority and clinical observer, he remained aloof and superior, and spoke in a tongue far removed from lifelike speech. But the higher his song the more likely his fall. Lofty poetic flights threatened to attract the Antipoet, who enjoyed tumbling his opponent from the heights by pelting him with coarse chunks of Life, mocking, laughing, deriding, deflating his pretensions. On such occasions poems become a battleground. While all this is going on the speaker's utterance may seem peculiar and confusing, even trivial, to readers brought up on Milton, Wordsworth, Tennyson, Eliot—indeed, most English poetry. But what emerges is poetry nevertheless. All this battling, contradicting, canceling out, and self-mockery does not eliminate the poem line by line until it disappears. It adds line after line, and in doing so creates its own peculiar message.

The message of all these battles and twistings is, in part, "I, the maker of these poems, am troubled about the value of poetry, but not so troubled that I don't delight in writing it, and I am uncertain about the style my poetic speakers should use." In a very real sense this is the important message of many Auden poems from 1930 well into the 1940's. What the speakers in those poems talk *about* (Freud, Marx, love, cultural sickness [discussed elsewhere]) is often less important than what they reveal by *how* they speak. In extreme cases what these poems mean and what their speakers say is completely unlike. While the Poet may speak solemnly about cultural decadence, and the Antipoet taunt him for mouthing pompous pretensions, the poem itself may steadily show Auden's concern about the distance between Art and Life and his uncertainty about what to do about it.

But the split between Art and Life, simply by being examined, threatens to become too serious, too important. Described as a man set upon by doubts, Auden begins to sound like some anguished Romantic guiltily destroying his special gifts. Discussion so far may suggest that he rejects a heroic and exalted dedication to Art for heroic and exalted opposition to it. The full truth is much more complex. Though his doubts about Art are real, Auden is no more the agonized antiprophet than he is an orphic seer. As Antipoet he would mock the one as loudly as the other. Both are alike in imagining the poet to be some heroic figure, struggling magnificently against heavy odds to utter something Important. Just such pretentiousness is the Antipoet's main enemy. Auden's Antipoet is not so much against the artist, the Romantic, or the serious as against the pretentious. Auden is temperamentally the sort of man who can instantly notice the ridiculous side of everything. For people of this sort, blessed (or plagued) with a comic eye, every earnest human act may appear hilarious, the more earnest the more hilarious. They always detect the silliness in every solemn speech, dignified act, or venerable object or institution. They can never for long pretend that life is anything but fundamentally and helplessly preposterous. Among the slogans that help explain Auden's poetry, "I hate *pompositas* and all authority" (*LLB*) is even more important than "Art is not life" (*CP*). So if pompous claims about Art's sacred purpose are silly, so are smug pronounce-

ments of the opposite sort. Gifted with comic sight, Auden seldom fails to
notice how ludicrous is the sober Poet talking about anything in exalted terms.
He must be brought down to recognize the innate foolishness of all human
behavior, especially the absurdity of those who take themselves too seriously.
To the Antipoet goes this educational task, and his deflating procedures are
various. Sometimes he openly mocks or abuses the Poet; more often he parodies
or burlesques. Sometimes the mere threat of his appearance seems to frighten
the Poet into suicidal antics. This happens when the Poet, in the midst of
solemn statements, ingenious analyses, sober diagnoses, authoritative classifica-
tions, pontifical judgments, suddenly seems to remember the Antipoet invisible
in the wings, watching his performance with a fishy eye. Nervously listening
for backstage snickers, the Poet, embarrassed by his own posturing, may suddenly begin to burlesque himself. "I am not really this pompous fool, this earnest
bore, this smug poseur my performance suggests," he implies. "It was all a joke.
I was fooling. It was an elaborate hoax, a comic parody you mistakenly took
seriously. Look!" And he flies a bit higher, elevates diction and syntax a notch,
and, sure enough, the heroic turns mock. We see it is all a farce. The Poet,
destroying himself, turns into Antipoet, while the poem cracks in half, its message
reverses itself, and the speech collapses around him in a comic heap—to the
bewilderment and confusion of many readers. Even more disastrous than this
are those times when the Poet unintentionally turns comic. He falls by rising,
of course, since for him the way up is always the way down. If he steadily
ascends increasing heights of solemnity, at some point he will soar into silliness.
Sometimes he does accidentally fly too high, and wax, feathers, and all plunge
into unintentional comedy.

Though poems may be nearly destroyed by these curious antics, Auden's
destructive acts never reflect a temperament masochistically and soddenly bent
on self-destruction, driven by some grim death wish. Quite the opposite. Auden
was never a poet of defeat, continually emphasizing the gaping abyss, evil, the
skull beneath the skin, getting perverse joy from self-torment and pleasure from
despair. In an age when many have said no to life Auden has usually said yes.
Even the Auden we see in the early poetry fits Louis MacNeice's description:
"Who have felt the deathwish too,/But your lust for life prevails. . ." Auden's
distrust of human pretensions in himself as well as in others is not a negative
but a positive thing. Pomposity and authority, the enemies, dwell only amid
the illusion that life is more certain than it is, that more is known about it
than can be known. Thus the Poet, attracted to certainty, is forever tempted
to turn away from confused Life to those twin certainties pessimism and
optimism. In opposing this, the Antipoet's destructive violence (even though
a poem may be ruined by it) is nearly always an act of healthy common sense,

vigorous reality attacking the smug illusions of those who believe life to be either better or worse than it really is. The inflated optimist who sings "I'll love you, dear, I'll love you/Till China and Africa meet..." must be brought down (*CP*). But so must those who believe the world to be a bleak sink of disgust and despair. Attacks on doom and neurotic despair, in fact, are more common in Auden's poetry than attacks on effusive optimism. Optimists often appear rather lovable innocents, deserving a gentle mockery. After all, soon destined to encounter those inescapable "Furies.../With claw and dreadful brow," simple naïfs may be treated kindly (*N*). But the smugness of despair receives harsher treatment. Auden's Antipoet vigorously attacks narcissists who, crying they are not worthy, turn their faces to the wall.

Auden's compulsion to note the ludicrous in every solemn action, then, appears healthy rather than sick. Even the most casual reader, though he may not understand the change, will discover suddenly a great wave of liveliness sweeping across a poem when the Antipoet takes command. Suddenly, in the midst of often funereal surroundings, of dismal prophecies and prognoses of defeat, life asserts itself. High spirits, even joy, break forth. Auden comes alive when his Antipoet appears. His spirits rise, his speakers become delighted with their own vitality, energy, cleverness, intelligence. Their ostensible malice often turns kindly and sometimes becomes a disguise for love. His sober Poet holds life in check, suppresses high spirits, stifles health and joy. His favorite speeches are about cultural sickness. When the Antipoet bursts forth filled with lively abuse and ebullient skepticism, his very presence shows that life is good. If the Antipoet distrusts Art, his mockery of it is still a healthy mockery that in attacking anything too soberly Important is affirmative rather than the opposite. And since the Antipoet speaks poetry, he makes Art by championing Life. The resulting poetic object, therefore, does not carry a message of grim despair from its battlefield, but asserts the value of both Art and Life, and especially of the struggle between them....

Auden's early poetry can be very confusing for even the most skillful readers. Even internally consistent poems can be puzzling enough, with their variety of speakers, allegorical landscapes, and private allusions. When inconsistent, they almost defy description. But since much of the complexity, and nearly all the inconsistency, is caused by the hostility of... Poet and Antipoet, these terms now make it possible to describe more fully... the enormously complicated situation in these early poems. Schematic description will best simplify the complexities. If individual poems, though internally coherent, can contradict each other, let us consider the numerous possibilities for confusion in Auden's early work. His temperament is split into two forces or personae, Poet and

Antipoet, each with its own style, beliefs, inclinations, predispositions, and habits. Within the allegorical landscape of these early poems are three classes of people who speak: the sick, the well, and the neutral observers. How may these five elements be combined?

First, a sick speaker may appropriately use

1. the Poet's voice
   —straightforwardly to confess and analyze his own sickness.
   —pompously to indicate indirectly his sick foolishness.
2. the Antipoet's voice
   —to reveal his own clownish sickness or banality.
3. awkward and contradictory combinations of the Poet's and Anti-poet's voices
   —to reveal his own confused sickness.

Second, a healthy speaker may appropriately use

1. the Poet's voice
   —to analyze or denounce sickness and suggest a cure (but he must avoid the dangers of pomp and pretentiousness).
2. the Antipoet's voice
   —to denounce and abuse the sick and show by his manner the healthy vigor of life (but he must avoid appearing foolish or banal himself, and he must avoid making what he attacks appear trivial by his comedy—or seem a complete spoof).
3. awkward or contradictory combinations of the Poet's and Anti-poet's voice
   —never (except to mock the Poet by mimicry. In this case the Poet must be clearly identified as one of the sick. If the Poet speaks as one of the healthy, accurately analyzing sickness, and is then mocked or parodied, the poem collapses).

Third, a neutral speaker may appropriately use

1. the Poet's voice
   —to analyze, describe conditions, and suggest cures (but he must avoid the danger of pretentiousness and unintentional self-parody).
2. the Antipoet's voice
   —only at its mildest (though he may be permitted enough wit and verbal dexterity to indicate his intelligence and rhetorical skill).

3. awkward combinations of the voices
   — never (except when mimicking the frivolous or banal sick,
   and even this is dangerous).

Charts and lists may be unattractive substitutes for exposition, but I believe
this one provides an outline of the major complexities of personae in Auden's
poetry from about 1928 to about 1935, though it comes nowhere near ex-
hausting all of them. Given his own temperamental fluctuations and this involuted web of subtleties in his personae, it is hardly surprising that time after
time Auden sails along the edge of disaster and often falls over. I do not imply,
of course, that he purposely, or even consciously, fashioned the tangle of
dramatic alternatives outlined above. Many things (some perhaps inadvertent)
contributed to its growth: his almost compulsive habit of allegorizing nearly
everything he touched, from nouns to entire volumes; his continual use of
speakers separate from himself; his uncertainty about the role of poetry itself.
All these and other temperamental inclinations and gifts produced this almost
fantastically complex poetic situation, filled with the possibility of suddenly
dropping into an abyss of self-contradiction. . . .

Inconsistent and contradictory poems are appropriate if their speaker is
sick, and therefore purposely made to look awkward and incoherent. In all
other cases such poems are simply flawed. The *author* is disorganized and contradictory. Distinguishing between the two is not always easy. The most notori-
ously unclear case is the ode that begins "Though aware of our rank and alert
to obey orders. . . ." Joseph Warren Beach, a perceptive reader, spent eight
pages of his book mulling over the puzzle of this poem before he tentatively
advanced a conclusion. He decided reluctantly (but rightly I think) that the
speaker is not Auden, but one of the sick. Auden is outside the monologue,
more knowing than the speaker, healthier, showing some contempt for him.
Yet Beach's problem — and everyone's — is that Auden's partisanship is too faint
(indicated almost entirely by private myth details described in Chapter One).
Since the speaker alternates awkwardly between the Poet's solemnity and the
Antipoet's foolishness, no one who assumed Auden to be the speaker could
decide for certain whether the speech or the mockery of it is the message.
But if we assume the speaker to be sick, then the poem's contradictions are
appropriate. This will explain why the speaker's pompous solemnity contrasts
ludicrously with his clownish slips:

Your childish moments of awareness were all of our world, . . .

At night your mother taught you to pray for our Daddy. . . .

To stand with the wine-dark conquerors in the roped-off pews,

>   Shout ourselves hoarse:
>   "They ran like hares; we have broken them up like firewood. . . ."
>
>   (CP)

Interpreted this way the poem shows Auden standing outside the poem laughing at the speaker's performance. But this is certainly not clear. Even a careful reader could think Auden agrees with the speaker and thereby reverse the poem's message. Apparently we are expected to discover, without external comment, that the speaker is unreliable, that the truth (or most of it) is the opposite of what he says. Yet his unreliability is so faint as to be scarcely discernible. Maybe Auden simply miscalculated (which is easy enough to do in such a case). Or he may have written the poem for his friends, for whom faint clues were enough. Or he himself may have wavered, unable to decide how foolish the speaker was.

If we decide that "Though aware of our rank and alert to obey orders. . . ." is a consistent poem whose consistency fails to be clear, what are we to think of poems where the speaker's reliability is never established, even by ultrasubtle clues? "Not, father, further do prolong/Our necessary defeat. . ." is an interesting case of this. The poem seems to contain a sick speaker solemnly requesting the quick destruction of his illness. But how is the poet related to this speaker? If the poet stands apart (neutral or one of the healthy) all flaws in the poetry—bad lines, pompous diction, exaggerated hysteria, farcical behavior—reflect appropriately on the sick speaker. But if the poet approves of the speaker, or if speaker and poet are identical, all such lapses are either breaches of decorum or failure of craft. I think this particular poem begins with Auden speaking as Poet, soberly petitioning for health. But in trying to maneuver his grave formal speech through some extremely involuted Anglo-Saxon syntax he stumbles into unintentional comedy:

>   These nissen huts if hiding could
>   Your eye inseeing from
>   Firm fenders were. . . .
>
>   [*The Orators*; all further references to this
>   text will be abbreviated as *O*.]

With some minute changes indicating that this comedy was intentional, Auden could, without changing a word of the quoted lines, make this utterance appropriate. The speaker could be made into one of the comic sick, or into a healthy Antipoet parodying the pompous Poet. But without such indications the speaker's flaws are the author's flaws. Auden makes a mistake. The poem flounders. His Poet steps across the border between high dignity and comic pomposity, and decorum is broken.

"Consider this and in our time. . ." is a slightly clearer case. The speaker here is the Poet, neither sick nor healthy, but a neutral observer. Exalted and omniscient, he looks down on a sick culture. His language, extremely formal and rigorously abstract, borders on the pedantic. Describing a hotel dining room, he uses an idiom even Cowper might have blushed at. Through the window he sees

> insufficient units. . . .
>
> constellated at reserved tables
> Supplied with feelings by an efficient band
>   (*CP*):

that is, while people eat, musicians play. Elsewhere the diction, though still stiffly formidable, may be accepted as proper for this very learned and correct Poet, who never calls a mountain a mountain if its proper classification is "massif," who says that clouds "rift," and speaks in phrases such as "life's limiting defect" and "derelict works." All these the tolerant reader might swallow, forgiving the Poet for being a bit of a stuffed shirt, but noting in his favor that he is unbending enough for a few happily low-brow clichés: "admire the view," "leisurely conversation," "within a stone's throw" (*CP*). But what are tolerant readers to think later on, when the idiom suddenly becomes undeniably pompous on the one hand and hilariously undignified on the other?

> And mobilize the powerful forces latent
> In soils that make the farmer brutal
> In the infected sinus, and the eyes of stoats
>   (*CP*),

the speaker says at one point. Do what with the soils? we exclaim. *Mobilize* their *forces*? To infect what? Sinuses and stoats' eyes? Can we accept this as serious speech? Can Auden, who later made high comedy out of just such incongruous juxtapositions, have stumbled accidentally into this preposterous style? If we believe so, our credulity will soon get a further buffeting. Juxtapositions that follow are even more fatal to solemnity. After plunging from lofty dignity to sinuses and stoats' eyes, the speaker next frightens the sick with the bogey of a destructive "rumour. . . horrifying in its capacity to disgust," a rumor likely to become for them "A polar peril, a prodigious alarm." In an earlier version this mock-heroic utterance was then followed by a stanza that continually demolished the stuffy speaker's decorum. And as his Poetic mask fell away, to our great surprise we discovered underneath something of a gleeful, naughty urchin issuing slangy low-brow threats ("The game is up for you"; "It is later than you think"). He also showed a leering fascination for queer neurotic symptoms, especially sexual, and was not above making everything comic by purposely linking together the most unlikely incongruities. For instance, among his list of doomed neurotics were those "Who are born nurses, who live in shorts/Sleeping with people and playing fives" [*Poems*; all further references to this text will be abbreviated as *P*]. The speaker, who began as a Poet, turned into an Antipoet. Can Auden possibly have fallen unintentionally into such comic circumstances? I think the answer is yes—that is, at *first* the comedy was unintentional. Once it began, Auden purposely continued it. The first lapses seem clearly unplanned. And even at the end the poem struggles bravely to maintain some vestige of its formal idiom and Poetic persona, as though retention of both were part of the original plan. The disaster occurs, I think, because though Auden as Poet is forced to be solemn, elevated, and seriously concerned with large weighty matters such as the evolution of cultural collapse, he wears this mask somewhat awkwardly. While he is fully behind it when the poem opens, it is somewhat askew. The manner is not native to him and he gets it just slightly wrong. The formality is misplaced in an epithet or two, the tone is faintly too high, gravity rises into pomposity, pedantry replaces correctness, colloquial idiom slips in to mar the finish. The contrast between the too-high and the mundane inadvertently threatens to create the very incongruities at the heart of the mock-heroic. But when the Poetic speaker steps accidentally across the line separating the formal from the comically pompous, Auden begins to revel in the new possibilities. His exuberant Antipoetic tendencies, longing to burlesque pretentiousness, take over. Whenever his own speech releases a great deal of verbal energy, Auden's Poet is in danger. High spirits begin to creep in, and Auden may begin to play with the medium. "Watch this," he says, in effect, as he makes the Poetic speaker perform an even more daring locution. Another step and all will be burlesque. In the early poetry Auden often takes that step, by mistake or by yielding to temptation. Then the Poet, with his dull gray decorum, disappears. The Antipoet takes command. The stage is filled with clowning, parody, self-mockery, and verbal play of all sorts, while the Poet's message gets reversed.

The clearest case of Auden stepping across the line from Poet to Antipoet occurs in "The Argument" section of *The Orators*. The speaker, a sick gang member, begins solemnly enough, in prose not very different from much of Auden's rough-rhythm poetry. His monologue, with its free association, broken rhythms, and high serious tone of desolation, owes something to Eliot. Obvious echoes and borrowings from him appear throughout: "Speak the name only with meaning only for us" (*O*). But very soon this tone becomes compromised and the persona confused. No sooner do lists of neurotic behavior appear than Auden's own healthy exuberance begins to show through the mournful gravity of his sick speaker ("one writes with his penis in a patch of snow 'Resurgam'"), while delight in cataloguing queer sexual behavior makes it particularly difficult for him to keep a straight face ("a douche for the unpopular member," *O*). Behind the sober speaker the author's laughter becomes increasingly obvious.

And once Auden the irrepressible comic breaks the solemn decorum, no matter how inconsistently, every utterance becomes suspect. The more sober it is the more hilarious it seems: "Theories inter-relating the system of feudal tenure with metabolic gradients" (*O*). Did Auden intend this to be comic? It seems almost impossible that he did not. But whatever he intended when he began this section of *The Orators*, by the time his speaker gets halfway through his monologue Antipoet has replaced Poet. We are confronted by a purposely comic prayer, containing an unbroken string of ludicrous invocations: "O Goat with the Compasses, hear us," "O Marquis of Granby, hear us," "George, we beseech thee to hear us," (*O*). This is something more than a sick narrator, in character, being foolish. Auden's Antipoet, after turning the Poet into a parody of himself, has simply run away with the performance.

A substantial portion of Auden's early work hovers on this line between solemnity and self-parody, an uneasy balance between Poet and Antipoet, so that in a single poem each may get the upper hand more than once before the end. In such cases the message, as well as everything else, seesaws from black to white and back again. In a sense the message has been destroyed. That is, the poem's opening message has been reversed by the end. But in another sense positive and negative messages blend to produce some third thing. For instance, when personae switch back and forth from Poet to Antipoet in "Under boughs between our tentative endearments how should we hear . . ." the final message is not just the opposite of the original one. It is something less than a complete reversal, some partial modification of what the speaker tries to make us believe. The poem begins with a highly serious clinical Poet, a speaker still present at the end, where in regal tones he informs us of his compassion for doomed neurotics: "Let each one share our pity, hard to withhold and hard to bear" (*CP*). But these lofty Poetic sentiments are offset by an earlier description that displays something more like comic glee at the neurotics' plight: "their mind's constant sniffling,/Their blood's dulled shuffling." Along with an effective colloquial pun ("Fathers in sons may track/Their voices trick") these witty deprecations sound very much like the Antipoet, delighting in clever images, wordplay, and abuse. This identity is confirmed when the new voice tells us how the sick "May creep to sumps, pile up against the door, crouching in cases" (*CP*). Certainly this is not the same speaker who finds his "pity" for these neurotics "hard to withhold and hard to bear." The Antipoet, drawn by the smell of joking, wordplay, and neurotics, is loose again. He does not sympathize with the Poet's pretentious royal forgiveness, and his brief appearances in the poem modify whatever the Poet tells us.

The best-known of Auden's confusing pieces, the "Address for a Prize-Day," is simply another case of shifting persona, probably unparalleled for creating an almost incredible tangle of irreconcilables. If the reader insists on making the "Address" coherent and consistent, he must decide whether Auden agrees with the schoolmaster speaker, whether he mocks him, or whether he can somehow manage both to mock and agree at the same time. Professor Beach, after considerable head scratching, decided that Auden agrees with the speaker, but mocks him to take the curse off his serious message. If this was Auden's intention he certainly fails disastrously. A fool's message is a foolish message, unless he is of the divine Fool sort, and Auden's schoolmaster is any-thing but that. Neither is he one of Auden's later speakers whose self-mockery establishes the honesty and humility of his own position. The "Address for a Prize-Day" is much more complicated than either of these possibilities. It is in fact such an unbelievable mixture of irreconcilable personae and messages, all given life with such attractive impetuosity, just as though the whole thing made perfect sense, that in a perverse way it succeeds in spite of itself. What could be more delightful, in a way, than Auden's boisterous audacity in pre-senting this amazing collection of comic self-contradiction for our solemn perusal. The poet who reminded the public that "he must beg/Permission now and then to pull their leg" (*LLB*) pulls hard here—though the final joke, I suppose, was in publishing it in *The Orators* as the opening piece, where its position suggests a seriousness and direction it certainly lacks. As written originally (surely for Isherwood and the Gresham's School friends), it must have been a more intelligible joke, simultaneously parodying a Gresham's schoolmaster, schoolboy life, and Auden himself as a solemn Poet. The schoolmaster is an awkward combination of Poet and Antipoet, a foolish mixture appropriate only for fool-ishly sick speakers. But the speaker cannot be a simple example of the foolish sick since he also presents Auden's familiar sober message about cultural decadence. When the speaker sometimes burlesques his own message, Auden's solemn themes appear silly too. Yet since Auden purposely laughs at his own Poetic messages elsewhere, even this behavior might still leave the speech in-ternally consistent if no further reversals appeared. But they do appear. This speaker does not seem to *know* that his message is foolish, and thus his speech becomes inadvertently an attack on himself—Auden's old enemy—a certain type of public school mentality. (At the end it is the masters who are "to die without issue," stuffed into the stoke hole under the stairs by healthy boys, *O*.) If this direction were consistently maintained, the malicious joke would be that, patently foolish as he is, the speaker believes himself healthy. But this message also collapses when Auden's delight in verbal mannerisms, clever inven-tions, and bizarre behavior so animates the speaker that his foolishness occa-sionally disappears and we come to admire his skill and wit. In short, "Address for a Prize-Day" is anything but a coherent social message. Put simply, the irreconcilable elements are these: The speaker is certainly not the author, but neither is he consistently anything else. Sometimes he speaks as Poet, sometimes as Antipoet, and each of these voices contradicts and reverses the message of the other. Auden could not make up his mind. Put in ideational terms, he could not decide what he believed. One part of him (The Poetic part) may have believed that "Address for a Prize-Day" should be a coherent artifact, with the sick speaker uttering a message that called for the destruction of others but implied that he should be one of the first to go. But another part (the Antipoet), caring little about artistic coherence, simply loved to clown, burlesque, parody, and play with words whenever he could. Neither part is subdued, controlled, or subordinated to the other in "Address for a Prize-Day," and as a result we see Auden's own temperamental inconsistency pulling the speech to pieces. Most of *The Orators* displays this sort of behavior.

Auden's early plays, *The Dance of Death* (1933) and *The Dog Beneath the Skin* (1935), are also fatally compromised by Poet and Antipoet battling for control—though in both the Antipoet wins easily. If we must decide finally whether *The Dance of Death* is a statement of or a parody of Auden's familiar evolutionary, death wish theme, surely we must choose parody (with a parody of Marx added). More accurately, the play wavers between social message and self-parody. Again in *The Dog Beneath the Skin*, whatever the authors' Brechtian beliefs about the viability of music hall drama, the play's social satire is hopelessly undermined by its vaudeville treatment of cultural ills. In this burlesque atmosphere, most evils become mere peccadillos, deserving no concern more urgent than laughter at their absurdities. Some deserve no concern at all. They are simply the unimportant subject for vaudeville gags. Part of this may be the mistake of excess. Jokes designed to take the curse off a solemn message may simply get out of hand and bury or destroy the message instead. But surely this does not explain everything. From the play's beginning the authors never seem totally interested in issuing their grave messages about a decadent world. Despite their persistent portrayal of illness and queer behavior, the play's atmosphere is generally benign. The world is all right, the play says; all this sickness is here to show how healthy and inventive and full of high spirits the authors are, and also presumably you the audience, who laugh. The social message seems to be there to make the comedy go rather than the other way round. Leaving the theater, the audience might well feel that the authors found their world not only acceptable but good fun. From time to time, in *The Dog Beneath the Skin*, the Poet puts in an uneasy appearance, but the Antipoet carries the day.

Auden's failure to unify personae and maintain decorum does not mean that each inconsistent creation is completely bad, or that his consistent works are always good. Many readers will surely prefer inconsistent Antipoetic poems to consistent ones featuring an overly pompous Poet. Occasionally we may

rejoice when the Poetic speeches, growing tiresomely solemn, are shattered
by the Antipoet leaping on stage to clown around. Better a flaw in decorum
than a stuffed shirt Poet. In any case flaws are not fatal to art. Even the worst
of Auden's early work usually exhibits great verbal energy, and verbal energy
is the *sine qua non* of poetry. He may sometimes lose control, but at least there
is an energy that needs controlling, and its mere presence is the most promising
omen in the work of a beginning poet. Nevertheless Auden's incompatible
swoops from Poet to Antipoet raise important doubts about his early philosophical themes. Much can be made of Auden the penetrating social analyst,
who shows a profound understanding of both the sick and the healthy, and
who surveys all from an omniscient hawk's-view perspective. But most generaliza-
tions made about this "Auden" are not quite right. The early Auden scarcely
fits the image of that disapproving, sober cultural analyst built up by journalists
and public. One part of his temperament seemed profoundly content with life
as he found it, and when he spoke as a grave cultural diagnostician and activist
leader, he sometimes had to invent personae whose earnest disapprovals were
so alien to some of his own inclinations that he could scarcely keep from
burlesquing them. Auden the social critic is only part of the total Auden. There
is also an Auden who mocks social criticism. The messages in the early poetry
are not merely inconsistent, then, but sometimes the complete reverse of each
other. And these contradictions, since they clearly do not all occur accidentally,
show something else about the early Auden. He often cared more about the
liveliness of the total verbal performance than about philosophy, ideas, social
themes, or his role of cultural critic. (In the long run, of course, this must
be true for any good poet. Auden ruined some early poems by wrecking his
speakers in order to play with their speech. But the skills learned from this
made him a much greater poet later on.) His contradictions also raise interesting
questions about the status of all his early themes. Subtle parody never deviates
far from a straightforward treatment of the thing parodied. Without changing
a single word, in fact, a sober speech can be parodied merely by placing it
in a spoofing atmosphere. Such an atmosphere can be created by the simple
knowledge that a given writer is a parodist, a leg-puller, a wit. When we know
this we always have to look twice at everything he says, to make sure the
clever jokester is not laughing up his sleeve while we earnestly mistake his parody
for its solemn opposite. Auden's open parody of his own themes creates this
atmosphere of doubt, and the careful reader will proceed cautiously. How
seriously did Auden and his friends take some of those completely solemn poems,
the ones with decorum intact, where the Poet dominates throughout? Since
some poems show that Auden and his friends occasionally thought of the Poet's
high-serious persona as a joke, is it not possible that in some others where

the tone was diligently sober, the diagnosis oracular, the Poet's authority awesome, that these made the spoof even more hilarious? How often was Auden privately laughing at his public solemnly pondering those enigmatic utterances that apparently embodied grave profundities. Sometimes, surely, he pulled the audience's innocent leg. But whatever the prevalence of this (and it is interesting to notice that self-parody appears especially in those works most openly directed to the attention of Isherwood, Upward, and Warner), the Antipoet's appearance, briefly or in full performance, throughout the early years, shows Auden's wavering inability to take seriously either his Poet's messages or style.

Auden's own response to his early poems, ten or fifteen years later, shows something worth looking at briefly. When he went back over his youthful work in order to put together *The Collected Poetry*, Auden apparently found some of the early solemnity even more comic than before, and this brought forward his latter-day Antipoet in full force. His playful, irreverent, flippant, comic hand often shows clearly in *The Collected Poetry*, causing some of the things that upset Beach. This is especially obvious in titles given to early poems originally identified only by Roman numerals. Twenty-six of the thirty selections from *Poems* (1933) turn up in *The Collected Poetry* with new titles. Of these twenty-six titles, eleven are unmistakably comic, and nine others are probably comic. Only six are too bland or enigmatic to raise a smile. Of the eleven definitely comic titles, at least eight are quite obviously comments made by the Antipoet on rereading the old utterances of the Poet: "The Questioner Who Sits So Sly" (*CP*), "Something Is Bound to Happen" (*CP*), "Venus Will Now Say a Few Words" (*CP*), "We All Make Mistakes" (*CP*), "Make Up Your Mind" (*CP*), "Do Be Careful" (*CP*), "Such Nice People" (*CP*), and "Two's Company" (*CP*). Though inconsistencies appear in some, all eight poems are written mostly in that solemn voice and high idiom of the early Poet, gravely surveying his world and time and dismayed at finding both bad. To the Auden of 1945, whose Antipoet found his world good, the early dismay a fashionable pose, and the solemn high style pretentious, these poems apparently seemed unintentionally comic, as his new titles indicate. The best example probably is "Doom is dark and deeper than any sea-dingle . . . ." Many readers, responding to its elegiac tone (rare in early Auden) and to its general suggestions of exile, alienation, and fall from brightness, regard this as Auden's best early poem. It contains no inconsistencies in persona or lapses in decorum. Nevertheless, to this rather poignant poem, pleading for a wanderer's safe return to a forsaken homeland, Auden affixed his flippant comment for title: "Something Is Bound to Happen." This remark suggests that the poem's pathos is maudlin, its situation probably melodramatically contrived, and its poignance sentimental. Found guilty of pretentious bathos, both Poet and protagonist are condemned by the

Antipoet in Auden. Full of brisk healthiness, he looks with disdain on their self-indulgent suffering and flips at both the unsympathetic title, which says by its tone, "Cheer up, buddy, something is bound to happen." The solemn Poet receives an equally deflating puncture from the title of "Watch any day his nonchalant pauses, see. . . ." Completely grave, the speaker in this poem tells of an outwardly poised neurotic, whose inner terror makes his every action a precarious balance between "shocking falls on razor-edge" (*CP*). This mighty sufferer and his somber biographer are cut down to minuscule size by an Auden who sees the posturing of each as comic. "We All Make Mistakes," he says in the title. To the sober, indecisive bumbler who speaks in another poem, Auden says, "Make Up Your Mind" (*CP*). In still another title, he remarks ironically of neurotics the Poet once took seriously, "Such Nice People" (*CP*). The most attractive of these titles (if I understand it correctly) is the one affixed to that puzzling ode from *The Orators* originally subtitled "To My Pupils" (*CP*). Turning to this baffling piece of schoolboy mystification (probably after he had first gone through the earlier *Poems*, making wry comments), Auden in his late thirties may have said to himself, with amused exasperation, "For God's sake which side am I supposed to be on," and left the last eight words as its title. If this guess is wrong, the other alternative, reflecting a similar amusement, is that he addresses his readers in the title, saying to them, "Guess which side I am supposed to be on."

Titles from *The Collected Poetry* provide an amusing insight into Auden's habit of noticing the ridiculous in every pretentious speech, particularly his own. But I am not claiming that the Antipoet of 1945 provides evidence for the existence of an Antipoet in 1928–35. That earlier existence needs no support from such after-the-fact evidence. Auden apparently took his Poet more seriously in 1928–35 than he took him in 1945, but the Antipoet is very much alive in both periods and frequently cavorts through the early poetry. *The Orators* (though it has little artistic value) provides an endlessly fascinating insight into just what sort of unique person Auden was behind that Poet's mask he so often donned for his early performances. The more one ponders *The Orators*, the more striking becomes its real oddity and queerness, and attractiveness too. A great deal of it resembles the free association of an irrepressible clown, mimic, and wit. Ebullient energy runs around everywhere, and a fantastic inventive imagination. In every corner are pack-rat collections of gifted wordplay, half-finished constructions, and odds and ends of situations. The whole book resembles a mixture put together by some irresponsible, precocious, and very talented schoolboy. We almost seem to get a glimpse into the wordy storeroom of an artist's unconscious, where constructions lie about every which way and energy, disconnected from order, rushes from side to side assuming a variety of strange shapes. To understand the later Auden fully, readers must immerse themselves in the Auden that could make *The Orators*. (Erudite comparisons to the works of Rimbaud and Blake probably just obscure the book's nature. The most important model, I would guess, was Mortmere, that endless schoolboy saga.) That all this untidy, attractive rush should somehow lie behind or beneath the grave, responsible, authoritative Poet is most significant. The puzzling behavior of many later poems can be explained as the result of this irrepressible energy, baffled, gagged, and banished with great difficulty, bursting through. . . .

The Sea and the Mirror is Auden's first masterpiece, more daring and exciting than *New Year Letter*, and larger than later comic poems that equal it in brilliance (perhaps only "Bucolics" exceeds it). No part of Auden's temperament is excluded from *The Sea and the Mirror*. His highest Poet, his lowest Antipoet all have their perfect and appropriate speech. More important, his mixtures of Poet and Antipoet, from Prospero's flawless middle style to the high comic speech of Caliban, surpass anything of this sort he had done before. In Prospero, Poet and Antipoet blend again to produce a speaker directly descended from *New Year Letter* and the Narrator of *For the Time Being*. In many places the three speakers are identical:

> When I am safely home, oceans away in Milan, and
> Realise once and for all I shall never see you again,
> Over there, maybe, it won't seem quite so dreadful. . . .
> > *(The Sea and the Mirror, CP)*

> Who
> That ever has the rashness to
> Believe that he is one of those
> The greatest of vocations chose,
> Is not perpetually afraid
> That he's unworthy of his trade. . . .
> > *(New Year Letter, CP)*

> We look around for something, no matter what, to inhibit
> Our self-reflection, and the obvious thing for that purpose
> Would be some great suffering.
> > *(For the Time Being, CP)*

The speaker in these passages is an intelligent educated man whose native formal idiom in relaxed moments becomes an easy, supple, middle-style soliloquy (still more declamation than conversation). Colloquial speech mixes with modestly correct syntax and learned vocabulary. On occasion he may rise to a high style or, when more playful, skillfully parody, mimic, joke, and clown – all without losing the authority and dignity of his self. As Prospero he can speak with high poetic artificiality (". . . and with your first free act/Delight my leaving; share my resigning thoughts/As you have served my revelling wishes. . ."). Or with colloquial ease: "In all, things have turned out better/Than I once expected" (*CP*). Or with playful comedy: "You, I suppose will be off now to look for likely victims;/Crowds chasing ankles, lone men stalking glory. . ." (*CP*). Or with affectionate mock-stiffness: "Stephano is contracted to his belly, a minor/But a prosperous kingdom" (*CP*). Poet and Antipoet are again united in a single personality, who seems larger, more lifelike and attractive for their being there. The unification produces in Prospero's speech a poem surpassed by nothing Auden had made before. By 1944 Auden had become, like Dryden, complete "master of the middle style" (*CP*).

The startling contrast between Prospero and Antonio is even more remarkable for the fact that Antonio speaks a style almost identical to Prospero's own, in the voice Auden had developed in *New Year Letter*. How can Auden create such unlike personae out of the same style? The answer lies in something observed before. Antonio, detached, looks at "others" with contempt. Prospero, detached, looks at them with love. Antonio's Poetic voice scornfully analyzes the ills, follies, and flaws of others; his Antipoetic voice mocks them with cruel jokes. Parodied and mimicked, their actions and idiom look fatuous:

> Two heads silhouetted against the sails
> — And kissing, of course — well built, but the lean
> Fool is quite a person, the fingernails
> Of the dear old butler for once quite clean. . . .
>
> (*CP*)

The tone of voice is heavily sarcastic. Prospero's Poet, detached from the "others" only by being more intelligent and articulate, mostly analyzes his *own* follies and shortcomings. When he mocks others, he does so with the awareness that they and he share the same sort of foolishness – the inevitable absurdity of being human. His mockery is the mockery of love. Turned inward the Poet's analysis and the Antipoet's mockery create a persona tolerant and affectionate. Turned outward the very same Poetic analysis and Antipoetic mockery create a persona a bit smug, contemptuous, and too knowing. Magnificent in Antonio where decorum demands it, this persona is not very attractive in earlier poems where it seemed to be Auden. Prospero's humility and self-mockery are always attractive. The rhetorical style of both may be the same. Their personae are near opposites.

Stephano is another mixture of Poet and Antipoet. The poet in him, though his intelligent analysis is not wrong, is just a shade too high, so that his formality becomes comic, especially set against his low subject: "Embrace me, belly, like a bride;/Dear daughter, for the weight you drew . . ." (*CP*). His Antipoet is low ("Wise nanny, with a vulgar pooh," *CP*) and makes him seem silly. Stephano descends from those sick speakers in the very early poems, made appropriately foolish by an awkward combination of Poet and Antipoet. The difference now is that Auden's compassion has increased. The intelligence of his Poetic voice and the humbling self-mockery of his Antipoetic make Stephano more attractive than not. He may be foolish, but he is not deluded.

Several removes further from Prospero's middle style, the Antipoet performs alone in the song given to Master and Boatswain. Its downright meter and perfect rhyme, its balladlike pattern, straightforward idiom ("We drank our liquor straight"), and literary parody ("The nightingales are sobbing in/The orchards of our mothers . . ." *CP*) assert the claims of the Antipoet as average sensual low-brow against the literary pretensions of elegant and highfalutin Poets, such as the one who precedes him in Alonso's speech. The magnificent success of Alonso as Poet is, in fact, more striking in some ways than the middle and low styles of Prospero and his inferiors. Though Prospero's speech is probably Auden's best middle-style performance, and the speeches of Stephano and the others appropriate and nearly flawless, Auden had successfully done these kinds of things before. But in Alonso's speech the high Poet's voice, often reached for but usually missed, succeeds better than ever before. Alonso's persona is that of a Prospero removed from the library (where over after-dinner brandy and cigars, indulgent and relaxed, he speaks to a beloved friend) and placed on stage before a formally dressed audience. No matter if the "Dear Son" opening suggests a letter or fatherly talk, Alonso, every bit the courtly rhetorician, puts on a deliberately high-style public performance. By greatly elevating the Poet, by dropping the Antipoet's mockery but retaining some of his wit and jokes, Auden creates a persona whose elegant language and clever tropes are an appropriate display of rhetorical skill by a master orator:

> So, if you prosper, suspect those bright
> Mornings when you whistle with a light
> Heart . . . .
> the park so green,
> So many well-fed pigeons upon
> Cupolas and triumphal arches . . . .
>
> (*CP*)

For once Auden has combined his own temperamental tendencies to produce a speaker of truly remarkable elevation. Alonso is a high Poet, who takes himself,

but particularly his performance, seriously. But the formal locutions set against
wit and cleverness, the very things that make other speakers seem foolish, in
Alonso become the marvelous constructions of an orator so confident of his
rhetorical skill that he dares to range outward to the borders of mock-heroic,
knowing that fully in control he will never slip over. If his delight in his own
skill shows through, we delight with him. Only a short distance separates serious
Alonso from comic Caliban, but that is the distance between heroic and mock-
heroic speech. Alonso provided Auden with just what the Poet in him had
yearned for all along: a verbal performance in the grand manner where wit
and cleverness would enhance rather than defeat the elevated idiom, where
all Auden's delight in rhetorical skill for its own sake could be appropriately
indulged in a high-style performance.

The Poetic performances of Gonzalo and Sebastian are lesser achievements,
partly, I think, because unless they were to be indistinguishable from Alonso's,
their rhetorical range had to be limited. As a result, though each speaks appropriately and well, their poems are not as exciting and dazzling as Alonso's.
In both, Auden eliminates the daring near-comic cleverness that distinguished
Alonso's speech. Except for one unlikely lapse in Gonzalo ("I whose interference
broke/The gallop into jog-trot prose . . ." *CP*) both are nearly pure sober Poets,
and Sebastian is particularly high:

> O blessed be bleak Exposure on whose sword,
> Caught unawares, we prick ourselves alive!
> Shake Failure's bruising fist! Who else would crown
> Abominable error with a proof?
>
> (*CP*)

These are dangerous heights. This speech is not supposed to be mock-heroic,
yet such questions cry out for Antipoetic answers that begin: "Dear Sebastian,
your splendid query deserves a plain reply. A great many unscrupulous sorts,
given the proper chance, would be only too happy to crown Abominable error
with . . ." But Auden's Antipoet is out of sight here. The allegorical images
Sebastian plays with are not used to mock himself or anyone. His rhetorical
embellishments are closer to metaphysical practice than is usual in Auden's
writing:

> The lie of Nothing is to promise proof
> To any shadow that there is no day
> Which cannot be extinguished with some sword,
> To want and weakness that the ancient crown . . . .
>
> (*CP*)

Perhaps the sestina form itself, with all those rhyme words relentlessly reappearing to limit the possibilities for every line, urges its repetitious sobriety on Sebastian.

Two other Poetic performances are interesting for different reasons. Miranda's villanelle, sometimes said to be a charming song of touching innocence, is nothing of the sort. The language in this intricate contrivance is hardly that of an innocent whose discourse falls accidentally into poetry: "her venomous body/Melted into light" (*CP*). Nor is the speech at all straightforward ("My Dear One is mine as mirrors are lonely") or unself-conscious and unliterary ("As the poor and sad are real to the good king" *CP*). The poem seems completely successful, but the speaker is not Shakespeare's Miranda by a long way, or an ingenuous country lass stumbling on the world. It is Auden as Poet, a highly learned, highly proficient, highly articulate Poet, putting on an extremely skillful exhibition in a game with very difficult rules. The Poet speaks not as Miranda, but as Miranda might speak could she analyze and conceptualize her emotions, realize her unrealized innocence, carefully silhouette herself against the wide world she does not know, and clearly articulate all these in an extremely sophisticated manner completely foreign to her. The entire poem is a wonderfully successful illusion. If Miranda really spoke in character she would sound much more like Trinculo than like the villanelle-speaking persona in her own poem. Triculo's poem is something of an Auden anomaly, at least a very rare poetic species at this stage of his career. In Trinculo's speech Auden writes one of his very few unmocked, unparodied, plain-style poems in a manner similar to Blake or Frost. Trinculo is simple and ingenuous, a completely defenseless and open man, whose life (making the performance even more difficult for Auden) is one of pitiable suffering. All these features require a style and forbearance from mockery alien to the temperament Auden displays nearly everywhere in previous work. In no earlier poem has any neurotic speaker completely escaped his detached mockery or clinical scrutiny. But Trinculo is loved, not judged, pilloried, or even classified. No Antipoet scoffs at him. No Poet dissects his psyche or turns his fears into pompous inflations. The poem is written as though Auden's Poet had suddenly become a Blake. Auden's signature shows clearly ("a laughter shakes/The busy and devout"). But there is an unusual limpid simplicity:

> On clear days I can see
> Green acres far below,
> And the red roof where I
> Was little Trinculo.
>
> (*CP*)

Since other poems in this style, with a similar persona, begin to appear later, I will postpone discussion of them. It is enough to note here that Auden's success with Trinculo demonstrates his increasing technical mastery. That he should succeed so well with the unlikely Trinculo persona adds considerably to the dazzling achievement of his entire performance in *The Sea and the Mirror*.

For who would have thought that the creator of Trinculo's innocent sad song could also have produced Caliban? Caliban's speech is Auden's great chance to let Poet and Antipoet move completely away from their quietly harmonious middle style to surfeit themselves at their outer limits. By great good fortune he discovered a situation in which just such splendid indulgence is appropriate, so that the reader can cast aside puritanical critical scruples and dive in. The performance is everything. Transferred into dull homiletic prose, Caliban's thesis would scarcely hold our interest for half a page, certainly not for the thirty-some pages of his monologue. The speech itself, though in prose, is not much different from Auden's poetry. Its rhythms are like those in his syllabic verse, and its syntax and diction are those of his familiar Poet, allowed an elevation beyond his wildest dreams. At the same time the Antipoet practices every verbal trick in his vast repertoire. Grandeur and slapstick merge in one gigantic mock-heroic performance, the explosive start of the high-comic style soon to dominate Auden's poetry. And of course the performance itself carries a message at least as important as what Caliban talks about. The style of this remarkable Auden persona tells us a great deal about his creator—about his joyous delight in grandiose verbal oratory, about his awareness of his own skill and his own foolishness, about his belief in the value of such Art and his delight in the Life which makes it possible. Caliban talks explicitly about all these things, but what he says is scarcely important. *How* he says them so clearly carries its own message about Auden's values and beliefs.

The Sea and the Mirror is the culmination of the evolutionary line I have been tracing. All Auden's beliefs, his styles, voices, techniques come harmoniously together in this work. Not only do Poet and Antipoet merge, but form and content, Art and Life, philosophy and craft merge too. In *The Sea and the Mirror*, the speakers' subjects and the message of their performances are the same. Through much of the 1930's, while Poetic speakers might *say* that life was grim, its inhabitants sick, and its culture moribund, their performances, so often filled with an exuberant healthiness and worldly delight, sometimes denied what they were saying. While Antipoet speakers might *say* that Life was more important than Art, their delight in Artful performances belied what they said. Furthermore when Poet and Antipoet appeared together in many poems, they often unintentionally fought each other to a standstill, while the message of both speaker and performance collapsed around them helplessly filled with self-contradiction. In *The Sea and the Mirror* all these divergent forces meet, are fused together, and produce a single coherent, unified creation. What the speakers talk about and how they talk about it, their matter and their manner, carry the same message. Stated imperfectly, this message is that Art and Life are utterly unlike, that the Aesthetic is different in *kind* from the Ethical (and both are different from the Religious), yet each is necessary to the other. Prospero talks openly about this. Antonio, Stephano, Gonzalo, Alonso, Sebastian, Trinculo, and of course Caliban, do the same, while lesser figures (Ferdinand, Master, Boatswain, Miranda) talk about the relation of Art and Life without knowing it. And the manner of everyone carries the same message: that Art and Life, while unlike, are both valuable. All this is most clear in Caliban's address, of course. His very manner of speaking shows (1) that he values nothing more than an unashamed Artistic performance, as far from Lifelike speech in its open contrivance and indulgent artifice as the Poet can make it, (2) that he values non-Art at least as highly as Art, and from this point of view mocks his own Poetic exhibition with all his Antipoetic skill, and (3) that he unifies these contradictory values not by logically resolving their conflict, but by simply accepting their paradoxical relationship as a delightful part of human existence. In this first of Auden's high comic performances, where Poet and Antipoet careen far out from the middle, what the speaker says and what he shows by his performance are the same. After this all Auden's best comic poems carry Caliban's message about Art and Life, but their speakers, with this message securely embedded in their style, are free to talk about whatever they wish.

FREDERICK BUELL

Auden After the Thirties

In *Another Time*, Auden continued a poetic development first evident in the sonnets and the "Commentary" in *Journey to a War*: an increased ease in writing a fully public, cultivated verse and a dramatic widening of intellectual and literary interests. A new, freer use of ideas emerged in the play with poetic summaries of historical movements in "Commentary," "September 1, 1939," and "Epithalamium," and the work of a variety of writers is expressed in more complexity than merely their inclusion in the Marxist or neo-Mortmerian drama of conflict between an ally and an enemy; writers and their ideas are fictionalized, dramatized, and appraised in a series of specifically literary poems, including both the famous elegies on Yeats, Freud, and Toller and the poems of Voltaire, Pascal, Rimbaud, and Melville. Accompanying this change is a gradual reappraisal which is a coda to Auden's political interest of the thirties and prelude to the "middle phase," in which, to the disillusionment of many of his admirers, he distanced himself from left-wing politics.

This transitional period was marked by experiment with a political attitude derivative principally from Rilke and Yeats; Auden was attempting to formulate a way in which a poet's voice could be of compelling political relevance without being subservient to any particular program for action. A review of Rilke's poetry gives an indication of Auden's thought:

> But Rilke's influence is not confined to certain technical tricks. It is, I believe, no accident that as the international crisis becomes more and more acute, the poet to whom writers are becoming increasingly drawn should be one who felt that it was pride and presumption to interfere with the lives of others (for each is unique

and the apparent misfortunes of each may be his very way of salvation); one who occupied himself consistently and exclusively with his own inner life; one who wrote

'Art cannot be helpful through our trying to keep and specially concerning ourselves with the distresses of others, but in so far as we bear our own distresses more passionately, give now and then a perhaps clearer meaning to endurance, and develop for ourselves the means of expressing the suffering within us and its conquest more precisely and clearly than is possible to those who have to apply their powers to something else.'

This tendency is not to be dismissed with the cheery cry "defeatism." It implies not a denial of the impulse to political action, but rather the realization that if the writer is not to harm both others and himself, he must consider, and very much more humbly and patiently than he has been doing, what kind of person he is, and what may be his real function. When the ship catches fire, it seems only natural to rush importantly to the pumps, but perhaps one is only adding to the general confusion and panic: to sit still and pray seems selfish and unheroic, but it may be the wisest and most helpful course.

The parody of those who "rush importantly to the pumps" is both a form of sniping at the political enthusiasms of the thirties and a recognition of the fact that the peculiar stability in the midst of political tumult, a major quality of the Baldwin Era in England, has broken down; the time is now one of a crisis of more threatening order, a time when international war is in the offing, war that can no longer be isolated and idealized as were the early stages of the conflict in Spain.

In the elegy on Yeats Auden argues that

> poetry makes nothing happen: it survives
> In the valley of its saying where executives
> Would never want to tamper. . . .

Instead, what poetry can do is

> Still persuade us to rejoice;
>
> With the farming of a verse
> Make a vineyard of the curse,
> Sing of human unsuccess
> In a rapture of distress;

> In the deserts of the heart,
> Let the healing fountain start,
> In the prison of his days
> Teach the free man how to praise.

Both opinions stem from Auden's thought about Yeats; the former opinion is formed in argument with Yeats and the latter is a remark that makes a hopeful gloss on the Yeatsian phenomenon of the poetic curse, suggesting that mere distress can become at least "a rapture of distress" when put into poetry. Auden's imitative and interpretive ability is crucial to the success of his poems on writers; the imitation corresponds as well to Auden's own peculiarly literary shopping about for a new political stance, and this becomes clear in "September 1, 1939" in the way Auden makes use of Yeats, both of his bitter audacity of reference, his calling on the famous dead in a tone both cavalier and off-hand yet urgently intense, and of his rhetoric of affirmation from the bottomless abyss of a poetic curse. Like "Spain, 1937," this is an occasional poem related to a historical situation (September 1 was the date of the fascist invasion of Poland); now, however, the "today" is not the time of the struggle but rather a time of a hateful, vicious, distorted, and hopeless normality, and the just are no longer united and capable of meaningful political action.

The *New Year Letter* is the first major statement of Auden's re-evaluation of politics (or, in other terms, recantation of his old commitment). He speaks directly to the question in the second part of the poem:

> We hoped; we waited for the day
> The state would wither clean away,
> Expecting the Millenium
> The theory promised us would come,
> It didn't. Specialists must try
> To detail all the reasons why;
> Meanwhile at least the the layman knows
> That none are lost so soon as those
> Who overlook their crooked nose.

Shortly thereafter, in *For the Time Being*, the tombstone is dropped over the recent grave by the admission of Herod, who, although a liberal and thus a figure of parody to Auden in his thirties phase, now stands for the political man in general: "I object. I'm a liberal. I want everyone to be happy. I wish I had never been born." The change is fast and a complete about-face; the reader is left asking what happened.

Biographically, several things did happen. First, Auden emigrated to

America, self-consciously choosing the role of the literary exile and leaving behind a disgruntled English literary group. That breaking off old literary ties was a principal reason for Auden's move is indicated by a comment of Cyril Connolly: "He reverts always to the same argument, that a writer needs complete anonymity, he must break away from the European literary happy family."

To leave this family behind and to educate himself in the anonymity of New York City shows considerable courage and self-awareness on the part of the poet in Auden; although he was cutting himself loose from a major source of his popularity and previous creativity, he was doing what was necessary for his poetic growth, not only in disassociating himself from the moribund movement of the thirties in England, but also in schooling himself in a new privacy from which he could reevaluate both man's relation to society and man's relation to God.

Second, Auden experienced a religious conversion; this gave him an intellectual position from which to reevaluate his former "beliefs." Instead of renouncing all he had experienced and thought, Auden had the good sense to rework this material into a new context, first into the *New Year Letter*'s idea of a double focus, and then to observe:

> The various "kerygmas," of Blake, of Lawrence, of Freud, of Marx, to which, along with most middle-class individuals of my generation, I paid attention between twenty and thirty, had one thing in common. They were all Christian heresies; that is to say, one cannot imagine their coming into existence except in a civilization which claimed to be based, religiously, on the belief that the Word was made flesh and dwelt among us, and that, in consequence, matter, the natural order, is real and redeemable, not a shadowy appearance or the cause of evil, and historical time is real and significant, not meaningless or an endless series of cycles. . . .
>
> I have come to realize that what is true in what they [the "heretics"] say is implicit in the Christian doctrine of the nature of man, and that what is not Christian is not true; but each of them brought to some particular aspect of life that intensity of attention characteristic of one-sided geniuses (needless to say, they all contradicted each other), and such comprehension of Christian wisdom as I have, little though it be, would be very much less without them.

Even though Auden's conversion represented a major reevaluation of his past, one remains skeptical of Auden's new-found "answer," because it seems to tie up reality and thought, as did Auden's other "answers," into such a neat and final package; Christianity had intellectually "one-upped" Blake, Freud, Lawrence, and Marx by including and harmonizing them all within its intellectual frame-work. Nor is Auden's statement of his personal experience with this new alterna-tive to frivolity wholly convincing: "And then, providentially—for the occupa-tional disease of poets is frivolity—I was forced to know in person what it is like to feel oneself the prey of demonic powers, in both the Greek and the Christian sense, stripped of self-control and self-respect, behaving like a ham actor in a Strindberg play." The image of the ham actor and Auden's knowledge of the traditions behind the fear he feels—he began his swerve toward faith by reading theology, in particular Kierkegaard—as well as the difficulty of pic-turing him as the "prey of demonic powers," create a doubt about Auden's alteration beyond role-play by the influx of the irrational and the divine. But perhaps the conversion of any socially adept, articulate, and sophisticated man would always seem suspicious to the world, and, in any case, the question of Auden's faith may well lie permanently beyond the reach of literary criticism.

Auden's conversion can in one way be fruitfully considered by criticism: although to evaluate the authenticity of the immediate experience is impossible, one can ask if it contributed to the development not just of new ideas, but also of a more judicious way of using these ideas, a new and more fully realized poetic voice. That Auden's major poetry—both his most ambitious longer poems and his most satisfying shorter ones—came after his conversion indicates this; more important still is that, after Auden's initial and often unsteady experimenta-tion with religious poetry, he developed a verse of baroque playfulness and comic meditation that has remained to the present day his major poetic voice.

One of the most effective ways of tracing Auden's development as a poet is to consider how successfully his poetic language, which always involves some implicit or explicit deprecation of itself as such, manages to refer to forms of truth that exist outside language. The Mortmere mode, with its privacy and aggressive parodic undercutting of both reality and itself, did not strive to achieve any firm outside reference. Poems like "Out on the lawn I lie in bed" attempted to check the Mortmerian fantasy and ground themselves in a utopian drama, which had for its basis the systems of Freud and Marx; the greatest danger in this attempt lay in the fact that, despite Auden's effort to achieve a nonpropa-gandistic, parabolic art, he involved himself too often in a logical and tonal inconsistency, in that he tried, after exposing the deceptiveness of poetic language, to assert instead a quasi-poetic utopian myth as truth. *Letters from Iceland* managed to solve the dilemma temporarily, by creating for itself a mythic, holiday world that was neither devoid of social reference nor forced to negate itself through parody; "Spain 1937," however, was a reversion to former problems because poetic language and political reality were finally antagonistic. Similarly unsatis-factory are a number of Auden's early attempts at an explicitly religious literature;

for example, "Returning each morning from a timeless world" and even "The Meditation of Simeon" are tonally uneasy; there remains an antagonism between playfulness of rhetoric and idea and religious motivation, between virtuosity and spiritual earnestness. The poem of the "middle period" most totally successful and revealing of the poetic voice of the later poetry is the narrator's closing speech in *For the Time Being*: it represents the development of what can be called an explicitly secular voice, one that takes the human, conditional world for its theme and remains comically humble in the knowledge of its own pro-visionality. Two aspects of this voice can be isolated: first, it creates a tone that resolves in itself both public reference and private community, and, second, it achieves a new and more satisfying indirect fusion of the poetic language with extrapoetic truth, of fiction with a reality beyond fiction.

Most striking about the narrator's voice is the sense of a public privacy—the assertion, in the public world, of the intimacy of a small group. Auden has found a voice that can inclusively and intimately make use of the pronoun "we"; in sketching in the typical detail of the conditional world which reemerges just after the celebration of Christmas, he indicates a world of profoundly and comically shared experience. In the uncomfortably prosaic, one finds, if it exists anywhere in contemporary Western society, the point for the communion of mankind; the attempt of Auden's later verse to bring poetry as close as possible to the language of prose is an attempt with implications for not only the form but also the tone and content of his poetry. In this shared world, Auden's vir-tuosic talent for seeing life in terms of all that is already stylized assumes a positive function: in the stereotype wittily rendered Auden finds one of the surest points for social cohesion in a world where philosophic and spiritual unity is lacking. Thus, the narrator's witty rendering of all the irritations and failures of the temporal world does not become, as does much of the earlier poetry, a display of exhibitionist wit; exhibitionism is tempered to a deeper comic affection for all the familiar imperfections of the world.

What lies behind the achievement of this voice of public privacy is not difficult to determine; Auden has discovered for himself a complex and yet not internally antagonistic poetic identity. He adopts the persona of the dis-comfited bourgeois, suffering from the 8:15 and living in a world without meta-physic or effective religion; at the same time, he brings to bear on this world a civilized, somewhat aristocratic wit, that of a highly cultured man living in an age of humorous barbarism. The two identities are then united in a marvelous-ly rich way: the assumption of a bourgeois identity is an act of affectionate humility for the man of wit and learning, which then allows that educated wit the pleasure of turning vulgar reality into baroque and comic form. Even when Auden attacks his new social enemy, the managers, it is from this complex standpoint; the managers are the figures whom all members of a bureaucratic society suspect and dislike, but Auden attacks them by means of a wit that juxtaposes them to their far more impressive and awesome forerunners, the rulers of an aristocratic era. This attack has none of the stridency of a rebel rejecting his society; both the revolutionary hostility to the bourgeois world and the revolutionary dream of a classless society have been abandoned in favor of a complex expression of comic, personal, yet generally shared dislike. What emerges is a paradoxically Arcadian attitude: the detail of the managers' world is sketched in with an irony that so enjoys itself and the communal attitudes it expresses, that one feels the very flaws and commonness of this world to be part of an ideal order. This partly mythic, partly real realm is precarious, being only one step from international disaster; at the same time, as long as it remains within moderate bounds, it indicates, as do limestone landscapes, a faultless world.

That Auden is able to remain so comfortably and lovingly within this realm of flawed flawlessness and mythic realism depends on his new definition of the sphere of poetic language and its relationship to extrapoetic truth. What is implicit in the tone of later poems is explicit in the narrator's closing speech in *For the Time Being*; both the human world and the world of poetic language exist in an affectionately, frivolously, and profoundly ironic relationship to divine reality. The ironic relationship is not a divisive one; on the contrary, it is one in which "God will cheat no one, not even the world of its triumph." The poet works with a medium that is hopelessly corrupt; not only has language been debased in a world of "mass education and mass media," but is also in essence a medium of artifice and fiction. As such, language cannot refer in any direct manner to truth; to bear witness to truth, poetry must be, as Auden argues in his T. S. Eliot lectures of 1967, "indirect and negative." More explicitly, "sanctity, it would seem, can only be hinted at by comic indirection, as in *Don Quixote*." In this way, the resources of language can be utilized and simultaneously qualified without a necessity for the disturbing self-retraction of much of Auden's work; its conditional nature, underscored by a comedy of sheer linguistic play, hints at a realm beyond the merely conditional. Thus the self-deprecating imagination can exercise itself to its fullest without disturbing what is ultimately real and ultimately nonpoetic.

This theory of the relationship of secular language to divine truth has not taken Auden beyond poetic pose and experimentation with ideas into some final kind of belief; he has found in it, however, the most successful solution to a persistent problem in his poetry. Whatever that outside truth may be, it holds generally true that a subtlety of reference to it makes the poem of particular aesthetic interest; as much as possible, Auden's notorious schoolmasterly voice disappears in favor of a process of indirection that becomes almost satisfying in and of itself. In poems like the narrator's last speech in *For the Time Being* Auden most nearly achieves his goal: the sacred is preserved almost intact outside the poetry, and, within, one finds realized a verbal and intellectual pleasure so pure that one feels as if the lowly human faculty of mere enjoyment had been somehow ennobled. Because of the lowliness of this chief source of pleasure in Auden's work, he will always be criticized; for the same reason he will always be admired.

WENDELL STACY JOHNSON

Auden, Hopkins,
and the Poetry of Reticence

Frost's. . . is not the speech of dream or of uncontrollable passion . . . One is aware of strong, even violent emotion behind what is actually said, but the saying is reticent, the poetry has, as it were, an auditory chastity.

Poems, like many of Donne's and Hopkins', which express a poet's personal feelings of religious devotion or penitence, make me uneasy.

These comments by W. H. Auden, in *The Dyer's Hand*, are complementary and consistent, just as they are consistent with Auden's remark that Americans are generally "far more reticent" than Englishmen about showing their deepest feelings. They are consistent, as well, with Auden's telling friends how much he valued reticence. To him it meant, in part, the refusal to speak in public or write specifically about those matters he considered the most private, that is, emotions involving sex and religion. The poet whose apparent lack of reticence on at least the second point most bothered him—the poet to whom he felt closer than to Frost or Donne, who of course influenced his verse more—was Gerard Manley Hopkins.

A number of critics have noticed in passing how the early Auden in particular both imitates and parodies the style of Hopkins—his ellipses, inverted syntax, and oddities of diction. As John Fuller comments, the poems of the late twenties

From *Twentieth Century Literature* 20, no. 3 (July 1974). Copyright © 1974 Hofstra University Press.

show "the impact of Hopkins and Eliot at its most extreme." But, like Monroe
K. Spears and Richard Hoggart, he recognizes the manner if not always the
matter of Hopkins in the later verse as well. Hopkins' voice is probably more
audible in some of this verse than Auden, who had as a young man lovingly
parodied the cadences of the "Deutschland," fully realized.

After a certain point in his career Auden wanted to give up imitating
Hopkins; the exclusions he made in editing his own poetry suggest that as
well as other decisions. The most striking instance, perhaps, is a poem that
has struck most critics as crucial in his career and life, the one that virtually
every commentator cites as showing the influence of Hopkins. This poem,
"Petition," represents a major omission from both *W. H. Auden: A Selection
by the Author* and *Selected Poetry of W. H. Auden.* The first word in Auden's
verse prayer is an echo, addressing God as "Sir," in imitation of Hopkins' usage
in his sonnet that begins, "Thou are indeed just, Lord." In the original, unpublished, draft the manner of Hopkins appears even more clearly:

> Sir, no man's enemy, forgiving all
> But negative principle of darkness, Will
> His treacherous inversion, are everywhere
> In desert as the hot extravagant glare
> As flash on hills, warning of physical death,
> Upon all surfaces, above, beneath,
> At all times several yet always one
> A gymnast's rhythm at Athens, or then
> A celibate and certain faith at Tintern.

The ellipses, omitting "who" or "you" in the third line and the article in the
fifth line, are purely Hopkinsian; Auden's alliterative phrase in the ninth line
is another, if fainter, echo. In this first handwritten version of the poem there
is a central section of ten lines—in which, unfortunately, many words are quite
illegible—that was apparently rejected before the poem saw print, and here,
too, the style of Hopkins is evident: the passage includes such elliptical, half-
rhyming and alliterative phrases as, "where men leave club" and "sleek in cab"
to characterize the empty lives of "the big towns."

"Petition" has been taken, fairly, to predict Auden's conversion. If it need
not be read as a Christian poem—although its Freudian and aesthetic concerns
by no means prevent such a reading—it is nonetheless a moral poem, the point
of which conforms perfectly to the incarnational Christianity of Hopkins. In
more lines from the unpublished draft, it prays God to forgive "the intricate
sin,/Mind's shame of its bodily origin." To many nominal Christians the idea
might be suspect, but to the Jesuit who celebrated earthly beauty this would

be the heart of the moral and religious matter: proud mind subdued to incarnation. For a moment, at least, Auden suggests here not only the style but also the substance of Hopkins: the ethical substance but not the personal mode, not the mode of "Thou are indeed just, Lord."

To the question why Auden chose to omit "Petition" from the selections of his verse, there is no clear answer. There may be several true answers. The one false answer would be that he no longer either admired Hopkins' poetic style or accepted his dogmatic belief. To the end of his life he was influenced by the one and subscribed to the other. Still, he was bothered by Hopkins' confessional verse—verse that is in one essential unlike "Petition," which is, after all, an observation on the human situation and a prayer for all mankind— and he may have deliberately tried to avoid following a model that could lead him into writing such verse.

For Auden, Hopkins was a major poet. He uses those words in his 1934 *Criterion* review of E. E. Phare's *Gerard Manley Hopkins*, where he also mentions parenthetically that he "became interested in Hopkins through reading 'Spring and Fall.'" It seems significant that "Spring and Fall" is one of the few Hopkins poems that are not explicitly Christian. Rather, it is a poem about childhood and mortality, possibly echoing Matthew Arnold's lines "To a Gipsy Child by the the Sea-shore" and surely, like Arnold's poem, pointedly inverting the ideas of Wordsworth in his "Immortality Ode." (Of course, it *is* Christian by unmistakable implication, since the words in the title come to mean not only the seasons but also an adamantine source and the Fall of Man.) Just as significant, it is unlike the "Deutschland" and most of the Hopkins sonnets in being a relatively impersonal dramatic monologue. The central figure in the poem is a little girl, not Gerard Manley Hopkins.

Clearly, the poems of Hopkins that made Auden uneasy were those dealing directly, or too nearly so, with either erotic or devotional feeling. This is very much a matter of critical principle. The 1934 review comments that "The Bugler's First Communion" "suggests a conflict in Hopkins between homosexual feelings and a moral sense of guilt." It asks, "Does 'The Bugler' fail because the guilt is unacknowledged, and "The Portrait' ['The Portrait of Two Beautiful Young People'] succeed because it is transformed into the unspecified moral danger which he fears for the subjects of the poem." The key critical word here is *transformed*. Deep-seated emotions, so Auden the critic insists, must be changed into a fictive form, a poet's lie that is for everyman more true than truth. "The truest poetry is the most feigning," he argues in the title and the text of a later poem. He once warned a group of undergraduate women that if a boyfriend sent his sweetheart a really good love poem he was probably more interested in writing than in her. (He also admitted that he needed to be in love with someone in order to write; erotic feeling was often, for him, as much a poetic inspiration as an end in itself.)

In his critical theory about reticence and feigning—as, no doubt, in anyone's theory—there is a large element of individual temperament. Not that Wystan Hugh Auden the man feigned his feelings or beliefs. Quite the contrary. He insisted quietly on being himself and openly going his way. At Swarthmore he took a good-looking young sailor to an academic party; at Smith he arrived in the classroom wearing slippers. And there was no attempt in either instance to shock or to pose, any more than there was when he avowed his Christian faith and was discovered to be a regular churchgoer who took communion and sang the hymns loudly. He never advertised. But for him it was essential that one know who one is and be who one is. Yet, he did not confuse what one is as a person with what one is as a poet.

A familiar way of perceiving literature, especially modern literature, is to consider the problematic relation, the distinction, the tension between person and poet. Ellmann's study of Yeats is an admirable instance of the method, one that explores an ambiguity in the very word "person," implying both an essential being and a mask. No recent writer has been more aware of the problem than Auden. As a private person—at least, as a middle-aged man in America—he was reasonably open: he would no more try to disguise his sexual inclination than he would announce to the newspapers and television stations that he had "come out of the closet," and he would no more hide his Christian belief from friends Jewish or Calvinist, atheist or agnostic, than he would allow himself to be photographed at prayer. As a critic he insisted that poetic truth is literally untrue, that the direct expression of deep personal feeling cannot succeed. What of Auden as a poet?

Hopkins, person and poet, was an especially interesting figure for him. Like Auden, he was homosexual. Like Auden, he was a catholic Christian. In Hopkins' poetry the erotic feeling finds only indirect expression; religious devotion often appears in the direct form of spiritual autobiography. Not all the first-person-singular verse is truly that: "The Windhover" moves at once from "I," the viewer whose heart stirs, to the object of vision; and the "I" becomes hardly more than a means to make the reader see. But in the first part of the "Deutschland," in at least some of the devotional verse, and in the later dark poems, the so-called terrible sonnets, Hopkins carries a Victorian tendency toward nervous self-revelation even further than Tennyson has. These are the passages and poems that made Auden uneasy.

Uneasy, certainly, because of a strong personal concern for reticence, not only a critical theory as to the impersonality of successful art—that theory trace-able from Keats through Eliot. (This modern critical tendency, by the way, is suggested by the names under which writers have published their work: the early William Butler Yeats soon became W. B. Yeats, and readers have not been on first-name terms with T. E. Hulme, I. A. Richards, T. S. Eliot, *or* Auden.) Like Arnold and Eliot, Auden wanted no biography to be written and wanted none of his personal correspondence to be published. With Auden, this was clearly a matter not of shame but rather of style.

The strategies, like most poetic strategies, were difficult. To write with conviction and to feign, to be morally true and yet true to one's art, which means artifice, is difficult. The younger Auden often generalized on the condition of humanity, giving sharp point to his moral comment by bringing in the topical and the metaphorical rather than a largely fictionalized self. If there is a self in his earlier verse, it is likely to be a clownish figure who merges with the idea of fallen, foolish, and yet infinitely significant Man—the central figure of Christian comedy, which Dante introduced as himself. Auden's commitment to Christian comedy, in both the large literary sense and the narrow popular sense, leads to what some critics, especially Leavis' more humorless followers, condemn as wisecracking; for Auden, as a Christian poet, every person including the speaker in a poem—and of course himself outside the poem—is both silly and of cosmic worth, and so there can be no total distinction between the flippant and the absolutely serious. When, later, he wrote love poetry, that too moved from the particular persons and emotions to a sense of the human predicament. Auden's finest love poem, "Lay Your Sleeping Head, My Love" (formally entitled "Lullaby"), which was in fact written for a particular young man, although the reader cannot know that, is about the paradoxical reality of love in a radically imperfect world. It is even less biographically specific than "Dover Beach."

The strategies a poet conventionally follows in dramatic and narrative works allow him more easily to be reticent. So Browning, stung by John Stuart Mill's remarks on the "morbid self-consciousness" of *Pauline*, turned to monologue. So Auden wrote plays, oratorios, ballads, verse stories. But, from the beginning of his career, it was evident to critics and other readers that his was a lyric voice, both musical and individually expressive. His favorite way of reconciling lyricism and a remarkable personality with the generalizing mind and with his reticence was to shift poetic focus from person to place: either to the actual or to metaphorical city and countryside. He had a strong sense of place and loved maps and geographical description (a fact that had a good deal to do with his delight in the fiction of Tolkien). His sense of geographical place, furthermore, became a trope for his sense of social place: he was always a democrat but never a leveler, for he believed in the necessity for, and respected the persons in, various levels of society, insisting that to know who you are means to know your place. A place, then, could be a social situation for him, or even a person in a situation, just as the dying Yeats in Auden's elegy is a disordered city.

For Auden the out-of-doors, too, takes on human significance while it remains real and external in a more social and perhaps a more specific sense than it does for the early Romantics. "Paysage moralisé" makes the point, but it is more evident and possibly more effective in the collection of geographical poems called *Bucolics*. These poems on landscape manage to convey an emotional reality, that of his inner experience, by focusing on objects; and this, too, is a successful strategy. Finally, in some very late poems, Auden speaks directly, almost for the first time, about his own life. But he does so, characteristically, by indirection, by describing the house where he lives. About love secular and divine he remains reticent.

Hopkins' apparent lack of reticence was something that Auden could account for, no matter how ill at ease it made him, largely by recalling that Hopkins' intensely personal poems were sent to friends and not published in his lifetime. What is more, as Auden said, Hopkins had virtually no friends to whom he could express his innermost feelings except in verse. "To seem the stranger lies my lot, my life," the converted, alienated poet wrote, thinking of his closest friends and family. Auden, too, like Hopkins, felt the talented person's urge to "express himself" (he knew it was the worst thing a would-be poet could attempt to do): to and for *his* friends he wrote not only verse epistles and at least one verse parody of a pornographic story but also love letters and comments on his religious faith (for instance, that he considered the doctrine of the Atonement as officially preached a morally offensive idea). But, unlike Hopkins, he was a publishing poet and a public figure.

In the elegy on Yeats, whom he disliked as a man, Auden declares that the dead poet has become his poems. This is what, for the world at large, he wanted to do: to be known not as a man bad or good but as poems bad or good—for the world at large, but not for those he loved personally. Auden once spoke in an offhand way of cannibalism: he said he wished he could be, after his death, quite literally eaten by his friends. He wanted to remain a part of them, not only as a poet, but as a public man. A quite early poem, "Who's Who," admits the actual identity of reticent public person and passionate private being. "Some of the last researchers even write/Love made him weep his pints like you and me." The poem ends with a wry comment: the one this great man loved answered some of his letters "but kept none." Probably all of Wystan Auden's letters of the past three decades have been kept. He wrote a good many, some of them with the direction, "This is for you alone," and the request that they be shown to nobody else. If those for whom he cared and to whom he wrote honor his wishes, the private letters—unlike those of Hopkins—will not be published.

He admitted that he was shockingly disorderly in everything—his clothes, his household, sometimes in his behavior (if "stood up" or denied a glass of beer with his lunch)—everything except his poetry. His reticence was meant not simply to protect his privacy but to protect this ordered self.

JOHN BAYLEY

Only Critics Can't Play

Even more than with most poets there is a gap between Auden and his critics, or rather between the way his poetry works and the things that we find to say about it. From its earliest beginnings the iconography of his poetry has always depended on a seeming system of correspondences – abounding intellect, theory and appetite for metaphysical and scientific systems transforming themselves in and through the poetic scene into fantasy and play, the fashionable and the sociable. But to get inside the poetry by winding it back, as it were, into this world of theory and abstraction, does not help.

For the fact is that Auden's poetry can no more be "serious" than life can be, and thus it resembles life far more than its author thought it ought to, or could. There is no need to labour Auden's almost obsessional preoccupation with the difference between art and life "we *may* write, we *must* live," and his stress on the divided self of the artist, the man who must sit apart, wrestling with the glum realities of existence, while the poet can enjoy himself as he pleases, giving tight-lipped orders to imaginary underlings (his crafts and vocabularies), arranging sensational displays and explosions and "spending, what would otherwise be a very boring evening indeed, planning how to seize the post office on the other side of the river." But in fact, just as the formidably "with it" iconography of his poetry melts into its social and performing being, so its "contraptive" aspect, its "halcyon structures," bring us by the best route into the middle of the ordinary human scene, the lives that poets and ourselves have to lead. Yeats wrote, "in dreams begin responsibilities." In spite of Auden's specific denial that life is in any sense a game, there is no doubt that in his poetry morality begins in the games of fantasy.

This is as much as to say that Auden's poetry, like that of other great poets, not only *is* a world but joins on at every point to the open world – the

From *W. H. Auden: A Tribute*. Copyright © 1974, 1975 by George Weidenfeld and Nicolson, Ltd.

civitas or *res publica* — in which the literate and responsive are dwelling or attempting to dwell. The point was admirably made by John Fuller in his *Reader's
Guide*, when he stressed the comprehensiveness of the Auden microcosm; and
the same emphasis is given in two very recent American academic studies —
Frederick Buell's *Auden as a Social Poet* and Richard Johnson's long essay called
Man's Place, which explores Auden's anthropomorphization of the world of
nature. Both are scholarly attempts to integrate the Auden canon, demonstrate
the processes of development and assess comparative achievement. To these
one might add François Duchene's *The Case of the Helmeted Airman*, which,
in spite of an appalling misquotation in the actual epigraph of the first two
lines of "Consider this and in our time," has some pertinent things to say about
the change in poetic attack and meaning which began in *New Year Letter*.

Yet since in order to make their critical points they have to take the poetry
seriously, these, with other critics, are bound to remain outside the curiously
intimate and Alice-in-Wonderland world of its logic and impact. And I can
think of no other poet in whose case this particular phenomenon is so marked.
Keats is perhaps the nearest parallel, for Keats too has critics who concentrate
on what might be called the projectional side of his poetry — the attempt at
working out, or at least the adumbration, of important Romantic myths in
Endymion and *Hyperion* — and are silent on its extraordinarily complex, vulnerable
and in some ways almost embarrassingly sensuous realities. There is nothing
embarrassing about Auden's poetic world, at least not to most people, and
as a poet he has little in common with Keats, except this elusiveness — this
tendency to by-pass in the act what is implied in the project.

Professor Johnson speaks of the "apparent failure" of *The Age of Anxiety*,
"which attempts to treat the phylogenic and ontogenic history of man both
as a series of landscapes and as a series of narratives growing out of a dramatized
situation"; and he concludes that the work "suffers from a confusion of spatial
and temporal form." It shows the way Auden's poetry works that Professor
Johnson follows this up in a footnote with an odd afterthought — that the "allegorical expansion of images and plot requires a more complex metrical unit
than the alliterative line, perhaps the Spenserian stanza?" — and then comes to
the disarming conclusion: "Yet I am far from certain *The Age of Anxiety* is a
failure." Neither am I, but I wholly sympathize with Professor Johnson's feeling
as a critic that it ought to be. His comments reveal, in passing, something of
real interest: the difference in Auden between craftsmanship — always immacu-
late — and the almost slickly throwaway conception, like "phylogenic and ontogenic history," which is indeed in some sense there, but as kind of distraction
and an earnest of magic, the mystic passes of the conjuror's hands.

If *The Age of Anxiety* is, so far from being a failure, among Auden's most
dazzling achievements, it is not because of its powers of "phylogenic and onto-

genic" diagnosis but because Auden hit on a new way of using a metre—and for English alliterating and accentual rhythm a totally unexpected one—to convey dramatically the interplay of daydream, self-deception, and self-awareness. Rosetta's daydreams of English landscapes and country houses are extraordinarily funny and touching—they surprise us into feeling: yes, that is what we feel, our inchoate selfhood is rendered with all the precision, economy, and humour of great art. I want to offer two critical ideas on this aspect of Auden's poetry, particularly in the development of his later poetry.

First, taking a hint from Auden's essays, I would try to join up the family aspect of the poetry with the deliberately monsterish—high camp monsterish—techniques which it latterly cultivated. The directness and common sense of the essays often conceals, I believe, a more subjective relevance than their apparently objective judiciousness would allow. Reflecting on Max Beerbohm in an essay called "One of the Family," Auden wrote:

> The great cultural danger for the English is, to my mind, the tendency to judge the arts by the values appropriate to the conduct of family life. Among brothers and sisters it is becoming to entertain each other with witty remarks, hoaxes, family games and jokes, unbecoming to be solemn, to monopolize the conversation, to talk shop, to create emotional scenes.

This constitutes a real threat, he goes on, to art "which cannot be governed by the rules of social amenity." Nonetheless, in some curious and remarkable way, Auden did so attempt to govern his own art, and increasingly so as time went on. Horace, true, was one of his background models, but another—both for his art and the effect it has on us—was Wagner:

> If we are to get the full benefit of Wagner's opera, we have simultaneously to identify ourselves with what we hear and see on the stage—'Yes, all that is me'—and to distance ourselves from it—'But all that is precisely what I must overcome.' If we can do this then we shall find that, just as Milton was 'of the devil's party without knowing it,' so Wagner, equally unknowingly, was on the side of Reason, Order and Civilization.

Now, of course Auden "knew it" perfectly well; but the point is that he understood that the kind of art he had at his command works on us in extremely oppositional, divided, and devious ways. No one is a better example of the total moral effectiveness of an art which is not only didactic but actually uses didacticism as a plaything, a family gambit. In an essay on Walter De la Mare, whom he deeply admired, he quoted Santayana's comment: "Every artist is a moralist though he needn't preach." Though Auden works on us very differently from Wagner it is equally by remote control. His Wagnerian properties, so to speak, are assertions and arguments, dogmas and distinctions; he seems to harangue and even to hector us by a kind of double bluff: "the more assertive I am the more we both know it is a game, with the rules of the game, and as you come both to perceive the point of rules and to relish them—so you will find yourself on the side of Reason, Order and Civilization. . . ."

And so in spite of his caveat about art and family life, Auden's art really depends on something very like it. But it is, let me hasten to add, family life on an international scale—there is nothing provincial about it. Not only can any number play, provided they have a proper knowledge of and enthusiasm for the English language, but the rules of the game, which are in many ways eccentric, extensible, and unexpected, are actually designed to favour those who have no instinctual or socially conditioned grasp of them. No artist has known so well the secret of mixing what might seem the irredeemably cosy, with what is ageless and confident, with unindulgent authority—the authority of the Maker in the compelling late poem of that title. It would not be out of place to compare this remarkable gift for international intimacy, which Auden as an artist possessed, with the powers of Tolstoy for achieving intimacy with the reader, especially in *Childhood* and in *War and Peace*. In *Boyhood* Tolstoy has a category of persons who *understand*: they may not be very good or clever (indeed Nekhlyudov, the future hero of *Resurrection*, who is both good and clever, is not one of them) but they have instinctively grasped the rules and seen what the game is about. One does not have to be of the English upper-middle class to see the point of Auden's game and to play it with him.

One does, perhaps, have to cherish a dislike for the grosser aspects of modern realism in art. The television play, the modern drama, much modern beat or pop-art verse exert in common a brusque dismissal of anything resembling family understanding, appealing instead to some sort of peer group ethos or, more characteristically, to the solitary ego who has no time for the conventions and rules which are required by a family's need for privacy and forbearance.

This brings me to my second point. It is often said that while early Auden was very influential with other poets, his later poems were usually considered by them (Berryman remarked as much) as isolated, eccentric, fuddy-duddy, and off the beam. Some kind of defensive stance may indeed have been important to such poets, because the continuing potency and authority of Auden affected them more than they knew or were prepared to admit. For Lowell and Berryman turned themselves into American family poets, a different species from the English kind, but none the less owing practically everything to it.

Of course Auden was not in their sense a confessional poet: he never gave us any revelations about his schooldays, sex-life, intimate friendships, or relations with mother and father, all of which, and especially the last, have been Lowell and Berryman's stock-in-trade. So what is Auden's relevance to poets who wish to tell us how things are with themselves, and to reveal the modern dilemma by showing how they personally in their lives have coped or failed to cope with it? I think the short answer is that he continued up to the time of his death to give them a sort of confidence, and a convention to operate in, which, however they modified it, would not have existed without him.

My point is that just as "naturalism" is itself a particular use of selective conventions, so this confessional and personal poetry is really a question of tone, a scale whose whole range Auden explored before it was used by confessional poets for their purposes. Auden created a completely authoritative and idiosyncratic world, loaded in the thirties with private menace and public dread, where the political, social, and personal anxieties of an age were mimed by agents and portents who "talk to your admirers every day."

> By silted harbours, derelict works,
> In strangled orchards and the silent comb
> Where dogs have worried or a bird was shot. . . .

The naturalism here is of course in that mixture of dread and desire which is the almost universal human response to imagined catastrophe, and which makes Auden's poetry of the thirties seem in retrospect as comprehensive and accurate in reflecting its time, as Tennyson's poetry reflected his. From this authority everything in later Auden naturally follows: the method remains the same. As I remarked in a book called *The Romantic Survival*, Auden showed how an intensely private world "could be brought right out into the open, 'eclecticized,' and pegged down to every point of interest in contemporary life." No wonder the influence was so great, not only showing the way to a poet like Berryman but making it difficult for him to escape. (Berryman reminisces in one of the *Love and Fame* poems that he didn't want his poetry to sound like Auden, but in that case what was it to sound like?) There is no doubt that the right use of Auden enabled him to be infinitely contingent and infinitely personal, while at the same time making of the *Dream Songs* a "halcyon structure" which was pure art and not actuality, however totally it appeared to imprison itself in the actual.

Founded as it was on Auden's genius, the paradox is yet not one of which we are conscious in Auden's own poetry. It may be the very completeness of the naturalism in which Berryman set about grounding his personal myth that makes us feel in the end boxed in by him, and that, meticulous as his art's awareness of common and contingent living seems to be, it is not in fact "earthed." By demonstrating its art so openly, on the other hand, and asserting its bonds of metre, its curiosity of phrase and search of vocabulary, Auden's later poetry joins itself effortlessly to life, shows us that it is indeed the game which counts most as the basic human activity, not personal myth or private confession.

A light masterpiece like "The Fall of Rome," in *Nones*, illustrates this as well as anything. Its appeal begins instantly in incantation and image, and goes on to reveal meaning that is both sharp and heavy with common sense and open to public verification—a meaning ultimately outside the poet—in a sense in which the historical fantasies of Lowell's *Notebooks*, for instance, do not strike us as being. The games and devices invented by Auden as a poet are played by us as members of the public, whom they can both delight and instruct, in the daily world and not in the world of poetic vision, the world into which the flower-bells of Rilke "endlessly prolong themselves." Such a world as Rilke's is of course the critics' joy: their exegesis matches his myth in taking itself seriously, and it was because of this that Auden had characteristically mixed feelings about him. Rilke is a poet of the elsewhere, as Lowell and Berryman in their different ways are too; and for Auden, as for Hardy, that was always only a region to be desired and imaged from outside, as happens in the concluding stanza of "The Fall of Rome."

> Altogether elsewhere, vast
> Herds of reindeer move across
> Miles and miles of golden moss,
> Silently and very fast.

LUCY S. McDIARMID AND JOHN McDIARMID

Artifice and Self-Consciousness
in The Sea and the Mirror

Auden's "guess," in 1966, was that *The Orators* sprang from an "unconscious motive...to exorcise certain tendencies in myself by allowing them to run riot." In similar language Auden has written of Goethe:

> The work of a young writer—*Werther* is the classic example—is sometimes a therapeutic act. He finds himself obsessed by certain ways of thinking and feeling of which his instinct tells him he must be rid before he can discover his authentic interests and sympathies, and the only way he can be rid of them forever is by surrendering to them.... Having gotten the poison out of his system, the writer turns to his true interests....

In Auden's own career expulsion of the poison does not occur only in *The Orators*; for him, repudiation of "certain ways of thinking and feeling" is almost a ritual. His long poems, especially, are often exorcisms of the imagination. In *The Age of Anxiety*, a night of intoxicated excursions to idyllic landscapes and remote islands ends with the return to a drab New York in the middle of World War II. Abandoning fantasy, the characters are "reclaimed by the actual world where time is real and in which, therefore, poetry can take no interest." In so recent a poem as "City Without Walls" the same pattern recurs. A neurotic voice drones on in insistent alliterative lines for twenty-one stanzas, rehearsing the horrors of "Megalopolis," before daybreak ushers in the ordinary, a new voice whose "Go to sleep now for God's sake" silences the self-indulgent

From *Contemporary Literature* 16, no. 3 (Summer 1975). Copyright © 1975 by the Board of Regents of the University of Wisconsin System. University of Wisconsin Press, 1975. Originally entitled "Artifice and Self-Consciousness in Auden's *The Sea and the Mirror*."

imagination. After its vision of the nativity *For the Time Being* also lets us down with a thump in reality, "where . . . Newton's mechanics would account for our experience,/And the kitchen table exists because I scrub it."

The Sea and the Mirror is unusual among Auden's poems because it begins with disenchantment. Some "therapeutic act" has preceded the poem. The characters of *The Tempest* appear as they would after Shakespeare's play, and are introduced by a stage manager: we are behind the scenes of the illusion from the start. Of all people, the stage manager is most likely to know that the world of art is only a temporary, artificial suspension of ordinary life:

> The aged catch their breath,
> For the nonchalant couple go
> Waltzing across the tightrope
> As if there were no death . . . .

And Prospero, when he appears, has already decided to dismiss Ariel. Each successive character, in fact, is relieved that he is no longer deluded. As Sebastian says: "I smile because I tremble, glad today/To be ashamed, not anxious, not a dream." Although there is no single questing figure, *The Sea and the Mirror* could be seen as a search for solid ground to end on. Each speaker seems to be saying, "At last! Reality!" The poem consists of a series of endings, or to use Auden's metaphor, attempts to leave a theater. But whereas in *The Orators* and *The Age of Anxiety* the illusion is clearly broken from, the theater left behind once and for all, in *The Sea and the Mirror* substantiality is elusive, and recedes before the speakers as they seem to move closer to it. Deliverance comes only with the acknowledgment that we are always on stage.

The Sea and the Mirror shares its pursuit of the real with its source. Auden's work is subtitled "A Commentary on Shakespeare's *The Tempest*," and perhaps it is best to see its status as derived from that of *The Tempest*'s own self-commentary—Prospero's speeches after the masque ("Our revels now are ended") and after the dramatic action of *The Tempest* ("Now my charms are all o'erthrown"). Both instances of *The Tempest*'s self-reference end on a note of concession, as one world gives way to another. The masque gives way to the greater substantiality of the world of conspiracies and murders, as that world will itself some day "Dissolve/And . . . leave not a wrack behind." The distancing of the masque caused by the intrusion of Caliban's plot provides the occasion for the distancing of life. In the epilogue the real world's dependent position mirrors art's, and the audience's Prospero's: "As you from crimes would pardoned be,/Let your indulgence set me free." Each speech places the play and, by analogy, life, in a series of worlds all alike conceding their insubstantiality and dependence on the next.

The Tempest is distanced by *The Sea and the Mirror* as the masque was by Prospero's speech, but of course *The Sea and the Mirror* is no less poetry itself than "Our revels now are ended." That is, the distancing *The Sea and the Mirror* provides does not make it "life" to *The Tempest*'s "art." Rather, the relation suggests, like Prospero's speeches, a greater consciousness of artificiality: the movement toward truth is actually the movement toward greater awareness of artifice. If we assume the whole poem to be a commentary on a previous performance of *The Tempest*, then each of the three main sections—"Prospero to Ariel," "The Supporting Cast," and "Caliban to the Audience"—is simultaneously more real and yet more artificial than that which preceded it. The only thing that is real, according to *The Sea and the Mirror*, is our own artificiality—"our incorrigible staginess," Caliban calls it.

Each section acts as a *Verfremdungseffekt* [alienation effect] for the previous ones, distancing successively *The Tempest*, Prospero, Antonio, and the beginning of Caliban's speech. The estranging of one section by the next is subtlest in the shifts of setting that occur, yet the changing context of *The Sea and the Mirror* is one of its most important features. Monroe Spears writes, "There is the implicit setting of a theater, after a performance of *The Tempest*," and John Blair, "The poem takes place in no space." Although before the main body of *The Sea and the Mirror* there is a brief preface spoken by "The Stage Manager to the Critics," he does not locate himself in space, and he does not literally "introduce" Prospero. A Roman numeral I comes between the "Preface" and "Prospero to Ariel" to separate the two speakers and their worlds. There is no single answer to the question, where are these people, because each one sees himself, and therefore *The Tempest*, in different ways.

Prospero, the first speaker, seems to be beginning where Shakespeare left off. He is addressing Ariel, and begins, "Stay with me, Ariel, while I pack," so one assumes he is in his cell on the island. One of his last lines—"Here comes Gonzalo/With a solemn face to fetch me"—implies that the whole world of the last pages of Shakespeare's play is still around him. Prospero asserts a number of times that over the years on the island he has acquired self-knowledge, and speaks in sadder-but-wiser tones:

> Now, Ariel, I am that I am, your late and lonely master
> > Who knows what magic is;—the power to enchant
> That comes from disillusion.

His previous life is a "dream" from which he is now waking. But in spite of his new understanding, Prospero's "space" is not significantly different from that of *The Tempest*. Auden's Prospero differentiates himself chronologically, but not ontologically, from Shakespeare's. *The Tempest* for Prospero is merely the past. The segment of his life recorded in *The Tempest* covers what Prospero might call his "escapist" period, but it is nonetheless on a continuum with the present. He does not see the life he is entering as different in status from the life he is leaving.

In the first speech of "The Supporting Cast, Sotto Voce," Antonio refers to sails, passengers, and crew, and sees the other characters "Dotted about the deck," so he is apparently on the ship going back to Italy. His world is not part of Shakespeare's play but exists through an imaginative extension of that world. Prospero had said, "I'll promise you calm seas, auspicious gales," and Antonio begins, "As. . .the sky is auspicious and the sea/Calm as a clock, we can all go home again." From Antonio's greater physical distance, *The Tempest* looks somewhat insubstantial. Antonio's first tercet, with its reference to Circe ("As all the pigs have turned back into men,") casts doubt on the nature of events at the end of *The Tempest*. There is something witchy about Prospero, and although the magical high jinks are supposed to be over, the last scene was suspiciously artificial. In fact, Antonio's language imputes to *The Tempest* the status of a work of art. What is really art has, he thinks, been disguising itself as life:

> it undoubtedly looks as if we
> Could take life as easily now as tales
> Write ever-after. . . .

Miranda and Ferdinand seem to Antonio about as lifelike as lovers on a postcard: "Two heads silhouetted against the sails—And kissing, of course." He goes through the cast by type—"The lean Fool. . . the dear old butler"—and analyzes *The Tempest* with the aesthetic detachment of a critic:

> the royal passengers [are] quite as good
> As rustics, perhaps better, for they mean
>
> What they say, without, as a rustic would,
> Casting reflections on the courtly crew.

Prospero is merely the arranger of a *nature morte* ("Your grouping could not be more effective,") and the finale of *The Tempest* is the fragile, temporary effect of a spell: "given a few/Incomplete objects and a nice warm day,/What a lot a little music can do."

As *The Tempest* begins to seem like a painting, a *tableau vivant*, or even a Shakespearean play, it recedes from the world of *The Sea and the Mirror*. Like Prospero in his farewell to Ariel, Antonio is saying, "That wasn't real, this is." Although Auden's Prospero professes to feel as if he were awake after a dream, and sober after drink, the world he imagines around him is still that of the play; he has not even left the island, but is still packing his bags and chatting with Ariel. Antonio never gives a name or status to *The Tempest*'s world but the names implied by his images—*tableau vivant*, magical spell, fairy tale—all emphasize its artificiality. Whatever it is, it is not life.

Caliban gives this artificial status a name—*The Tempest* is a play. More than suspiciously fictive or masquerading as life, *The Tempest* was a work of art from start to finish. His speech is entitled, "Caliban to the Audience," so the status of *The Tempest*, as well as his "space," is implicit in the title. Now, at any rate, we are in a theater after a performance of *The Tempest*. The audience, "having dismissed [their] hired impersonators," are faced with someone who does not impersonate but appears as his real self. Caliban presents himself as life after art. Caliban's understanding of his context, or "space," is the third stage in what we can now see as a progression defined by increasing awareness of the fictive status of *The Tempest*. In the final paragraphs of his speech Caliban will come to see his own status, too, as artificial.

There is a progressive self-consciousness in the style of the three main sections that works in tandem with the growing sense of artificiality. Prospero's style is as little conscious of itself as a style as he is aware of any touch of artifice in *The Tempest*. Style and setting both glide unnoticeably into the "real." Casual and colloquial, the speech is full of such ordinary phrases as, "Stay with me," "Thanks to your service," "I don't know," and "To you that doesn't matter." The meter, syllabic verse of thirteen and eleven syllables alternately, is as unobtrusive as the language. In a sentence like, "So at last I can really believe I shall die," the diction and cadences of the spoken language fit easily into the meter. Although a reader is of course aware that this is not an exact transcript of spontaneous speech, the conversational tone and frequent reminders of Ariel's listening presence ("You, I suppose...") do give the impression that we are overhearing whatever Prospero has to say to Ariel.

Antonio, by contrast, makes himself conspicuous through his style. His voice dominates the second part of *The Sea and the Mirror*. "The Supporting Cast, Sotto Voce" consists of ten speeches by the rest of the cast as they evaluate their particular disenchantments. With the exception of Antonio, all are grateful for the awakening Prospero has sponsored. Antonio darts out from hiding and inserts himself in the lulls between their eloquent and sincere speeches to sing a mocking refrain. His stanzas—symmetrical in their form and in their variations—are like flourishes, waves of a plumed cap, that call attention to the speaker. Each stanza echoes the lyric it follows only to pervert its imagery and mock its sincerity. After Ferdinand's love sonnet, for instance, comes the response:

> One bed is empty, Prospero,
>   My person is my own;
> Hot Ferdinand will never know
> The flame with which Antonio
>   Burns in the dark alone.

Alonso's discussion of kingship and government is countered by the lines:

> One crown is lacking, Prospero,
>   My empire is my own;
> Dying Alonso does not know
> The diadem Antonio
>   Wears in his world alone.

And so for ten stanzas Antonio tells us, "My will is all my own," "My person is my own," "My nature/language/audience/empire/compass/conscience/humor/magic is my own." Antonio is the source of a pattern so obtrusive we begin to see the "supporting cast" as more subject to Antonio's spell than Prospero's.

Just as Antonio was sufficiently aware of artifice in *The Tempest* to see the play as a tale or a picture, so he speaks in a style conscious of itself as a style: each stanza is perfect for its place, specially contrived to follow a certain lyric, and all repeat the identical five-line form. (The final stanza has one extra line, as if Antonio were penning an extra swirl under his signature.) The style of the stanzas, with their insistent, identical rhymes and their circumambulating pattern, is distinctly artificial. Prospero's lines might seem to suggest overheard speech, but Antonio's stanzas are consciously crafted poetry. Although they are addressed to Prospero, his presence is not suggested in this part as Ariel's was in the first section; *we* are Antonio's real audience. In the pattern of repetitions with variations set up by the refrain there is a nascent awareness of an audience to appreciate the craftsmanship. This awareness, however, does not break through the surface until the third part of *The Sea and the Mirror*.

Antonio may be a dashing villain with wavy mustachios, lurking in corners and popping out, conscious of his kinship with Richard and Edmund, but Caliban outdoes him in "staginess." With Caliban, the style of *The Sea and the Mirror* recedes even further from some conversational norm. He is, of course, *on* a stage, like a performer, while Antonio is only on the boat going home. Caliban is histrionic, florid, and extreme. He enters like a soft-shoe dancer waving his boater and twirling his cane. His smile—and he is grinning hard— has two layers, one for the audience and one for himself. As a performer he must smile to entertain, but as a stylist he is conscious of his own artifice and enjoys it. His sentences are full of superfluous phrases which add no nuances of meaning but serve only to display the performer's agility. He comes onstage acutely conscious of his audience. Here is part of his first sentence:

> If now, having dismissed your hired impersonators with verdicts ranging from the laudatory orchid to the digusted and disgusting egg, you ask, and, of course, notwithstanding the conscious fact of his irrevocable absence, you instinctively *do* ask for our so good, so great, so dead author to stand before the finally lowered curtain and take his shyly responsible bow for this, his latest, ripest, production, it is I—my reluctance is, I can assure you, co-equal with your dismay—who will always loom thus wretchedly into your confused picture, for. . . .

Caliban may not be a hired impersonator, but he is certainly a voluntary one. After distinguishing himself from actors, he proceeds to take on a series of roles (the audience, Shakespeare, himself), announcing after the first that he is returning for the moment to his "officially natural role." The phrase is an oxymoron—does Caliban mean that "officially" his role is to be "natural"? Is he still Shakespeare's Caliban, who allegorically represents "nature" to Ariel's "art"? Or does he mean that he has officially—i.e., for the sake of his audience—a "natural" role, a basic, unartificial self, to which he will return between impersonations? Either way, the word "natural" still refers to something artificial. If the self to which he returns is merely a role, there is no "natural" self, but only a series of artificial ones. Caliban is conscious that even his "official" self is a "stagy" one, that while he may be removing one hat with the right hand and slowly putting on the next with his left, he is never bare-headed.

This "stagy" presentation, a sequence of "acts" rather than a single speech, is suggestive of a progression in the poem's ideas. If all modes of personation are equally artificial, there is no such thing as an objectively real self. With each successive section of *The Sea and the Mirror*, more of life comes to be seen as subjective. A gradual shift of focus away from objective reality is implicit in the change of setting from island to stage, and the change of style from colloquial to artificial. The increasing complexity of structure in the various sections—from Prospero's casual musings with their brief lyric interruptions to Caliban's "baroque profusion of distinctions and elaborations" is evidence of the will's growing readiness to choose, to determine, and to create its world. As the poem develops, the characters' beliefs about the relative strengths of objective and subjective reality shift from Prospero's deterministic view of the world to Caliban's existentialism. Viewing Prospero and Antonio at first as characters in a play, Caliban clings to a belief in his own reality. Only at the very end, in a moment of vision and humility, does Caliban come to consider himself just as artificial as the others, and acknowledges with confessional relief his "incorrigible staginess."

The division of life into mutually incompatible escapist and naturalistic realms is implicit in Prospero's chief linguistic habit, the pairing of opposites. The balance of clauses in his second sentence – "share my resigning thoughts/As you have served my revelling wishes" – is an emblem of the way Prospero thinks. A few lines later his syntax and cadences make the same contrast between a world where revelling is the predominant mood and wishing the customary form of mental activity, and one where all thought is sober: "Ages to you of song and daring, and to me/Briefly Milan, then earth." The prevalence of pairs – shadow/substance, dream/wake, drunk/sober, moonshine/daylight, smooth song/rough world – suggests that Prospero's world, like his language, is polarized. The lyrics Prospero bursts into at intervals during his speech – "Could he but once see Nature," "Sing first that green remote Cockaigne," and "Sing, Ariel, sing" – are another instance of the separation of "song" from "thought," as if the two modes were the "songs of Apollo" and the harsh "words of Mercury."

In Prospero's scheme of things Milan is objective reality, immutable fact – a world in which no human choice or act of will can be effectual. Trapped in this prison, the child Prospero felt like a "sobbing dwarf/Whom giants served only as they pleased." The grotesque extremes of this vision of the relation between parent and child imply a world defined by its power to oppress. Only in magic, which the child practiced "To ride away from a father's imperfect justice," were choices possible. Prospero's exile on the island was a brief sojourn in a fantasy land of freedom. All the subjective, world-creating activities associated with the island – magic, art, language – seem incompatible with a return to Milan: "But now all these heavy books are no use to me any more, for/Where I go words carry no weight." When Prospero thinks of schooling himself for the real world's suffering, he sees speech as his biggest temptation:

> When the servants settle me into a chair
> In some well-sheltered corner of the garden,
> And arrange my muffler and rugs, shall I ever be able
> To stop myself from telling them what I am doing, –
> Sailing alone, out over seventy thousand fathoms –?
> Yet if I speak, I shall sink without a sound
> Into unmeaning abysses. Can I learn to suffer
> Without saying something ironic or funny
> On suffering? I never suspected the way of truth

> Was a way of silence where affectionate chat
> Is but a robber's ambush and even good music
> In shocking taste. . . .

Music, "affectionate chat," and "saying something ironic or funny/On suffering" are all detours from the silent, stoic "way of truth." His speech itself is a last indulgence, a "something ironic or funny/On suffering" before the passive suffering begins.

Although Prospero claims to have recognized that art offers us an "echo" and a "mirror," his speech ends in "song" rather than "thought," and the lyric itself belies the recognition. Prospero is still thinking in the same polarities as he imagines Ariel

> Entrancing, rebuking
> The raging heart
> With a smoother song
> Than this rough world. . . .

Art is still a kind of lullaby for Prospero, and life unpleasant. His last words are a plea for Ariel to sing to him as "Trembling he takes/The silent passage/Into discomfort."

In Part II, as I mentioned above, the grateful comments of the "Supporting Cast" are countered by Antonio's denials: "I am I, Antonio,/By choice myself alone." More self-conscious than Prospero, Antonio is also conscious, as Prospero is not, of the power of choice in the world, his ability to affect if not to control reality:

> To wear my fashion, whatever you wear
> Is a magic robe; while I stand outside
> Your circle, the will to charm is still there.
> As I exist so you shall be denied. . . .

The antiphonal pattern of speeches and stanzas demonstrates formally the intractability of will which Antonio's opening speech states explicitly. There are two structures in tension in "The Supporting Cast," one the circular dance of Prospero's plan, the other the dance broken by Antonio's refusal to join. The cast all acknowledge themselves to have been the swaggering "extravagant children" Prospero called them, and in appropriate poetic forms describe their joy at having "received a second life." Miranda says, "we/Are linked as children in a circle dancing," and without Antonio's speech or refrains the characters form such a pattern, linked through the marriage of the first and last, Ferdinand and Miranda. The speeches pair off symmetrically, making partners of the two lovers, the two drunkards, the false and true courtiers, and the two sets of friends. The hinge of the symmetrical pairs is the king Alonso, whose speech is about the "tightrope" or middle way between the sea and the desert, the "temperate city" precariously balanced between opposite extremes:

2 Ferdinand	Miranda	10
3 Stephano	Trinculo	9
4 Gonzalo	Sebastian	8
5 Adrian and Francisco	Master and Boatswain	7
6 Alonso		

(Numbers indicate the order of the speeches; Antonio's is first.)

Without Antonio, Part II would look like the dance Miranda describes, the circle of perfection, with the "children" linked together by Prospero's benevolent manipulations. Antonio's speech, coming first, ruins the geometric pattern; as he says, "I stand outside/Your circle." The stanzas which follow each of the nine speeches virtually unlink them, forming a counterspell to undo Prospero's magic. Every success of Prospero's—for instance, Sebastian's "I smile because I tremble, glad today/To be ashamed, not anxious, not a dream"—is countered by Antonio's equal and opposite verbal force. Auden does not have Antonio assert his will through silence, as Shakespeare did. In *The Sea and the Mirror*, the "way of silence" is Prospero's submissive way of truth; the way of choice is a way of speech.

If the power of speech is related to the power of will, then Caliban is living in a world of great freedom, since his address to the audience is half again as long as the rest of the work. From the vantage of his speech, patterns in the whole work can be seen which could only be dimly apprehended before. This most self-conscious section of the poem uses terms—audience, role, performance—which serve to clarify and explain the form of the whole poem. For instance, the awareness of an audience which was suggested by Antonio's language, with its flourishes and arabesques, is much stronger in the third section, since Caliban is on a stage.

In a similar way, the self-reflectiveness is very apparent in the third section, since that section reflects the whole poem in miniature. The structure of Caliban's speech, with its three "roles" parallel to the poem's three main sections in their growing subjectivity and self-consciousness, reveals the latent self-reflection in "The Supporting Cast." The shadowy presence of Prospero's choreography is obscured by Antonio's stanzas, but it is there *in potentia*. In its third section *The Sea and the Mirror* is so self-conscious that it refers almost exclusively to itself, but that self-reference is part of the poem's development. The opinions dramatized in the "roles" are seen as inadequate, even as Antonio deprecates

Prospero's achievement. In presenting even his own opinions as a role parallel to the other two Caliban reaches the ultimate degree of self-consciousness. *The Sea and the Mirror* follows to its logical conclusion the structure suggested by its conception: it is a work of art reflecting another work of art, and as it progresses it turns inward and reflects itself more and more. The "baroque profusion" of its final section is not random imaginative excess but an intricately executed pattern of accumulating subjectivity.

The audience whose "echo" Caliban speaks in his first role is like the one Brecht so disparagingly describes: "They stare at the stage as if spellbound." The magical term is apt, because the audience's life, like Prospero's, is polarized into golden and drab worlds. Its own daily life the audience describes as "the wearily historic, the dingily geographic, the dully drearily sensible," in wearily alliterated phrases. Art, like Prospero's island, is a realm of beauty and "freedom without anxiety," utterly separate from the "shambling slovenly makeshift" world. The "native Muse" is beautiful precisely because she is "other":

> We most emphatically do *not* ask that she should speak to us, or
> try to understand us; on the contrary our one desire has always
> been that she should preserve forever her old high strangeness, for
> what delights us about her world is just that it neither is nor possibly
> could become one in which we could breathe or behave. . . .

Hungry for its few glimpses of beauty, the audience is naturally indignant with Shakespeare for including "the absolutely natural . . . utterly negative" in *The Tempest*. It complains to him histrionically that the Muse's soirées have been spoiled:

> How *could* you, you who are one of the oldest habitués at these
> delightful functions . . . be guilty of the incredible unpardonable
> treachery of bringing along the one creature . . . she is not at any
> hour of the day or night at home to . . . .

The audience's extended social metaphor and fussy style—replete with Gallicisms and italicized phrases—expose its "role" as caricature, ridiculing the notion of a "real" life. Like Prospero, the audience devotes its final thoughts to Ariel, but in quite a different vein. We do not laugh when Prospero asks Ariel, the "unanxious one," to sing to him as he enters the world of discomfort; but when the audience reacts in horror at the thought that Ariel has not been confined at the end of the play we see through their indignant "bourgeois" reaction to Caliban's glee:

> We want no Ariel here, breaking down our picket fences in the
> name of fraternity, seducing our wives in the name of romance,

and robbing us of our sacred pecuniary deposits in the name of justice.

Through Caliban's sophistication the view which Prospero expressed in nostalgic sincerity is distorted into parody.

In his second "role" Caliban delivers "a special message" from Shakespeare to budding magicians. Like "The Supporting Cast," the message is constructed as a confrontation between choice and limitation. As a counter-manipulator, Antonio is limited by Prospero just as Prospero is limited by him. Antonio can "choose to wear [my] fashion," but not much more. The idea of choice is just being born in that section, and it is not yet powerful. Antonio's limitation is suggested by his reiteration—he can only say the same thing over and over again. The artist in Shakespeare's message can choose a lot more, and Caliban emphasizes choice in his first sentence: "So . . . you have decided on the conjurer's profession." The message is a fable in which an Everyartist has "heard imprisoned Ariel call for help," liberated him, and launched a promising career. He reaches a pitch of success but finally, tired of giving orders to Ariel, peremptorily frees him. Before his very eyes, refusing to go away, Ariel turns into Caliban, and the artist is forced to confront "a gibbering fist-clenched creature with which you are all too unfamiliar . . . the only subject that you have, who is not a dream amenable to magic but the all too solid flesh you must acknowledge as your own." Shakespeare's message ends on a note of admonition: Caliban and the artist must accept one another's necessary presence, keeping their "hopes for the future, within moderate, very moderate, limits."

The artist has complete freedom—up to a point. One aspect of life remains "not . . . amenable to magic," i.e. choice: the flesh. Flesh remains an uncontrolled alien outside of the domain of the spirit. Shakespeare, in Auden's opinion, still believed in some degree of determinism. In the next role, Caliban addresses the audience "on behalf of Ariel and myself," and the combination suggests a break with the notion that the fleshly Caliban is of a different ontological order than the spiritual Ariel. The two characters, though opposites, are now two aspects of the same realm.

Caliban presents his and Ariel's opinions in conscious parallel with the two previous roles. The third part of his speech is simultaneously itself and a reflection of itself; that is, it is both part of the third section of *The Sea and the Mirror*, and a reflection of that third section, as the other two roles reflect Parts I and II. The self-conscious presentation of the self is appropriate to this role's conception of living as role-playing. The waking to consciousness which is occurring as the poem develops is seen here as a "fall" from a fluid state into a condition of distinctions between fantasy self and real self, role and identity. The speech at this point is virtually explaining its own method: commentary has become self-commentary. Resistance to the utter subjectivity now implied takes the form of nostalgia, and this stage is characterized as a *loss of unawareness*:

> All your clamour signifies is this: that your first big crisis, the breaking
> of the childish spell in which, so long as it enclosed you, there was,
> for you, no mirror, no magic, for everything that happened was
> a miracle—it was just as extraordinary for a chair to be a chair as
> for it to turn into a horse; it was no more absurd that the girding
> on of coal-scuttle and poker should transform you into noble Hector
> than that you should have a father and mother who called you
> Tommy—and it was therefore only necessary for you to presuppose
> one genius, one unrivalled I to wish these wonders in all their endless
> plenitude and novelty to be, is, in relation to your present, behind,
> that your singular transparent globes of enchantment have shattered
> one by one, and you have now all come together in the larger colder
> emptier room on this side of the mirror which *does* force your eyes
> to . . . reckon with the two of us . . .

The clause dependent on the pronoun "which" is suspended in time, like childhood, for almost as long as the syntax can bear, though its own dependence as well as the grammatical necessity of a verb to follow "crisis" doom it to death from the start. The most fragile and vulnerable illusions of childhood—when, for Wordsworth, "the earth and every common sight/To me did seem apparalled in celestial light,/The glory and the freshness of a dream"—are carefully protected between dashes ("it was just as extraordinary . . .") within a dependent clause from the brutal realities of the indicative voice. After the suspension the words of the clause strain at the syntax before "is" breaks in with the unalterable facts of existence.

In a way, Caliban's central expository sentence recapitulates the same dis-enchantment that Auden is turning over in his mind in the whole poem—the breaking of the magic spell, the end of the play, the fall into self-conscious awareness. Plays end in infinite regress in *The Sea and the Mirror*: the whole poem follows some hypothetical performance of *The Tempest*; Caliban faces the audience after his performance in it; here, in simile, an audience faces Caliban and Ariel; and in the last pages of Caliban's speech, he and Ariel face themselves. The "larger colder emptier room" is literally where Caliban's audience is as it hears him speak, but the description is only a metaphorical explanation of their fallen state.

In the previous role Caliban and Ariel were servants to a master artist, and his decisions determined the nature of his life as well as his career. Here also they receive "fatal foolish commands," but what is determined is not merely the self but the world; we are artists not merely of our lives but of the whole context which surrounds us. This responsibility is seen as the beginning of a journey manifestly unlike the one Prospero mentioned. The "Journey of Life" requires no silent stoic submissiveness but a recognition of "three or four decisive instants"; the "way of truth" is a way of choices.

"Stagestruck" at all the possibilities before them, the members of the audience may become dissatisfied with their "minor roles" and attempt to avoid the complexities of a world whose nature is entirely subjective. They may, on the one hand, decide to try to put Caliban "in charge" and beg for release into the state Auden has called a "Hell of the Pure Deed." Longing for the simplicities of childhood, they will find themselves only in a "secular stagnation." Alternately those who want to live in a world beyond choice rather than before it will, according to Caliban, put Ariel in charge. Longing to be delivered from "this hell of inert and ailing matter," they create an equal and opposite hell of "the Pure Word," where "Everything suggests Mind." Those who insist on refusing the responsibility of their subjectivity get a world in which they are imprisoned rather than free.

After a final admonition to the audience, Caliban's efforts collapse in disgust and contempt, and he wishes he had had "the futile honour of addressing the blind and the deaf." The tone really reflects Caliban's frustrations with himself; the third role represented his own opinions, and he has nowhere to go. In a kind of hell himself, Caliban is not aware of the full implication of his own phrase, "officially natural role." His hell is the same as Prospero's and Antonio's, belief in one's own reality. Although he danced jauntily onto the stage with a sophisticated consciousness of his own style, he saw himself nevertheless as replacing "impersonators." They were art, he was life.

Then, in a quantum leap in consciousness of artificiality, Caliban distances himself from his own speech, comparing his function to a dramatist's and, implicitly, his remarks to a play. Although this is only an intensification of the movement we have seen all along, it is a turning point, because it is the first step toward acknowledging what Auden calls the "unnecessary" status of our lives. In seeing the remarks he had earlier contrasted with the speech of "impersonators" as themselves a play, Caliban recognizes that nothing is absolute; that in an infinite series of distancings all life could be seen as art. In a method appropriate to the idea of infinite regress Caliban creates similes within similes, never returning to the plane of the original tenor but entering deeper into the hypothetical worlds of the vehicles. As the status of Caliban's remarks appears to be getting more artificial, it is, paradoxically, getting closer to the truth. Moving through similes within similes, in the most tenuous touch with the world of the work, to the life on the other side of them, Caliban in a state of visionary receptiveness reaches the absolute.

The first simile, in which Caliban compares himself to a dramatist, begins as if it were an epic simile but turns into a narrative, and the world of the vehicle soon acquires independent importance. The original point of tangency is the frustration felt by both Caliban and the dramatist in relation to their audience. Any artist's "aim and justification" is

> to make you unforgettably conscious of the ungarnished offended
> gap between what you so questionably are and what you are
> commanded without any questions to become. . . .

We are "commanded," in the Sermon on the Mount, to become perfect: "Be ye perfect, even as your Father in Heaven is perfect." The artist must indicate our condition of estrangement from the truth and dramatize how "Wholly Other" the truth is. Somehow he must show us that although we are commanded to become perfect, perfection is outside our state of existence altogether. The audience's tendency to "interpret any sight and sound to their advantage" dooms this attempt to failure:

> for the more truthfully [the artist] paints the condition, the less clearly
> can he indicate the truth from which it is estranged, the brighter
> his revelation of the truth in its order, its justice, its joy, the fainter
> shows his picture of your actual condition in all its drabness and
> sham, and. . . the more sharply he defines the estrangement itself. . .
> the more he must strengthen your delusion that an awareness of
> the gap is in itself a bridge. . . .

The audience will resist acknowledging their "unnecessary" status and the distance of the Necessary from their own lives. The only solution for the artist is to

> give all his passion. . . to the task of "doing" life. . . as if it lay in
> *his* power to solve this dilemma—yet of having at the same time
> to hope that some unforeseen mishap will intervene to ruin his effect,
> without, however, obliterating your disappointment, the expectation
> aroused by him that there was an effect to ruin. . . .

If the audience is going to take the play to their own advantage, they will have to be shown how artificial the play is. If the "effect" is "ruined," they will be conscious of it *as* an "effect," a display, a scene—something collapsible. The interruption is not important in itself but in its power to distance what it interrupts. The play's artificiality will be exposed, and the audience will be made conscious of dramatic illusion as an illusion.

Caliban never returns to the tenor of his simile; he never returns, that is, to his own problems with his audience. As he enters deeper into the world of his simile Caliban speculates about the genesis of the "dramatist's" play, wondering what originally inspired his "imitative passion." The language in which Caliban poses his question implies a foreknowledge of the answer, since he is seeking

> some large loose image to define the *original drama* which aroused
> his imitative passion, the first *performance* in which the players were
> their own audience, the worldly *stage* on which their behaving flesh
> was really sore and sorry—for the floods of tears were not caused
> by onions, the deformities and wounds did not come off after a
> good wash. . . .(authors' emphasis)

Caliban cannot even use the word "life" because it sounds too absolute. In this context it might suggest a radical difference in status between whatever aroused the imitative passion and the imitation itself, and by this time Caliban is beginning to realize the utter artificiality of all we consider real.

The answer to Caliban's question must be a simile, since he was looking for an "image," and the world of the final simile becomes the context for the rest of his speech. Like its mother simile, it becomes a narrative, and the original point of comparison is forgotten as the world of the vehicle becomes the world of the speech. The vehicle, or answer—"the greatest grandest opera rendered by a very provincial touring company indeed"—is a performance full of mishaps, an "effect" ruined in every detail:

> Sweating and shivering in our moth-eaten ill-fitting stock costumes
> which with only a change of hat and rearrangement of safety-pins,
> had to do for the *landsknecht* and the Parisian art-student, bumping
> into, now a rippling palace, now a primeval forest full of holes,
> at cross purposes with the scraping bleating orchestra we could
> scarcely hear for half the instruments were missing and the cottage
> piano which was filling-out must have stood for too many years
> in some damp parlour, we floundered on from fiasco to fiasco. . . .

In his description of the "original drama" Caliban appeared to be distinguishing between art and life. He wanted an image for the performance in which tears were *not* caused by onions, deformities and wounds did not come off with washing, suicides could not take curtain calls, and so forth. It is paradoxical that his image for what he so carefully defines as *not* artificial is a play whose artificiality is obtrusively present. The opera is a succession of unforeseen mishaps and illusion-breaking incidents. What is really indisputably real, Caliban is saying, is our artificiality. To see life as a play is the logical next step after seeing one's own speech as a play, and the final stage in the progressive growth of awareness of subjectivity.

Caliban acknowledges his own personal artificiality and, in "contrition and surrender," dives into his own simile. The direction of his movement is reversed from that of his first appearance, when he stood in front of the "finally lowered curtain" and distinguished himself from "hired impersonators": "Our performance—for Ariel and I are, you know this now, just as deeply involved as any of you—. . . has been so indescribably inexcusably awful. . . ." Performing, in the simile, is tantamount to behaving or living, an activity in which Caliban acknowledges his imperfection. If life is also a bungled performance, it is one that constantly reveals its contingent, unnecessary state, that its landscapes are scenery, its clothes costumes, its music cacophony. All its attempts to pass itself off as absolute only show more obviously its insubstantiality.

The actors in the simile accept their failure: they stand "down stage with red faces and no applause," knowing that "no effect. . . came off." They give up when they "see [them]selves as [they] are," performers in a play, people whose lives are unnecessary. They give up assumptions about what performing can do, acknowledging that perfection, or reality, lies outside the zone of their endeavors. Caliban's pace slows, and his sentences become shorter and simpler as the buoyant self-confidence which had propelled his verbosity fails him: "There is nothing to say. There never has been,—and our wills chuck in their hands— There is no way out. There never was. . . ." Acceptance of their imprisonment in contingency opens the way to the truth. Resigning themselves to imperfection, they have a vision of Perfection:

> it is at this moment that for the first time in our lives we hear, not the sounds which, as born actors, we have hitherto condescended to use as an excellent vehicle for displaying our personalities and looks, but the real Word which is our only *raison d'etre*.

When Caliban's style picks up speed again, it has not changed; his "incorrigible staginess" is still there. But now he understands that in spite of estrangement from the truth

> we are blessed by that Wholly Other Life from which we are separated by an essential emphatic gulf of which our contrived fissures of mirror and proscenium arch—we understand them at last—are feebly figurative signs. . . .

In this new understanding of the metaphor of the stage, in which "all our meanings are reversed," Caliban is on stage and the more real world on the other side of the "essential emphatic gulf" is that of the Absolute, the Life which is defined in terms of its "otherness" from our own. As Caliban amplifies his vision in a succession of images, the rhythm of his prose builds up in a crescendo of progressively shorter sentences to the final restored relation. The "perfected Work," at first seen as if hazily from a distance, comes into closer focus:

> it is just here, among the ruins and the bones, that we may rejoice
> in the perfected Work which is not ours. Its great coherences stand
> out through our secular blur in all their overwhelmingly righteous
> obligation; its voice speaks through our muffling banks of artificial
> flowers and unflinchingly delivers its authentic molar pardon; its
> spaces greet us with all their grand old prospect of wonder and width;
> the working charm is the full bloom of the unbothered state; the
> sounded note is the restored relation.

This is the perfect vision of the "greatest grandest opera," whose coherences show off our structures as a "secular blur," and whose blooms expose our flowers as stage properties. At first the coherences "stand out" as if at the end of a broad avenue. Then the voice speaks, audible but still "through" the flowers to us. After the pardon is delivered, forgiving our pride for ever hoping to identify words with the Word, the distance is diminished: the spaces seem to reach out and greet us. The combination of the present participle ("working") and noun signifying a finished product ("bloom") suggests the reconciliation of process and product, performing and perfected Work. The musical note signifies the harmony of the restored relation between fact and value, artificial and real, man and God.

The short poems that stand outside the three main sections of *The Sea and the Mirror*—the Stage Manager's Preface, and Ariel's Postscript—are usually seen as "frames" for the "triptych" between them. One does feel a certain symmetry in their positions, but the lyrics are just as much phases in the poem's development as the three parts themselves. The Preface, the main part of the poem, and the Postscript form a progression crucial to the poem's meaning; they reveal how *The Sea and the Mirror* becomes what it describes.

Like the three inner sections as a whole, each lyric follows the pattern of a movement from art to life to some absolute which makes art and life both look insubstantial. The scene of Prospero's masque in *The Tempest* (IV.i) is perhaps the source of this pattern, as it develops from Ferdinand's association of the masque with paradise, through the disappearance of the masque, and finally the disappearance of life and art both in "Our revels now are ended." Prospero's speech lacks Auden's third term, however: Our "little life is rounded with a sleep," but it is not clear what, if anything, surrounds the sleep or whose dream we are. Auden's versions of this concession end facing heavenward, towards a life real because it is "Wholly Other."

The Stage Manager, for example, begins with Ferdinand's misconception. The circus he describes is a magical world, as suspended in time as the tightrope-walkers in space:

> The aged catch their breath,
> For the nonchalant couple go
> Waltzing across the tightrope
> As if there were no death . . . .

By contrast the audience's world seems more real; after the performance they drop with a jolt into time:

> We are wet with sympathy now;
> Thanks for the evening; but how
> Shall we satisfy when we meet,
> Between Shall-I and I-Will,
> The lion's mouth whose hunger
> No metaphors can fill?

In the last stanza circus and audience, art and life, disappear together, inverted in that leap of understanding which suddenly sees the world as a stage before an audience of angels. Auden does to Shakespeare's lines what the Stage Manager does to the analogy of stage and world—he juggles them around and juxtaposes words and images in an artful rearrangement which shifts our sense of value:

> this world of fact we love
> Is insubstantial stuff:
> All the rest is silence
> On the other side of the wall;
> And the silence ripeness,
> And the ripeness all.

The Stage Manager's final lines constitute a grammatical version of the changing conception of the real. The identity between subject and predicate signified by the verb "to be" fosters a gradual transformation, and the nouns progress successively from "this world" to "insubstantial stuff" to "silence" to "ripeness" to "all." Through a verbal recapitulation of concession, fact disintegrates before the silence which gradually emerges as the source of all value.

This inversion is the same one that Caliban expresses at the end of his speech: "all our meanings are reversed," and the "contrived fissures of mirror and proscenium arch" are understood as "feebly figurative signs" for the gulf between man and God. Caliban's imagery repeats the Stage Manager's, since he finds, on the other side of the proscenium arch, "the full bloom of the un-bothered state." In fact, Caliban makes the discovery which the Stage Manager's speech describes. Prospero's and Antonio's sections, in their expanding awareness, are stages in the approach to this discovery.

Ariel's song is the third and final recognition of insubstantiality. The most concrete of the three, it fully embodies the idea of concession, of acquiescence in one's insubstantiality. "Fleet persistent shadow," Ariel himself embodies the insubstantiality of *The Tempest*'s metaphors of clouds, mists, vanishing, fading and melting. Ariel's self-definition as a "shadow" suggests that the life which he reflects is substantial and real. From an expression of the dependence of art on life—"Helplessly in love with you,/Elegance, art, fascination,/Fascinated by/Drab mortality"—Ariel moves to an evocation of the ultimate powerlessness of both. Caliban and Ariel

> Can, alas, foretell,
> When our falsehoods are divided,
> What we shall become,
> One evaporating sigh, . . .

Ariel's song literally evaporates, its last syllable a weak echo of its penultimate word. Like the work it ends, Ariel's poem is a concession. With it the whole *Sea and the Mirror* concedes itself out of existence.

If *The Sea and the Mirror* is a distorted mirror of *The Tempest*, its distortions tell us something about Auden's habits of mind. Auden once wrote that *The Tempest* ends "sourly," and in a way *The Sea and the Mirror* explores the sourness. Shakespeare's Prospero twice "forgives" Antonio in language distinctly unfor-giving, qualifying his forgiveness the first time with the phrase, "unnatural though thou art," and the second time prefacing it with the parenthetic "whom to call brother/Would even infect my mouth." Caliban's hostilities to the master whose skull he wants to batter ("or paunch him with a stake,/Or cut his wezard") seem too suddenly converted to contrition and obedience:

> PROSPERO: As you look
> To have my pardon, trim it handsomely.
> CALIBAN: Ay, that I will; and I'll be wise hereafter,
> And seek for grace.

The Sea and the Mirror allows the two who rebelled against Prospero's authority in Shakespeare's play to have their say, and to have the last words.

More than anything else, Auden's "revisions" of Shakespeare reveal a new view of the relation between Prospero and Caliban. *The Sea and the Mirror* distorts *The Tempest* according to the stipulation that "the last shall be first, and the first last." The reversal corroborates Auden's complaints about *The Tempest* in his essay "Balaam and His Ass":

> *The Tempest* seems to me a manichean work, not because it shows
> the relation of Nature to Spirit as one of conflict and hostility, which
> in fallen man it is, but because it puts the blame for this upon Nature
> and makes the spirit innocent.

The structure of *The Sea and the Mirror* is a kind of Christian judgment, placing the proud Prospero in the lowliest position. As the speaker of the first of the three sections, he is the most naive and the least self-conscious. The beast Caliban, the final speaker, is the most sophisticated, and his self-consciousness ultimately leads him to the vision of grace which Shakespeare left him seeking. One could say that Auden has "put down the mighty from their seat,/And hath exalted the humble and meek."

The rereading of *The Tempest* is as Freudian as it is Christian. The fool is granted the vision of God, but this fool is "natural" in another sense. Shakespeare's Caliban may have trotted off stage obediently, but Auden's refuses to leave it. He is, after all, "the dark thing you could never abide to be with." From both Christian and Freudian points of view, Auden's interpretation of Caliban is reminiscent of his reading of another anarchic figure, Falstaff. The Hal of *Henry IV, Part II* does not come to terms with Falstaff and what he represents; he merely suppresses him with superior legal force. In "The Prince's Dog" Auden goes so far as to suggest that Falstaff is morally superior to Hal, "the supernatural order of Charity as contrasted with the temporal order of Justice symbolized by Henry of Monmouth."

Auden's dislike of Hal is his dislike of temporal justice, of moral compromise, of "a practical reckoning with time and place." Auden's feelings about Prospero are more closely related to his ideas about the artist. The structure of *The Sea and the Mirror* could also be interpreted as a deliberate incapacitating of the artist, who emerged successful at the end of *The Tempest*. Auden concluded *The Enchafèd Flood* with a similar abrogation, in words more normative than descriptive:

> We live in a new age in which the artist neither can have such
> a unique heroic importance nor believes in the Art-God enough
> to desire it . . . in which the heroic image is not the nomad wanderer
> through the desert or over the ocean, but the less exciting figure
> of the builder, who renews the ruined walls of the city.

In his "commentary" on *The Tempest*, Auden is grappling not with Shakespeare but with the idea of the artist's "unique importance." Although this is an idea which Auden associates with Romanticism, and with writers such as Tennyson and Rimbaud, it is really his own bogeyman, the escapism and solipsism he is exorcising in *The Orators*, *The Age of Anxiety*, and "City Without Walls." *The Sea and the Mirror* is subtler than those works because each character asserts his own disenchantment. The Prospero of *The Sea and the Mirror* seems to be the perfect hero for Auden: in wry, conversational tones and Kierkegaardian language he rejects magic for "the way of truth." But the characters in *The Sea and the Mirror* are often less wise than they appear. Only when Prospero is seen as the first character in a progression defined by increasing awareness is he properly·understood. As the poem moves from Prospero's confident declarations to Caliban's visionary receptiveness, it reveals two simultaneous motions, a movement inward toward full acceptance of subjectivity, and a movement outward toward freedom. Auden is following the dictum Yeats's death inspired him to express:

> In the prison of his days
> Teach the free man how to praise.

DAVID BROMWICH

An Oracle Turned Jester

This is the Auden canon as planned by Auden. The poet who was apt to deride "accurate scholarship" would nevertheless have been pleased with the editorial job: the *Collected Poems* supplies dates and variant titles, but otherwise keeps the apparatus to a helpful minimum, and is good to the eye and the touch. We shall have to wait for a promised second volume, *The English Auden*, if we want to read the canon as a palimpsest, compare the rubbed-out edges with the bold outline laid over them, and arrive at some conclusion about the poet's character. In the meantime Auden's literary executor, Edward Mendelson, wisely cautions us to regard Auden's final change of dress as indeed final. It is. But a few intractable spirits ought to remain on the scene to ask if this was not after all another disguise. In his foreword to the *Collected Shorter Poems* (1965), Auden defended revisions "as a matter of principle" by quoting Valéry: "A poem is never finished; it is only abandoned." The allusion is not quite candid. Valéry, who was by no means of Auden's party in these matters, saw the work of a poet as forming an activity of unbroken meditation. To decide what the public should see of the meditation was a secondary worry: a fragment might be as important as a completed poem. What could a poem be for Auden, on the other hand, if not the finished expression of feeling on a given occasion?

Auden generally revised for sentiment rather than sound and, without being an exponent of "pure sound," one may raise a simple enough objection. To play the sage or pedant, and chasten the record of an earlier renegade self, is never good for the character; the results, when it is a poet who does this, are seldom happy for the poetry; and Auden is an exception to neither rule. Poetry survives, he said in his elegy for Yeats, "In the valley of its making

From *The Times Literary Supplement*, Sept. 17, 1976. Copyright © 1976 by The Times Literary Supplement.

where executives/Would never want to tamper." Poets are the first to tamper. Consider the following inconspicuous change in "Paysage Moralisé":

> It is the sorrow; shall it melt? Ah, water
> Would gush, flush, green these mountains and these valleys,
> And we rebuild our cities, not dream of islands.

The altered version gives "It is our sorrow . . . ." It is an emphatic bit of scoring, and what is gained is emphasis. But the loss is very great: the poem has given up something of its tacit strength. "Our sorrow," it insists, "yes; all of us." What was implication is now statement. *Our* and *sorrow*, by the way, do not mix well as sounds. And *our* slows down the cadence, where, in the first version, it was slowed and then halted, as if stunned, only at *sorrow*, the last word of the first sentence of the envoy.

More painful and harder to miss is a change in the Yeats elegy itself. "O all the instruments agree/The day of his death was a dark cold day" has become "What instruments we have agree . . . ." Granted, we do not have all the instruments: to say so is perhaps a stroke for moderation and truth. But the poem has stopped singing. "This Loved One," a very early poem which Yeats anthologized, used to address a "Face that the sun/Is supple on." We are now to favour "Face that the sun/Is lively on." Here it is surely sound and sound alone that disturbs the revising poet. And we did hear a slight drone in the short vowel sounds: yet it seemed right for the mostly drowsy mood of these lines. The hopeless correction is a fine flower of poetic diction.

In the mid-1940's Auden began, in bracing moral tones and on every possible occasion, to lay down the laws of modesty proper to the poet. Poetry, he had said, makes nothing happen. Nothing, that is, in particular, nothing right away, nothing to bet on: so one might have gathered too from Robert Frost's perfectly balanced appeal for the poetry of griefs against the poetry of grievances. But Auden went considerably further than this. In prose and in verse, he gave perhaps the most limited description of the aim and use of poetry that has ever come from a major poet: in his ideal world poetry is among the more harmless indoor pastimes. And of course there is a matter-of-fact equability in this view of poetry, and it made a pleasant change from the climate of Yeats and Eliot. Very successfully, Auden became the virtuoso of modesty. In art as in life, however, modesty must never be confused with sincerity. There is something bullying in Auden's desire to ingratiate, and he is out to bully himself as well as others. Here one reaches the heart of his impulse to revise. For, more than most poets, Auden in every phase was concerned to be the useful man, the man society cannot dispense with: first as the voice from the tripod, then as the licensed jester. There was an element of pathos in his quest. And if one holds the full career in mind, one will see how pervasive was his fear of isolation: the revisions are issuing, not from a conflict between one manner and its successor, but from an anxiety, which has become almost a ruling passion, about manners in general.

"Human beings," announces the narrator of *The Age of Anxiety*, "are, necessarily, actors who cannot become something before they have first pretended to be it; and they can be divided, not into the hypocritical and the sincere, but into the sane who know they are acting and the mad who do not." What a very strange generalization. Play-acting, one might object, simply does not have so central a place in the lives of most of us. But to Auden the dictum seemed self-evidently true. Baudelaire writes somewhere of "the aristocratic pleasure of giving offence": equally aristocratic is the pleasure of having it in one's power to offend but holding back. And Auden's earliest role, in which he sought to offend all, and his latest, in which he offended none, were not markedly different in the demands they made on the player. Both entailed a steady awareness of the risks and attendant rewards of authority. The paradox that the word frames, with its rival connotations of power and trustworthiness, was not lost on Auden. Of his own uneasy stance he made his poetry.

The mark of his best early poetry is the widely distributed shock.

> Others have tried it and will try again
> To finish that which they did not begin:
> Their fate must always be the same as yours,
> To suffer the loss they were afraid of, yes,
> Holders of one position, wrong for years.

We once read of a similar defeat in "History to the defeated/may say alas but cannot help or pardon." But there it does not work. Auden's self-criticism as usual is disingenuous:

> To say this is to equate goodness with success. It would have been bad enough if I had ever held this wicked doctrine, but that I should have stated it simply because it sounded to me rhetorically effective is quite inexcusable.

In fact, the sentiment is consistent with everything Auden believed about history. The trouble is rather that these lines resist any historical context. They are brilliantly anonymous, the feeling they impart is far from local, and they should not have been kept for the end of "Spain."

Who are the "old gang" that must be killed off in Auden's early poems? Those, the poems continually assert, who have been possessed by a bad motive. The behaviour they are denounced for extends from the sinks of personal cowardice to the summits of political oppression. The drawing together of two vastly different sorts of corruption, that which comes of power and that which comes of fear, is an astonishing feature of Auden's ideology. In forty years it has not ceased to be a puzzling human lapse. Yet none of the poems connected with this lapse is without canonical status. And we can still read the ballad of "Miss Gee"—Miss Gee, who, being too meek to live and too thwarted, grows a cancer and dies—and we can applaud the flat pitiless gaze of the poet.

> They laid her on the table,
>   The students began to laugh;
> And Mr Rose the surgeon
>   He cut Miss Gee in half.
>
> Mr Rose he turned to his students,
>   Said, "Gentlemen, if you please,
> We seldom see a sarcoma
>   As far advanced as this."

Or perhaps we will shudder a little, and not for the reason the poet intended. It is such an odd choice of targets for an exercise in *nil admirari*.

Courage, or the courage of these particular convictions, together with an unworried pertinacity in the campaign to disgust, Auden learnt from D. H. Lawrence. To disgust on behalf of the truth was permissible since the truth, as Lawrence taught, was often in bad taste. The reader who wants a key to the attitude of Auden's early work and finds himself resisting those enjoyable but esoteric psychologists, Groddeck and Homer Lane, can do no better than to look up Lawrence's *Psychoanalysis and the Unconscious* and its sequel, *Fantasia of the Unconscious*. There he will come upon the Leader, the Group, the Wrecked Society, the Disease-Growing Neurotic, the War to the End of the Pure-in-Spirit. "The Wanderer" has its source in one of Lawrence's characteristic improvised arias, about the peace that belongs to the hero returning home. "Consider," with its celebration of the hawk's-eye view in which an absence of compassion is notable and to be admired, looks back to several passages loaded with *frisson*:

> We can see as the hawk sees the one concentrated spot where beats the life-heart of our prey. . . . Love is a thing to be *learned*, through centuries of patient effort. It is a difficult, complex maintenance of individual integrity throughout the incalculable processes of inter-human polarity. . . . Who can do it? Nobody. Yet we have all got to do it, or else suffer ascetic tortures of starvation and privation or of distortion and overstrain and slow collapse into corruption.

But Auden can touch us as Lawrence's crank manifesto cannot. And his moods of disgust take from the surrounding poems or lines a resonance not simply of disgust. One sees the moods, in the end, as frank confessions of weakness, of failure, of his own indebtedness to the system of illusions he hates and would dispel. For the band of heroic conspirators that dominate his work are plainly shadowed rather than shadowing, among the watched not the watchers. They as surely as Miss Gee are headed for defeat; but they of all others cannot accept it. Their fate reads out its sentence, simple and laconic like the end-stop of a line of verse, in poems that do not strike the tragic note yet have the tragic need to step quietly.

> For to be held as friend
> By an undeveloped mind,
> To be joke for children is
> Death's happiness:
> Whose anecdotes betray
> His favourite colour as blue,
> Colour of distant bells
> And boy's overalls.

Few of Auden's grateful readers have been tempted to solve the paradox of an angry poetry which is most confident and most beautiful where it is most cautious. The gratitude seems enough.

> I, decent with the seasons, move
> Different or with a different love,
> Nor question overmuch the nod,
> The stone smile of this country god
> That never was more reticent,
> Always afraid to say more than it meant.

Here at least one ought to trust the tale. Auden's poetry knows what its author sometimes forgot: that what it seeks to join—life and death, isolate heroism and the sense of community—must remain forever parted. There is nothing to be done. And this knowledge brings to Auden's early poetry its unique dignity and its air of self-sufficient and unappeased loneliness.

Much of what Auden wrote between "The Letter" (1927) and "On This Island" (1935) has kept its original vigour. The best of these poems, untitled at birth but eccentrically christened in their after-years, come back to the memory whole from the sound of their first lines: "From scars where kestrels hover"; "Again in conversations/Speaking of fear"; "Before this loved one/Was that one and that one"; "The strings' excitement, the applauding drum"; "Will you turn a deaf ear/To what they said on the shore"; "Since you are going to begin today/Let us consider what it is you do"; "It was Easter as I walked in the public gardens"; "This lunar beauty/Has no history"; "'O where are you going' said reader to rider"; "Consider this and in our time"; "Doom is dark and deeper than any sea-dingle"; "Hearing of harvests rotting in the valleys"; and the terrifying and unforgettable refusal to forgive a happy childhood, called "Through the Looking-Glass," which begins: "Earth has turned over; our side feels the cold,/And life sinks choking in the wells of trees." On these poems rests Auden's claim as one of the great inventors of modern poetry. Leafing through Robin Skelton's anthology, *Poetry of the Thirties*, and hearing Auden in poems as individually realized as MacNeice's "The Sunlight on the Garden" and Henry Reed's "Hiding Beneath the Furze," one feels his influence as an invigorating fact.

Auden is at his height perhaps only in *Paid on Both Sides*, the one verse drama of our time that is really verse and really drama. The Nower–Shaw feud gives Auden a sustained glimpse of the individual operating within the group, and the flaw at the heart of all human action is laid bare. We fight others in the name of ancestors whom we are fighting to escape. This is the trap. Our loyalty to all "Whose voices in the rock/Are now perpetual" is always necessary and always destructive. The self-imposed ailment is here treated humorously, and tellingly, as an appropriate emblem of sick ancestor-worship: the Doctor cures the wounded Spy by removing from his body an enormous tooth, which "was growing ninety-nine years before his great grandmother was born. If it hadn't been taken out today he would have died yesterday." And the final chorus is our nearest approach to an Auden credo.

> Though he believe it, no man is strong.
> He thinks to be called the fortunate,
> To bring home a wife, to live long.
> But he is defeated; let the son
> Sell the farm lest the mountain fall;
> His mother and her mother won.
>
> His fields are used up where the moles visit,
> The contours worn flat; if there show
> Passage for water he will miss it:
> Give up his breath, his woman, his team;
> No life to touch, though later there be
> Big fruit, eagles above the stream.

To move from this to the aggressive middle style of 1935–45 is a bewildering drop. Auden has become the good poet of responsibility: the vagueness is in the role, not the phrase, and no number of capital letters would save it. The style now is Dryden plus contemporary journalism. Stretches of *For the Time Being*, especially Herod's speech, are in the mode of Jean Anouilh's updating of Greek tragedy. Yet Auden's conspiratorial phase hints directly enough at his later courtship of the social muse: the progress has its logic. The missing link is, of course, *The Orators*, which one may hope *The English Auden* will reprint *in toto*. The Airman of that story makes his sacrifice not from strength but from weakness, and the drama reaches its climax in the "Letter to a Wound," where the wounded man's love for his own limiting defect allows it, after endless cossetting, to establish complete domination over his mental life. In Auden's view the case is representative—he printed the "Letter" separately in his first collected volume. And in the mid-1930's his poetry shows him growing steadily convinced that society is itself a conspiracy of weaknesses from which the individual cannot secede. By 1942 his conversion is wholehearted.

We must all live in a world that is the sum of all those things we cannot do. This is what Auden says, tirelessly, in every possible context. But his diagnosis has not altered. It is only that the prognosis has turned pessimistic. With a curious fidelity to his old beliefs, he was able to change sides without ever changing his mind. The lesson he discovers in Melville belongs properly to himself.

> Evil is unspectacular and always human,
> And shares our bed and eats at our own table,
> And we are introduced to Goodness every day,
> Even in drawing-rooms among a crowd of faults;
> He has a name like Billy and is almost perfect,
> But wears a stammer like a decoration:
> And every time they meet the same thing has to happen;
> It is the Evil that is helpless like a lover
> And has to pick a quarrel and succeeds,
> And both are openly destroyed before our eyes.

Society, the family, have triumphed, with all their capacity for evil: we can only give them our pledge. Sympathy is the gift Auden has come most keenly to desire in his poetry, and it is, he seems to think, a quality more nearly allied to prose than to poetry. In the run-on lines of his elegy for Freud he brings the which-side-am-I-supposed-to-be-on theme to a final resolution.

> But he would have us remember most of all
> to be enthusiastic over the night,
>   not only for the sense of wonder
>   it alone has to offer, but also
> because it needs our love. With large sad eyes
> its delectable creatures look up and beg
>   us dumbly to ask them to follow:
>   they are exiles who long for the future

> that lies in our power, they too would rejoice
> if allowed to serve enlightenment like him,
>   even to bear our cry of "Judas,"
>   as he did and all must bear who serve it.

Of Auden's "fellow-traveller" phase nothing need be said, since, according to his wish and the present volume, it never happened. In *Letter to Lord Byron* and *New Year Letter* we are overhearing a charming conversational wit who will doubtless be equally charming to readers a century from now. *The Age of Anxiety* is a long dull forced amusement dedicated and devoted to Betjeman. But there remain three poems, in a wholly new manner, in which one feels that Auden is writing at the top of his powers. The manner is that of the oracle who unhappily knows too much; the poems are "The Fall of Rome," "Under Sirius," and "The Shield of Achilles." The first of these has something of the spirit of Dryden's *Secular Masque*. For technical precision over a short distance it scarcely has a rival in Auden's work or in anyone else's. The American rhyme of *clerk* with *work* is cunning, and identifies the empire whose careless largesse Auden is elsewhere at pains to celebrate.

"Under Sirius" is a rhetorical flourish, executed in a single stroke, which warns the lazy epic poet Fortunatus of his coming disaster. "Improve the man," Auden says, here as elsewhere, "by giving him a good fright." This poem makes the grandest of all his gestures of veiled menace.

> How will you look and what will you do when the basalt
>   Tombs of the sorcerers shatter
> And their guardian megalopods
>   Come after you pitter-patter?
> How will you answer when from their qualming spring
>   The immortal nymphs fly shrieking,
>   And out of the open sky
>   The pantocratic riddle breaks—
>   "Who are you and why?"
> For when in a carol under the apple-trees
>   The reborn featly dance
> There will also, Fortunatus,
>   Be those who refused their chance,
> Now pottering shades, querulous beside the salt-pits,
>   And mawkish in their wits,
>   To whom these dull dog-days
>   Between event seem crowned with olive
>   And golden with self-praise.

"The Shield of Achilles," written perhaps under the influence of Simone Weil's "The Iliad or, The Poem of Force," mingles the grey world of the death camps with the thriving civilization depicted on the shield, until neither is quite recognizable and both seem appalling. Only Auden would play Cassandra to Achilles in this way. The anachronistic details are deftly managed and the poem is a careful tour de force.

Apart from these poems, *Paid on Both Sides*, and some lyrics in his first volume or a little after, Auden can be seen to best advantage in his songs. "Fish in the unruffled lakes"; "Now the leaves are falling fast"; "Underneath an abject willow"; "Make this night loveable" and, the poem to which it is sequel and counterpoint, "Lullaby": these are intent on themselves as true poetry must be. Yet the faithful reader of Auden will find such a list ungenerous, and he is right. A poet is someone who invents a new tone of voice. Early, middle, and late, Auden was busy doing so: in "Herman Melville," in parts of the Freud and Yeats elegies, in the calm equipoise and tact of *The Sea and the Mirror*, and in "Bucolics" and "Horae Canonicae," which are his unofficial farewell to the art. One may watch him "doing" Graves or Frost in poems as late as "Limbo Culture" and "Objects" (1957); but what was closest to him he learnt early, most of all from Hardy; and his typical poem like Hardy's starts from a meditation which must be idiosyncratic on a landscape which must be difficult. Hardy's "Where the Picnic Was" and Auden's "From scars where kestrels hover" are employing remarkably similar methods to remarkably different ends. "In Praise of Limestone," if not for its poetry, then for its criticism, survives as a testament of the healing power of things beyond the human thrall.

Auden frequently lacks the sounded or line-by-line concentration that one associates with the greatest modern poetry. But he has a subject uniquely to himself. This is the skeleton-key quest, the quest without a goal. The conventional detective story, he wrote in *The Dyer's Hand*, assumes a world in which "it is certain that a crime has been committed and, temporarily, uncertain to whom the guilt should be attached; as soon as this is known, the innocence of everyone else is certain." A work of art such as *The Trial*, on the other hand, assumes a world in which "it is the guilt that is certain and the crime that is uncertain; the aim of the hero's investigation is not to prove his innocence (which would be impossible for he knows he is guilty), but to discover what, if anything, he has done to make himself guilty." There are critics who will prefer to call this the Kafka theme or the Childe Roland theme. But, of our contemporaries, it was Auden who appropriated it most thoroughly and self-consciously.

It is the subtle and artful form of the confidence game which he plays artlessly in his revisions. It gives his anxiety free rein, without the indecencies

of simple exhortation, or the idiocies of confession. It presents in full figure
the threat of his nervous sense of duty and isolation: yet we feel the threat
as something named, informed by dramatic energy, and mastered. In a poem
of 1956 Auden received a definitive last word from his accuser. Society, the
Group, the Superego, the Other, had long since become the "they," impenetrable
and unreflecting and never to be questioned, whom Auden shares with Kafka
and Edward Lear. From "moonless absences you never heard of" they, who
have seen everything, are now asking for total surrender. And Auden, helpless
in their sight, wants the battle to continue and calls the poem "There Will
Be No Peace."

> There will be no peace.
> Fight back, then, with such courage as you have
> And every unchivalrous dodge you know of,
>   Clear in your conscience on this:
> Their cause, if they had one, is nothing to them now;
>   They hate for hate's sake.

But he had answered himself two decades earlier. The choice of weapons
is really no choice. It is mere reflex. And at last, as one of Auden's few inspired
revisions makes clear, we are the victims of our own survival.

> Clear, unscaleable, ahead
> Rise the Mountains of Instead,
> From whose cold cascading streams
> None may drink except in dreams.

We must make ourselves at home with whatever illusions of independence
we can salvage; hence the cheerful welcome accorded to belief as a value in
itself. The poems let one see how shrewdly and yet precariously, like the rest
of us, Auden built the church of self-knowledge on the rock of his own all-
too-human nature. While remaining an altogether distinctive moralist he was
himself in this sense a representative case.

WILLARD SPIEGELMAN

The Rake's Progress:
An Operatic Version of Pastoral

W. H. Auden once called Stravinsky "*the* great exemplary artist of the twentieth century, and not just in music." One aspect of Stravinsky's example that certainly would have appealed to Auden was his strong revisionary commitment to his musical heritage. In no other major composer do we find so many obvious homages to and reminders of his predecessors, and yet no other has so distinctly retained his own inviolable identity. Stravinsky's individuality results directly from the genius of his imitations; he is, paradoxically, most master when most sedulously a student. His feeling for (in Eliot's phrase) "the presence of the past" is most clear in *The Rake's Progress*, an opera that must be listened to with Mozart echoing in our inner ear. Stravinsky was inspired to his subject in 1947 by Hogarth's famous 1735 prints; on the recommendation of Aldous Huxley he asked Auden to write the story. Auden accepted the commission, and with the help of Chester Kallman finished the libretto in three months. Stravinsky set to work on the score, and the premiere was held in Venice in 1951.

Auden's and Kallman's libretto is to English poetry what Stravinsky's music is to the classical opera. In its intelligent evocativeness, *The Rake's Progress* is the exception that proves Auden's rule that "it is rare for the story of a successful opera to be interested in itself." I am concerned with *The Rake* as a twentieth-century version of pastoral, an effort on Auden's part to recapture the myths and language of an earlier, more optimistic world, and to examine that world from the perspective of our own. The opera is an Empsonian pastoral in two distinct ways: first, its basic fable explores the themes of paradise and potential rebirth; and second, the libretto is Auden's attempt to adapt certain poetic styles

From *Southeast Review* 63, no. 1 (Winter 1978). Copyright © 1978 by Willard Spiegelman. Southern Methodist University Press, 1978.

to the conditions of twentieth-century literary life, to imitate or parody older
models in much the same way that Stravinsky's music casts new light on earlier
operatic techniques. In its neoclassical form and language, *The Rake* is an act
of homage to the past as well as an admission that mere imitation can cope
only partially with modern artistic and moral dilemmas.

The story of a mélange of myths (a return to an Edenic golden age, the
bargain of Faust with Mephistopheles, and the death and rebirth motif of Venus
and Adonis), and fairy tales (the three wishes, the Ugly Duchess, and a new
version of Mother Goose herself). Like the score, the story evinces resemblances
to Mozartean themes; but since it accepts the fact that we live in an anti-heroic,
anti-pastoral age, it tries to reconcile them to present realities. It was natural
for Auden to make this examination in a libretto. For the modern poet, he
writes,

> opera is the last refuge of the High Style, the only art to which
> a poet with a nostalgia for those times past when poets could write
> in the grand manner all by themselves can still contribute, provided
> he will take the pains to learn the metier, and is lucky enough to
> find a composer he can believe in.

Opera is the only remaining "secondary world" to which the would-be heroic
poet has access, because the conditions of our primary world make it impossible
for him to use the grand style *in propria persona*, without some intervening filter.

Auden was still concerned with finding an appropriate style in his "Dedication to Reinhold and Ursula Niebuhr" from *Nones* (1951), the book compiled
immediately after *The Rake*. Looking back to the "golden hours" of youth and
happiness, he laments, like Yeats before him, both the passage of time and
the paucity of poetic styles which remain to him:

> [W]e would in the old grand manner
> Have sung from a resonant heart.
> But, pawed-at and gossiped over
> By the promiscuous crowd,
> All words like peace and love,
> All sane affirmative speech,
> Had been soiled, profaned, debased
> To a horrid mechanical screech:
> No civil style survived
> That pandaemonium
> But the wry, the sotto-voce,
> Ironic and monochrome:
> And where could we find shelter

> For joy or mere content
> When little was left standing
> But the suburb of dissent.

Not content to be merely "wry" and "ironic," tones of which he was certainly master, Auden spent his last twenty-five years exploring new means of achieving a civil style which would combine the wit of his occasional poems and the passion of his larger articulations. "The Truest Poetry Is the Most Feigning" (1954) demands grandiose gestures in poetry: "By all means sing of love, but, if you do,/Please make a rare old proper hullabaloo." More recently, in "The Horatians" (1969), Auden equated heightened emotion and the operatic stage: "the courts/of Grand Opera, that *galère*/of lunatics, power-famished/or love-ravenous, belting out their arias."

Auden was of two minds about the role of the librettist. In *Secondary Worlds* he says that "the job of the librettist is to furnish the composer with a plot, characters, and words: of these, the least important, so far as the audience is concerned, are the words." He cautions the writer against puns, double meanings, and long verse lines, and suggests that Shakespeare's "Farewell, thou art too dear for my possessing" is "unsettable, because there is no musical way of conveying the two meanings of *dear* as *precious* and *expensive*." Reminding us of Goethe's comment that opera is a succession of significant situations artificially arranged, he concludes his theoretical remarks by insisting that opera must be melodramatic, in both senses of that word, and must provide as many occasions as possible where people might sing. The emotional persuasiveness of music is, he says, axiomatically greater than that of words, and many operatic situations would be laughable if staged without music.

Auden's practice, however, in *The Rake*, does not square easily with his theory; he and Kallman created a libretto which is more literary, delicate, and even academic than he might later have deemed wise. In this opera, the librettists are ventriloquists, creating singing voices for their characters and speaking themselves through the language of their literary heritage.

The story parallels Hogarth's prints in a general way. Young Tom Rakewell receives a bequest from a distant uncle, delivered by Satan disguised as Nick Shadow. Tom agrees to employ Shadow and to pay his wages after a year and a day. They go off to London, abandoning Anne Truelove, the heroine, and Tom succumbs to the standard vices: drinking, gaming, and swindling. At Shadow's suggestion, he marries the bearded lady, Baba the Turk, to prove his freedom. He seeks prosperity, falls into debt, gambles for his soul with Shadow in the penultimate scene, and is saved from Hell by a reminder of Anne's love for him. Keeping his soul but losing his sanity, he ends his life in Bedlam, picturing himself as Adonis comforted by Anne as Venus.

The first act opens on a rural eighteenth-century scene with a highly stylized love duet:

> ANNE: The woods are green and birds and beasts at play
> For all things keep this festival of May;
> With fragrant odours and with notes of cheer
> The pious earth observes the solemn year.
> TOM: Now is the season when the Cyprian Queen
> With genial charm translates our mortal scene.
> When swains their nymphs in fervent arms enfold
> And with a kiss restore the Age of Gold.

This introduces a libretto full of verbal echoes and allusions, one which is a serious reconsideration of, and recommitment to, our literary tradition. The pastoral scene, under the touch of *Venus genetrix*, prepares us for the ritual awakening of Adonis by Venus in the final scene, but it also returns us to the concerns and language of neo-Augustan poetry. The new "Age of Gold" is announced in Latinate diction which refers us to Pope and Dryden, just as their poetry evokes Horace and Vergil. Moreover, despite Auden's advice that the words are the least important part of the librettist's art, it is clear that in a set-piece like this duet, which contributes nothing to plot or characterization, the words are in fact *all* that is important. "Pious," "solemn," "genial," and "translates" are used with Latin or archaic connotations which a listener must feel if he is to respond fully to the scene. We even hear a double meaning (precisely what Auden would theoretically have avoided) in "observes," suggesting both celebration and inspection or perception. The pastoral attitude and the pointedly eighteenth-century diction of the duet continue throughout the first scene. When Anne sings: "How sweet within the budding grove/To walk, to love," Tom answers: "How sweet beside the pliant stream/To lie, to dream." We are in the world of Pope's *Pastorals*. Of course, we expect an opera based on Hogarth to capture an eighteenth-century flavor in speech as well as in costume, setting, and music, but the depth and persistence of verbal imitation and echo suggest that Auden and Kallman are attempting something more serious.

We hear reminiscences of many English poets throughout the opera: a glance at even the most obvious allusions makes it clear that the librettists are forcing our literary past to speak directly to us. In Tom's opening soliloquy, for example, the hero entrusts himself to Fortune and rationalizes his actions. He ends with lusty optimism: "My life lies before me,/The world is so wide;/Come, wishes, be horses;/This beggar shall ride." With a Miltonic echo ("The world was all before them . . ."), Auden reminds us that Tom, about to make his bargain with Shadow, is virtually a fallen man. Unlike Adam, however, Tom is still self-deceived; the world that lies before him is a London of greed and corruption, but also, the line implies, a world in which redemption is possible.

In the next scene, when Tom catechetically recites that his duty is to "shut my ears to prude and preacher/And follow Nature as my teacher," he echoes the advice of Pope, Wordsworth, and others. Later, in I, iii, Anne's lines ("if love be love/It will not alter") rework Shakespeare's Sonnet 116 ("love is not love which alters when it alteration finds"). We hear Shakespeare again when Anne sings in the final scene: "Every wearied body must/Late or soon return to dust." This time, the change from *Cymbeline's* "golden lads and girls" emphasizes the distance between the magical, pastoral world of romance and our more ordinary, modern one. The pathetic closing lines of the scene—mad Tom singing "Weep for Adonis whom Venus loved," and the chorus replying, "Mourn for Adonis, ever young, the dear/Of Venus: weep, tread softly round his bier"—refer us to the essence of pastoral elegy (now viewed semi-ironically), especially to *Lycidas* and *Adonais.*

In addition to specific literary echoes, the text is filled with poetry appropriate to different characters. In the chorus of whores and roaring boys (I, ii), the deliberately jazzy syncopation complements the musical setting. The "Lanterloo" song, a mock Mother Goose ballad, combines ridiculous details ("an almanack in a walnut tree") with sexual ones ("Draw his sword and chop off her head"). Baba's patter-song (II, iii) is in Ogden Nash-like couplets; the irregular lines define the garrulous and bizarre bearded lady. At the auction (III, i), Sellem, whose very name is obviously meaningful, sounds like an eighteenth-century cleric:

> Truly there is a divine balance in Nature: a thousand
> lose that a thousand may gain; and you who are the
> fortunate are not so only in yourselves, but also
> in being Nature's very missionaries. You are her
> instruments for the restoration of that order we all
> so worship, and it is granted to, ah! so few of us
> to serve.

In "Notes on Music and Opera" in *The Dyer's Hand,* Auden says that "the golden age of opera, from Mozart to Verdi, coincided with the golden age of liberal humanism, of unquestioning belief in freedom and progress." By reminding an audience in the "age of anxiety" of earlier, golden days, and at the same time giving their story a distinctly modern edge, Auden and Kallman have written more than a simple pastoral imitation. Even though Auden regarded

opera as the only available genre for the poet's high style and for heroic characters, *The Rake* is filled with suggestions of doubt and irony. Indeed, the focus
at the heart of the text is double. The Miltonic allusion in Tom's first aria
balances the intimation of the opening duet that the hero and heroine are unfallen innocents in Eden. As a literate audience, we must respond to both ideas:
the authors wish us to believe for a moment in the possibility of a golden age,
if only in the reconstructed tableau in front of us. But they also insist that
the tableau *is* a fiction. The restoration of the Age of Gold of which Tom
sings is both magical and willful: it is with a playful "kiss" that the past is recalled.

Tom is neither a simple swain nor an unfallen Adam, not Hogarth's passive
Rake, but an ennui-ridden, twentieth-century youth. Auden himself has identified Tom's three wishes with three different philosophical categories (which
some critics view as parallel to stages in Kierkegaard's system). He calls the
bordello scene (I, ii) "*le plaisir*," and Tom's marriage to Baba "*l'acte gratuit*," an
almost existential assertion of free will (and an assertion, as well, of the Absurd
in human choice, the same absurdity emphasized by Tom's second choice of
the Queen of Hearts in the graveyard scene). Of the bread-making machine
(II, iii), Auden wrote to Stravinsky that Tom "*desire devenir Dieu.*"

The myth of progress itself, which, Auden reminds us, could be taken
seriously only in the age of opera, is exploded and satirized. Tom tells Nick
(II, iii) of his millenarian dream of prosperity: "I saw all need abolished by
my skill/And earth become an Eden of good will." His Utopianism is foolhardy:

> Thanks to this excellent device
> Man shall reenter Paradise
>   From which he once was driven.
> Secure from want, the cause of crime,
> The world shall for the second time
>   Be similar to heaven.

Tom's error is a predictably modern, liberal one; like Shaw and Brecht he thinks
that need makes man greedy and criminal, but the story tells us that humanity
is inherently fallen. Consequently, the opening duet undergoes still another
modification, as the possibility for pastoral innocence recedes into the fictive
past. Tom's optimistic language imitates eighteenth-century meliorism but
signifies his own delusions:

> Omnipotent when armed with this,
> In secular abundant bliss
>   He shall ascend the Chain
> Of Being to its top to win

> The throne of Nature and begin
> His everlasting reign.

Because of the outcome of his dream (the bread-making machine is a hoax) and because we, the audience, are living in the postliberal (and postoperatic) age, Tom's wishes are pathetic.

The pastoral myth so delicately affirmed in the opening duet is gradually modernized throughout an opera which refuses to grant our expectations about the course of pastoral. In his first outline for a scenario Auden describes the opening duet as "pastoral, *comme* Theocritus, of love, youth, country, etc. (perhaps mention Adonis here?)." In a letter to Stravinsky he writes that Tom's bequest should come from an uncle, not his father, so that "la note pastorale n'est pas interrompue," (i.e., a father's bequest comes by right, an uncle's by chance). The note may not be interrupted, but it is certainly blended with occasional dissonances. Truelove's fears about his prospective son-in-law add a highly realistic touch to the scene. Tom's soliloquy, already cited as proof of his fallen condition, indicates his self-serving casuistry; his later equation of Fortune and Shadow furthers our suspicions about natural innocence. Even styles of versification affect our response. Anne, with naïve optimism, sounds like Pope in *Windsor Forest*: "The joyous fount I see that brings increase/To fields of promise and the groves of peace." Tom, on the other hand, sings an aside like a frivolous song in a Restoration play:

> Laughter and light and all charms that endear,
>   All that dazzles or dims,
> Wisdom and wit shall adorn the career
>   Of him who can play and who wins.

In the second scene, we see a new Venus who balances the presiding *Venus genetrix* of the first. Together with Mars, she is worshiped by the whores and lusty boys in the bordello. John Blair has identified three types of Venus in the opera, each casting light on the others: pastoral, bawdy, and in the Bedlam of the last scene, heavenly. Mother Goose and London parody the Cyprian Queen and the rural charm of Scene 1. The very mention of "love" strikes at Tom's guilty conscience. He feels remorse but cannot act upon it. In a falsely pastoral note, Shadow tries to convince him, but pushing the clock back, that they have conquered time, but Tom still cannot ignore his sins.

In II, i, the bored rake demands variety in London. His recitative, "O Nature, green unnatural mother," rejects the world which was previously so fruitful and orderly. Tom's wish for inner illumination and his feeling for Nature as "unnatural" deepen the religious motifs already adumbrated. In a chilling image, he contrasts false glitter with the true light he seeks:

> I walk
> An endless hall of chandeliers
> In light that blinds, in light that sears,
> Reflected from a million smiles
> All empty as the country miles
> Of silly wood and senseless park;
> And only in my heart—the dark.

Tom desperately regards Nature as silly and tedious; his inability to perceive natural beauty is a sign of his own alienation from internal and external goodness.

The Christian motifs grow stronger in the following scene; Anne arrives in London, more saintly and determined than ever:

> Hear thou or not, merciful Heaven, ease thou or not
>   my way;
> A love that is sworn before thee can plunder Hell
>   of its prey.

Having discovered Tom's marriage to Baba, she laments the death of innocence "when spring was love" and Tom, sensing the irrevocable step he has taken, responds in an aside:

>   should I turn again,
> The arbor would be gone,
> And on the frozen ground,
> The birds lie dead.

The end is foreshadowed here, at his lowest moment; he is now without hope. The death of the pastoral world is announced by a reminder of "La Belle Dame Sans Merci" ("And no birds sing"), but Tom is wrong in thinking salvation impossible. Unlike Keats's Knight, he has not been entrapped by a Circean woman, but has acted freely; he can therefore help to redeem himself. The pastoral world exists, the librettists suggest, in the imaginations of the characters as well as the minds of the audience.

It is partly for this reason that they present us variations on the theme of paradise, from the opening and closing strains of rebirth, the Christian promise of redemption through love, to Tom's "secular abundant bliss" (II, iii), and Sellem's parody of it (III, i) through bibelots and trinkets. The climax of the ambivalent treatment of the pastoral and paradisal motifs comes in the final scenes.

At the end of III, ii, Tom is saved, by chance and by the revival of love (an echo of Anne's voice allows him to beat Shadow at cards) from the eternal damnation to which the Devil expects to bring him. Releasing his control over Tom's immortal soul, Shadow exits with a final curse: Tom will be forever mad. He retains his soul but loses his mind, and at the end of the scene, he pictures himself as Adonis waiting for Venus. This mock-mythologizing is painful: the promise of the opera's opening is ironically fulfilled, but now a true rebirth of Adonis and springtime does not occur.

The end is in Bedlam, the final resting place of Hogarth's Rake as well. The whole scene has a deliberately literary edge to it: no attempt to revive myths of nature in this age is futile, and almost egregiously comic. Both the moving spirit of true pastoral and parody continue. While the chorus sings of an unchanging, chaotic, and democratic Hell (like Milton's), without season, degree, or ritual (everything "in a common darkness set" recalls the universal darkness which buries all in Pope's *Dunciad*), Tom and Anne sing their final duet which, unlike their first one, employs the pastoral apparatus in a half-serious, half-mocking way. The lovers have been reunited, like Venus and Adonis, but elegiac beauty is undercut by its setting in an asylum. The opera offers two views of redemption, the more modern of which relinquishes sanity for happiness. The duet reminds us of the contrasts at the heart of the opera by deliberately juxtaposing two lines in the high, literary style with two which have a modern existential flavor:

> Rejoice, beloved: in these fields of Elysium
> Space cannot alter, nor Time our love abate;
> Here has no words for absence or estrangement
> Nor Now a notion of Almost or Too Late.

True pastoral ease is to be found neither in an Edenic countryside nor in progress toward a future Utopia, but only in death. Anne's lullaby, "Gently, little boat," which Auden subsequently included in *The Shield of Achilles* (1955), is an elegy for the dying Tom. The Christian and pagan strains of the opera are combined in the image of a world where the lion and the lamb lie down together, fulfilling the promise of springtime:

> Orchards greenly grace
> That undisturbed place,
> The weary soul recalling.

The ending of the opera is deliberately modern in its ambiguity. Despite the suggestions of Blakean innocence in Anne's lullaby, the theme of redemption is never satisfactorily resolved. We never know what happens to Tom's soul, and the myth of Adonis is modified by our knowledge that it is used to pacify the fantasies of a lunatic. The hero dies, overcome by grief and unable to maintain his illusions. He has paid for his excesses. The chorus of Bedlamites sings for his release, and, as he did in the first scene, Truelove brings us back to reality by reminding Anne: "my dear, the tale is ended now. Come home." Anne understands that "it is no longer I you need." The embodiment of Venus Urania or Christian Love is insufficient to save a modern madman, and the opera ends on a skeptical note about the adequacy of the pastoral myth.

In an epilogue, obviously inspired by the finale of *Don Giovanni* and by the stylized verses of Dr. John Hoadly on Hogarth's etchings, the men appear without wigs, Baba without her beard, and the ensemble moralizes in a jaunty, "wry" and "sotto voce" modern way. Baba warns the ladies that "good or bad,/All men are mad;/All they say or do is theatre," and Tom cautions against heroic delusions: "Beware, young men who fancy/You are Virgil or Julius Caesar,/Lest when you wake/You be only a rake." It is a lighthearted attempt to balance the pathetic elegiac ending with witty moralizing. Anne seems to think that Tom has been rescued:

> Not every rake is rescued
> At the last by Love and Beauty;
>   Not every man
>   Is given an Anne
> To take the place of Duty.

She is wrong, however, since Tom has only been partially saved (from the Devil's clutches); in both the primary and secondary worlds, we live by necessary fictions.

The final chorus repeats the earlier references to the Fall and the possible redemption of Man, but now the singers insist only upon the certainty of Work, our curse "since Eve went out with Adam." This witty epilogue forces us to examine the moral which the characters and their authors are preaching. Like his use of pastoral myth, the moralizing in Auden's libretto is meant seriously and comically at once. The story and poetry of *The Rake's Progress* evoke a past age when humanism, progress, innocence, and morality itself could be taken seriously. But the opera hopes in quiet ways for a future when human goodness, like Adonis, will be reborn in fact, and another golden age return. Until such time, there will be neither a High Style nor a proper hero for an aspiring poet, who will have to rest content with the secondary world which opera offers him.

EDWARD MENDELSON

Auden's Revision of Modernism

Auden was the first poet writing in English who felt at home in the twentieth century. He welcomed into his poetry all the disordered conditions of his time, all its variety of language and event. In this, as in almost everything else, he differed from his modernist predecessors such as Yeats, Lawrence, Eliot, or Pound, who had turned nostalgically away from a flawed present to some lost illusory Eden where life was unified, hierarchy secure, and the grand style a natural extension of the vernacular. All of this Auden rejected. His continuing subject was the task of the present moment: erotic and political tasks in his early poems, ethical and religious ones later. When Auden looked back into history, it was to seek the causes of his present condition, that he might act better and more effectively in the future. The past his poems envisioned was never a southern classical domain of unreflective elegance, as it was for the modernists, but a past that had always been ruined, a northern industrial landscape marred by the same violence and sorrow that marred his own.

Everything that is most distinctive about Auden can be traced to his absorption in the present: even, in what might seem a paradox, his revival of the poetic forms and meters that modernism had pronounced dead a few years earlier. Auden was able to find them still alive and well, and as effective as they had always been. In Auden's unbroken vision of history, the ancient discontents survived in contemporary forms, but so did the ancient sources of personal and literary vitality. Modernism, disfranchised from the past by its own sense of isolated "modernity," could bring its literary tradition into the present only as battered ironic fragments (as in Eliot) or by visionary heroic efforts (like Pound's) to "make it new." For Auden, it had never grown old.

From *W. H. Auden, Selected Poems: New Edition*. Copyright © 1979 by Edward Mendelson. Vintage Books, 1979. Originally entitled "Preface."

A laconic Old English toughness thrived in his poetry, as did an Augustan civility. One might even find, in the shape of Auden's career, traces of an ambitious recapitulation of a thousand years of European literary history: his earliest poems use the Icelandic sagas as their major source; then in the thirties Dante is heard insistently in the background of his work; followed by Shakespeare in the forties; and in the sixties, Goethe.

Modernism tended to look back toward the lost reigns of a native aristocracy; too often, it found the reflected glory of ancient "tradition" in political leaders who promised to restore social grandeur and unity through coercive force. Auden's refusal to idealize the past saved him from comparable fits of mistaken generosity. His poems and essays present the idea of the good society as, at best, a possibility, never actually to be achieved, but towards which one must always work. In Auden's poems from the thirties, this idea took form in a vision of history as the product of unconscious but purposive forces, of which social-democratic movements were potentially the conscious agents; one was free either to reject these forces or to ally oneself with them, but the choice was less a moral one than a choice between ultimate victory and ultimate defeat. Auden later renounced this view— which in any case he held less as a personal belief than as a scaffolding on which to build his poetry—and disowned the poems that expressed it. He came to understand history as the realm of conscious ethical choices, made personally and deliberately, and, if at all possible, in full awareness of their consequences. Whichever of these views Auden's political poems assumed, the poems consistently used the same basic technique. From the exhortatory "Spain" to the meditative "Vespers," Auden dramatized the unresolvable tension between personal wishes or fantasies (apocalytic fantasies in his early years, arcadian ones afterwards) and the claims and obligations of the social realm (which he designated "history" in the early poems, "the city" in the later ones). This drama of public responsibility and private desire is part of a tradition that extends back to Virgil and beyond, but by the early part of this century it had disappeared from English poetry. Auden revived it with the same confidence and exuberance he had brought to his revival of traditional poetic forms.

In short, the surest way to misunderstand Auden is to read him as the modernists' heir. Except in his very earliest and latest poems, there is virtually nothing modernist about him. From the viewpoint of literary history, this is the most important aspect of his work. Most critics of twentieth-century poetry, however, still judge poems by their conformity to modernist norms; consequently, a myth has grown up around Auden to the effect that he fell into a decline almost as soon as he began writing. Critics who give credence to this myth mean, in fact, that Auden stopped writing the sort of poems they know how to read; poems written in a subjective voice, in tones of imaginative superiority and regretful isolation. Auden's poems speak instead in a voice almost unknown to English poetry since the end of the eighteenth century: the voice of a citizen who knows the obligations of his citizenship.

Like Brecht in Germany, whose career offers the closest parallels with his own, Auden began with a brashly threatening manner that grew into an ironic didactic one. Both Auden and Brecht started out as amoral romantic anarchists; and both, around the age of thirty, adopted a chastening public orthodoxy — Christianity in Auden's case, Communism in Brecht's. Both came to prefer mixed styles and miscellaneous influences to the purity of the lyric or the intensity of the visionary tradition. Both collaborated with other writers (once even with each other) as no poet had done since the start of the romantic era. Unlike the modernists, both adopted popular forms without the disclaimer of an ironic tone. Each exploited the didactic powers of literature, but rejected the reigning modernist assumptions that granted primacy to the creative imagination or asserted the writing of poetry to be the central human act. Neither was afraid to be vulgar, and neither would entrust serious issues to the inflation of the grand style. Modernism was a movement populated by exiles, at home only in their art. Auden and Brecht were exiles who returned.

"Who stands, the crux left of the watershed" (dating from 1927, when Auden was twenty) is the first [poem] that Auden wrote in the voice he came to recognize as his own. For about five years afterwards, his voice retained something of the modernist accent he had learned from Eliot, and his poems used the free verse he had learned at the same school. These first poems often have the air of gnomic fragments; they seem to be elements of some hidden private myth whose individual details never quite resolve themselves into a unified narrative. The same qualities of division and irresolution that mark the poems also mark the world they describe, a world where doomed heroes look down in isolation on an equally doomed society. There is division also between the poems and their readers; the poems not only refuse to yield up any cohesive meanings, but adopt a recurrent tone of foreboding and threat: "It is time for the destruction of error," "It is later than you think." Auden's early readers missed the point when they inferred from the poems' elusive privacy the existence of a coterie who shared the meanings and got the jokes; Auden's friends were as much in the dark as everyone else. The elusiveness and indecipherability of the early poems are part of their meaning: they enact the isolation they describe.

The turn away from this early style, and from the manner and subjects of modernism, can be dated precisely. Auden prepared for it in the late spring of 1933, in a series of poems that expressed first the hope of a release from isolation and from the delusive wish for an innocent place elsewhere, and, finally, asked for the will and strength to "rebuild our cities, not dream of islands." Then, in June 1933, Auden experienced what he later called a "Vision of Agape." He was sitting on a lawn with three colleagues from the school where he was teaching, when, he wrote, "quite suddenly and unexpectedly, something happened. I felt myself invaded by a power which, though I consented to it, was irresistible and certainly not mine. For the first time in my life I knew exactly—because, thanks to the power, I was doing it—what it meant to love one's neighbor as oneself." Before this, his poems had only been able to celebrate moments of impersonal erotic intensity, which he called "love." Now, in the poem "Out on the lawn I lie in bed," prompted by his vision, he had praise for everything around him. He described as "lucky" ("luck" in Auden's vocabulary has almost the force of religious "grace") "this point in time and space"—that is, the immediate moment and his "chosen . . . working-place" where he had both friends and responsibilities. His earlier forebodings are transformed into a hymn of renewal; the mutual affections of his friends will have effects beyond the privacy of their English garden and will share in the strength that can rebuild the ruined city.

This jubilant tone could not last, but Auden's sense of public responsibility did. He now began to address his audience, rather than withdraw from it or threaten it; and his audience, amid the discontents of the thirties, was eager to listen. No English poet since Byron achieved fame so quickly. In plays that borrowed their techniques from the music-hall and the cabaret, in poems written in stirring rhythms with memorable rhymes, he hoped to "make action urgent and its nature clear." This proved to be less simple than he imagined. The urgency was vivid enough in his political poems, but the exact nature of the actions urged was never as clear as he might have wished. Readers felt free to find their own actions and attitudes endorsed in these poems, and Auden, recognizing this, began to face his own increasing scruples over his easy relations with his audience. He began to use "vague" as a strong moral pejorative; and the word seemed to apply to many of his own public statements, whose resonance and rhetorical force tended to overwhelm any objections that readers, or Auden's conscience, might raise against their content or their imprecision. In his most politically active years, in the mid-thirties, Auden constantly maintained an inward debate that led him to answer a public exhortation like "Spain" with the hermetic mysteries of a poem like "Orpheus," written at about the same moment. His love poems insisted on the fragility and transience of personal relations, while at the same time his public poems proclaimed a hope for universal harmony. Auden was never altogether happy in his role as poetic prophet to the English Left, and he was often most divided when he appeared most committed. As early as 1936 he sensed that if he were ever to escape the temptations to fame and to the power to shape opinion that led him to accept his role, he would have to leave England. His work in the later thirties records a series of exploratory voyages from England to Spain, Iceland, China, across Europe, finally to America, where, in 1938, he made his decision to leave both England and the role it offered, and to leave, he thought, forever.

When he arrived in America to stay, early in 1939, he set to work on what was virtually a new career, recapitulating his earlier one in a drastically different manner. He began to explore once again the same thematic and formal territory he had covered in his English years, but with a maturer vision, and no longer distracted by the claims of a public. Whether or not by conscious intention, each of the longer poems he wrote during his first years in America served, in effect, as a replacement for a long poem he had written earlier in England. Thus in 1928 he had written a Christmas charade, "Paid on Both Sides"; now, in 1941–42, he wrote a Christmas oratorio, "For the Time Being." In place of his 1936 verse-epistle to a dead poet, "Letter to Lord Byron," he wrote in 1940 a verse-epistle to a living friend, "New Year Letter." In 1931 he had invented a form for *The Orators*, a three-part structure, framed by a prologue and epilogue, with the first part spoken by a series of voices, the second by a single voice, and the third again by multiple voices; in 1943–44 he used the same form, with the central sequence inverted, for "The Sea and the Mirror." When he published the first of his collected editions in 1945, the later poems were all present and complete, while the earlier ones had been either dismembered into their component parts or dropped entirely. Similarly, the inconclusive ending of his 1938 sonnet sequence "In Time of War" — "Wandering lost upon the mountains of our choice" — was resolved at the close of his 1940 sonnet sequence, "The Quest," in the recovered peace of "The Garden." Even the way he made his living in America repeated a pattern he had followed in the thirties: in England he had taught at various schools until 1935 when he left to work as a free-lance writer; in America he taught at various colleges and universities until 1945, then once again took up his free lance.

His shorter poems emerged from the same process of remaking that gave form to the longer ones. Shortly after he reached New York he began to write in a compressed introspective style that corresponded to the gnomic privacy of his earliest poems but transformed the old aggressiveness into self-reproach. Auden's poems passed judgment on his earlier self and work with a severity that disconcerted his admirers (who complained only of his departure from England, which he seemed to think was the best thing he had done). But the change in his life was as deep and extensive as the change in his work. The restrained and chastened intensity of his first American poems was a sign of

his newly discovered commitment to the Anglican faith he once thought he
had outgrown in adolescence. In his first year in America he began attending
church; he returned to communion late in 1940. The equivocal political commitments of a few years earlier proved to have been rehearsals for a religious
commitment that was permanent and undivided, even if its later expression
became considerably more relaxed. The last of his longer poems, "The Age
of Anxiety" (1944–46), celebrates the personal triumph of his faith, against
all odds. There was a corresponding change in the commitments of his love
poems. In the thirties he had written of the transience of eros: "Lay your sleeping
head, my love," this century's most famous love lyric, praises a faithless and
unequal relationship, its inequality signaled by the very act of the conscious
lover's address to his unconscious partner. In the forties Auden wrote of a love
that was spousal and permanent, whose responsibility endured—as one title
put it, in a phrase from the marriage service—"In Sickness and in Health."

The shift from private to public concerns that occurred in Auden's work
in the early thirties occurred again in the mid-forties, although now he was
without ambition for social influence and lived in a country where poets traditionally had none. His departure from England proved not to have been a
rejection of all public roles, as he thought at the time, but a rejection of the
wrong ones. He now became an interpreter of his society, not its scourge or
prophet. Once again, as in England, he began collaborating on works for the
stage. From the late forties onwards he wrote moral parables in the form of
opera libretti, as in the thirties he had written political propaganda in the form
of musical plays. His greatest works in the late forties and fifties were his extended
meditations on the city, its historical origins and present complexities. An initial
exploration of the subject, "Memorial for the City," a poem prompted in part
by his experience of Germany in 1945, led to the extraordinary sequence of
"Horae Canonicae," where the events of a single day, among various urban
roles and personalities, are set within a framework encompassing vast reaches
of time. The sequence's passage from dawn to dusk corresponds to passages
from birth to death, from the rise to the fall of a city, and from the creation
to the second coming. Parallel with these urban poems are a group set in rural
landscapes: "In Praise of Limestone" establishes the theme, and the sequence
of "Bucolics" extends and develops it.

In the late fifties and sixties Auden turned to the more local significance
of a single dwelling place. In 1957, he bought a farmhouse in Austria as a
summer home (the first home he had ever owned) and began the poems that
grew into the sequence "Thanksgiving for a Habitat." While narrowing his
focus to his private hearth he retained his sense of historical and social extension;
each room of the house, like each landscape in "Bucolics," has its moral and

political analogues, and more often than not, is the occasion for a meditation on history.

In his final years his subjects narrowed still further, and he returned to a transformed version of the privacy of his first poems. He left America to return to England. A nostalgic note, absent since his earliest poems, began to enter his work once more. Still, as he had denied his earlier nostalgic longings by recalling the evidence of history ("The pillar dug from the desert recorded only/The sack of a city"), now he emphasized the imaginary quality of the past whose image he evoked by writing about it in the language of folk tales. He wrote again of a doomed landscape: not an external one, but the micro-cosmos of his own aging body. He directed his meditations on history to thanks-giving rather than analysis: if his last poems concern his doomed flesh they also celebrate the family and the age from which it sprang. He made explicit his gratitude to his literary sources. At the end, in "Archaeology," his last completed poem, he delved into an unknowably remote past, yet—as he pre-pared for his own exit from the world of time into an unknowable future—he concluded with an affirmation. History, he wrote, is made "by the criminal in us:/goodness is timeless."

Most criticism, however, has taken a censorious view of Auden's revisions, and the issue is an important one because behind it is a larger dispute about Auden's theory of poetry. In making his revisions, and in justifying them as he did, Auden was systematically rejecting a whole range of modernist assump-tions about poetic form, the nature of poetic language, and the effects of poetry on its audience. Critics who find the changes deplorable generally argue, in effect, that a poet loses his right to revise or reject his work after he publishes it—as if the skill with which he brought his poems from their early drafts to the point of publication somehow left him at the moment they appeared, making him a trespasser on his own work thereafter. This argument presupposes the romantic notion that poetic form is, or ought to be, "organic," that an authentic poem is shaped by its own internal forces rather than by the external effects of craft; versions of this idea survived as central tenets of modernism. In revising his poems, Auden opened his workshop to the public, and the spectacle proved unsettling, especially as his revisions, unlike Yeats', moved against the current of literary fashion. In the later part of his career, he increasingly called attention in his essays to the technical aspects of verse, the details of metrical and stanzaic construction—much as Brecht had brought his stagehands into the full view of the audience. The goal in each case was to remove the mystery that surrounds works of art, to explode the myth of poetic inspiration, and to deny any special privileges to poetry in the realm of language or to artists in the realm of ethics.

Critics mistook this attitude as a "rejection" of poetry, when in fact it was a recognition of its potential effects. The most notorious aspect of Auden's revisions, as of his whole poetic theory, was his insistence that a poem must not be "dishonest," must not express beliefs that a poet does not actually hold, no matter how rhetorically effective he finds them. In Auden's view, poetry could not be exempted from ethical standards of truth or falsehood: a poem could be a lie, and what was more serious, a poetic lie could be more persuasive in the public realm than lies less eloquently expressed. Words had the potential to do good or evil, whether their source was political discourse or the ordered images of a poem. Auden's sense of the effect of poetic language—like Brecht's sense of the effect of stage performance—differs entirely from the modernist theory that sets poetry apart from the world, either in an interior psychological arena or in the enclosed garden of reflexivity where poems refer only to themselves. Already in the thirties, Auden's political poems assumed they had the power to affect attitudes, and therefore indirectly to affect action; his later judgments on those poems made the same assumption, but from a very different moral perspective. In the first version of "In Memory of W. B. Yeats" Auden had written that time would pardon writers like Kipling and Claudel for their right-wing views; the implication was that the left-wing views held by Auden and his audience were consonant with the force of history and would need no forgiveness whatever. Auden soon found this less easy to believe than he did when he wrote it, and was less willing to encourage such complacency in his readers. He dropped the stanzas about Kipling and Claudel, and dropped entirely such poems as "Spain" where the "struggle" is more important than its consequences and goodness is equated with victory, or "September 1, 1939" where a rhetorical sleight-of-hand grants the moral value of just actions to the ironic "messages" of the isolated just. These poems are memorable enough to survive all of Auden's interference, and there are ancient and vigorous critical standards by which they must be judged great art; still, when Auden called them "trash which he is ashamed to have written" he was taking them far more seriously—and taking poetic language far more seriously—than his critics ever did.

Too seriously, most readers would argue. Yet the revisions Auden made in the forties, like the changes in his life and work, effectively put into practice the doubts he had experienced earlier. He had embedded an allegory of his mixed feelings into *The Ascent of F6*, a play written with Christopher Isherwood in 1936. The play traces the destruction of a mountain climber (Auden's dramatic representative), at the moment of his greatest triumph, as a result of the conflicts inherent in a public role his private terrors tempted him to accept. Auden avoided a parallel fate by leaving England for America at the height of his fame, and by working to expunge from his poetry the tendencies that he sensed might otherwise have destroyed him and his poetry together. Later he could write more tolerantly of the temptation to "ruin a fine tenor voice/For effects that bring down the house," but by that time, having defeated his public temptations, he had set out to conquer his private ones also. The poems he wrote in this period, in the forties and after, are less immediately compelling than his earlier ones, but more profound and more rewarding in the long term. His masterpiece is arguably "The Sea and the Mirror" (its nearest rivals may be "New Year Letter" and "Horae Canonicae"), whose longest section, "Caliban to the Audience," is the work he preferred to all his others. It had been the most recalcitrant in conception—he was stalled six months before he could work out its form—and the most pleasurable in the writing; and it confronted most directly and comprehensively the limits and powers of his art, and its temptations and possibilities.

JOHN R. BOLY

The Orators: *Portraits of the Artist in the Thirties*

Although it has been almost fifty years since it first appeared, Auden's *The Orators* is still a much appreciated but little understood work. The four alternately addled and sinister speakers of Book I, the introspective and doomed Airman of Book II, and the six occasional and parodic odes of Book III have each, to some extent, been separately glossed. But so far, no one has found the pattern in the carpet that shows how they all fit together. What Monroe K. Spears wrote of *The Orators* in his major study, *The Poetry of W. H. Auden*, still holds true today: "One constantly feels on the verge of discovering the key that will make the whole thing clear. Since thirty years have failed to reveal anything of the sort, one must conclude that this feeling is illusory." Spears's admission, as well as those of subsequent critics, is really a commentary on the limitations of purely textual criticism. When detached from its peculiar place in literary history, *The Orators* never has and never will make sense. When seen, however, in the context of what writers and especially poets were concerned with in 1932, it falls into a splendid, simple pattern. *The Orators* is Auden's literary manifesto of the thirties, and it was to govern his verse for the rest of that tempestuous decade.

There can be little doubt but that in *The Orators* Auden was primarily addressing the new generation of writers that had just emerged as a self-conscious group. The main dedication to Stephen Spender is followed by further dedications in the odes of Book III to Gabriel Carrit, Edward Upward, Rex Warner (through his little boy John), and to Auden's students at Larchfield School, Helensburgh. With the exception of one to students at Larchfield, all the dedi-

From *Twentieth Century Literature* 27, no. 3 (Fall 1981). Copyright ᵖ 1982, Hofstra University Press. Originally entitled "W. H. Auden's *The Orators*: Portrait of the Artist in the Thirties."

cations were to Auden's literarily ambitious Oxford acquaintances. The ill-fated decision to address this group stands, incidentally, behind the notorious complexity of *The Orators*. As understandably disgruntled reviewers noted, Auden's text is littered with slang, public-school esoterica, cryptic references, and private rituals. Few outside a very small circle would have known in 1932 who were Pretzel and Maverick in the first ode (schoolboy nicknames for Spender and Isherwood).

Auden's choice of audience was unfortunate because it diminished, not the literary quality of *The Orators*, but its influence. What Auden had to say to his old school friends was extremely important, and it remains so today. In 1932, a young English poet was faced with a dilemma. Liberals were outraged at Ramsay MacDonald's betrayal of the Labour Party, there appeared to be no real leadership in England, and the Depression had hit hard. So poets were expected, as they had not been expected since the days of Peterloo, to address contemporary social issues in a confident and authoritative fashion. Yet at the same time, poets were still poets. Auden and his young friends could not forget, though a few tried, the modernist innovations of T. S. Eliot in *The Waste Land*. Through the force of his example, Eliot had ushered in an age in which the poet was imprisoned within the fragmentary and perplexing impressions of his own subjectivity. As Laura Riding sadly noted in her *Contemporaries and Snobs*, all the post-Eliotic poet could hope to know was Tiresias' heap of broken images.

For the poets of Auden's generation, this dilemma of the thirties assumed a quite practical form. They wanted to be the Byrons and Shelleys of their age. But their modernist exemplum was Eliot's bewildered and enfeebled Tiresias. With the foresight and brashness so characteristic of him, Auden responded directly to this dilemma in the two thematic impulses of *The Orators*. In one, which informs the "Journal of an Airman," Auden shows how the modern poet can, if not escape, then at least make partial sense of a world fragmented through subjectivity. In the other impulse, which provides the structure for the entire work, Auden defines through parody and satire the limitations of the modern poet when dealing with social concerns.

Christopher Isherwood had translated Baudelaire's *Intimate Journals* in the early thirties, and when he showed this recent work to Auden, there was born the Airman of *The Orators*. In the introduction he later wrote to Isherwood's translation, Auden characterized Baudelaire's journalist as a type of the self-conscious modern everyman, struggling to order the chaos of his subjectivity. But unlike that other everyman, Eliot's wan and forlorn Tiresias, Baudelaire's journalist is possessed by a feverish vitality. Noting what we can now see was Baudelaire's influence upon Auden, the *London Mercury* (26 [1932]), wrote of *The Orators:* "It appears to be the work of an imagination without a mind—a far more complicated state than paranoia—working on fragments of knowledge and experience." In that operative phrase, "working on," Auden's reviewer had hit upon the precise point of thematic divergence between *The Waste Land* and *The Orators.* Auden's Baudelarian Airman, unlike Tiresias, is an active and even aggressive arranger of his subjective experience.

Evidently Auden himself had practiced such arrangements for years. In his early autobiography, *Lions and Shadows*, Isherwood recalls how during the late twenties he and Auden used to play "the *Waste Land* game." The idea was to string together bits of foreign languages, proper names, and private references—much as Eliot had done. But Auden introduced an important difference: "For Eliot's Dante quotations and classical learning he substituted oddments of scientific, medical, and psychoanalytical jargon." The Airman, with his technician's language and mechanistic metaphors, follows his author in this clinical mode. One would search through *The Waste Land* in vain for an image of perception as optimistic as this: "My first memories of my Uncle were like images cast on the screen of a television set, and maternally induced." Here, perception is not a hopeless mystery, as in *The Waste Land*, but an explicable and perhaps even adjustable process. Thus, as a response to Tiresias, whom Eliot called "the central consciousness" of his poem, Auden's Airman is not only more energetic, but also more calculating, analytical, and rationalistic. Instead of a despairing and enervate prophet, Auden chose as his model perceiver a self-possessed and tight-lipped technician.

Like any good technician, the Airman first plans what he is going to do, and then does it. The Journal begins with a rationalistic formula for dealing with the unruliness of one's subjective impressions: "A system organizes itself, if interaction is undisturbed. Organization owes nothing to the surveyor. It is in no sense pre-arranged. The surveyor provides just news." The system that the Airman mentions is man. The surveyor is man's *sensation*, which gathers sensory impressions. The organizer is man's *mind*, which arranges those impressions. Our phenomenological and neo-Kantian Airman thus announces at the outset that organization—the desired goal of understanding—results from an interaction between gathering sensation and organizing mind.

Having defined his method, the Airman proceeds in a businesslike fashion to its application. The most obvious thing about the Journal is also the most significant: every page is littered with organizational schemes. After some preliminary definitions, the Airman proceeds to a numbered list, six geometrical diagrams, a Mendelian hereditary chart, and several more definitions. He then relaxes for a moment by composing a sestina, and having in this way gathered strength he proceeds further to more definitions, an alphabet, a list of triads, a calendar of the week, more lists, more notes, more outlines, and so on. This frantic organization is exciting in its way, for it records an incessant warfare between mind and sensation. No sooner does the clinical mind of the Airman arrange a batch of impressions into an orderly scheme than along comes a fresh onslaught from sensation, and the mind must begin anew. Auden's response to the despairing and chaotic subjectivity of Eliot's Tiresias, then, takes the form of a technique or process of understanding. For want of a better name, this technique could be called skeptical probabilism. It is skeptical because the Airman's succession of rational schemes shows that he does not trust any of them very far. It is probabilist because his formulation of any schemes at all shows the Airman's provisional faith in their validity.

With the method of skeptical probabilism in mind, we can see for the first time just what is happening in the Airman's Journal. Commentators have long recognized that the Airman struggles against an announced "Enemy." But they have generally overlooked that the Airman, as Robert Penn Warren pointed out (*American Review*, 3 [1934]), is actually caught in the middle of a civil war. He does not have one enemy but two—the flux-mongers and the order-doctrinaires. Upon examination, these enemies turn out to be none other than allegorical versions of sensation and mind. The order-doctrinaires, who represent mind, like things tidy. They are respectable, educated, squeamish, and dogmatic city dwellers: Uncle Sam, the Oxford don, and the good ladies of the London Truss Club. It is characteristic of order-doctrinaires that they prefer expressions such as "I mean" and "quite frankly," and that they refuse to kiss a baby on the mouth. The flux-mongers, who represent sensation, like things rowdy. They are slovenly, ignorant, vulgar, and anarchistic savages: the invaders glimpsed on distant farms such as Arncliffe and Kettlewell, or the frenzied tribes at whom a fellow Airman fires his last, desperate drum of ammunition. In the allegory of the Airman's Journal, the Airman shuttles back and forth between these two opposing forces, mind and sensation, alternately trying to upset the complacency of the one and to discipline the unruliness of the other. He is, in short, a model skeptical probabilist.

As Auden noted in his 1966 Foreword, he adopted as one of his sources for *The Orators* a bizarre book, *The Coming War* (1931), by General Ludendorff. An ex-member of the German High Command, Ludendorff deemed it necessary to warn the Germany of the early thirties against an imminent Franco-Italian invasion. In a similar vein, the Airman strives to warn complacent mind, the order-doctrinaires, against an approaching invasion by obstreperous sensation, the flux-mongers. This goes on throughout the Journal, and all is well. But at the end, the Airman discovers a set of attack plans. According to this fiendish plot, anarchy is to be unleashed by the flux-mongers through such devices as accusing leading citizens of vicious looks, and by having girl guides mob vicars at the climax of their sermons. The Airman panics at the awful news, but it really is no news at all. Sensation is always trying to overwhelm and disrupt the arrangements of mind. A few days before the attack, the Journal mysteriously ends, so that Auden's allegory of understanding, like its human subject, remains unresolved.

Auden responded directly to Eliot's despairing predicament of subjectivity, then, but not in the way one might expect. Indeed, as a dialogue within the modern tradition, the confrontation between Tiresias and the Airman qualifies as one of the great neglected oddities of modern literature. We can imagine on one side the sere and withered Tiresias, elegant in his Laforguian detachment, subtle in his Bradleyan sophistication, dazzling in his Eliotic erudition, an imposing literary precedent and an intimidating philosophical adversary. On the other side stands the Airman with his bumptious schoolboy energy, his language out of some technical manual, and his cookie-cutter schemes and diagrams. It would be tempting to dismiss the whole affair as premeditated horseplay, as to some extent it is, except that Auden is rarely more serious than when playing the lunatic. The Airman's skeptical probabilism stands behind the vitality, fearlessness, and curiosity that are distinctive of Auden's best social poetry.

Having dealt with the side of the thirties dilemma that involved the poetic tradition, Auden had then to deal with the other side, which involved the historical situation of the Depression. Granted that poets wanted to address social ills and political problems, what implications did the Airman's skeptical probabilism have for them? As a method, skeptical probabilism was utterly indifferent to subject matter. The poet was free to talk about anything he desired—tramlines, power lines, or unemployment lines. But though it delivered the poet from the chaos of his subjective impressions skeptical probabilism did not deliver him from subjectivity itself. The poet was still every bit as trapped as Tiresias within the prison of his own being. Consequently, he could talk about anything he liked, but only as a private individual with a limited point of view. This is, of course, exactly what Auden did in the years after *The Orators*. His poems about contemporary issues—"A Summer Night," "On This Island," "Lullabye," "September 1, 1939," and the long poem that concluded the decade, *New Year Letter*—habitually place before the reader a human and finite speaker, firmly located in time and space.

Such an accepted limitation of the poet, however, ran counter to the usual practice of the thirties poets. In their eagerness to ignore the curse of Tiresias, Auden's contemporaries tended to adopt the disembodied voice of a megaphone at a rally or a crowd at a parade, a loud strident voice that was supposed to prove the speaker's detachment, objectivity, and unquestionably righteous authority. So uniform is this voice that political poetry from the thirties is probably easier to recognize than any other kind of poetry written in our century. Consider the following passages:

> They walk home remembering the straining red flags,
> And with pennons of song still fluttering through
>   their blood
> They speak of the World State...
> All you that have a cool head and safe hands
> Awaken early, there is much to do...
> I see the house of the future, and men upstanding,
> men not fearing the sack.

Only a handful of experts would be able to identify these passages as the work of Spender, Day Lewis, and Rex Warner. But any student of modern literature could place this verse in the thirties.

The authoritative voice adopted by the thirties poets is essential to *The Orators* for in the Journal, as well as in the other two books, Auden in effect cautions his contemporaries against this voice. Who were poets, after all, to lead and to redeem England? When we first meet the Airman, he would be right at home among the bold new writers of *New Signatures* and the later *New Country* in that, like them, he is convinced of his calling to save society. And like them, his great problem is to justify that call. Accordingly, the Airman invents a fantastic genealogy that bypasses his real parents, he eschews contact with other people, he plays preposterous jokes, and, above all, he is an airman. Flying enables him both literally and figuratively to look down upon his fellow beings, an activity he accepts as a sovereign privilege. As a result of the reminiscent essay, "A Literary Transference" (*Southern Review*, 6 [1940]), Auden's indebtedness to Hardy for the Airman's hawk's-eye vision is well known. But it is less frequently noted that Auden, even in the early thirties, rejected this viewpoint as well as its dangerously arrogant presuppositions for the poet. The early poem "Consider," for example, begins with an Airman's perspective, high in the clouds. But it ends by hurtling both speaker and audience back down to earth. The reason why is suggested in one of the poems that Auden contributed to *New Country*, "Me, March, you do with your movements master and rock." A long song, the poem rejects the hawk's-eye vision because it ignores the reality of all that is human and particular.

It comes as no surprise, then, that in the course of his Journal, the Airman is gradually brought down to earth. This would-be redeemer comes to the startling realization that he is not so superior after all. A perambulating textbook of psychosomatic ailments, the Airman suffers from fainting spells, kleptomania, and paranoid delusions. He tries to conceal this condition, but these attempts are stymied by his kleptomaniacally rebellious hands. Significantly, the Airman is not worried about the ethics or the psychology of the situation, only the consequences: "If the enemy ever got to hear of it, my whole work would be nullified." That is, if his readers ever guessed the poet's humanity, then his career as an authoritative propagandist would be finished. (Earlier in the Journal, the Airman had made plans to drop leaflets from his craft.) But as always in Auden, the horrid truth will out. The Airman's denied humanity at last rises up in the climactic and most fascinating passage of the Journal, the dream at the end.

The dream goes as follows. The Airman sees his lover, the mysterious E, being put to death on the far bank of a deep river. He rushes to save E, yet the Airman cannot cross the river because the young boatman has his back turned. Desperately the Airman screams at the boatman, but his cries are drowned by the howls of a nearby crowd.

A classic study in self-repression, the dream reveals that the Airman is split into two opposing halves. The Airman's private self, which wants to save E, is repressed by the young boatman of his public self, which heeds the roaring crowd. In later editions, E is referred to as he, so it is likely that the Airman is trying to conceal a homosexual affair, or at least his longing for such an affair. As an authoritative thirties poet, to do otherwise would mean certain failure for his Messianic mission. After a few days, however, the Airman realizes that his dream, with its enforced reminder of his inescapable humanity, means the end of his social redeemership: "The true significance of my hands. 'Do not imagine that you, no more than any other conqueror, escape the mark of grossness'." The mark of grossness, the curse of individual and subjective humanity, was what the thirties poets were reluctant to admit.

As we turn from the Journal to the other two books of *The Orators*, we are in a good position to see the beautifully designed structure of the entire work, a structure that has proven elusive for the last fifty years. All three books confront the problem of what the post-Eliotic poet should do in times of social crisis. Book II, which occupies the center of the work, shows the provisional intellectual schemes of the Airman and his discovery of human individuality. Here we find Auden's answer to the dilemma of the thirties poet, as well as his primary portrait of the artist. The other two books, which flank the Journal, break down this harmonious union into its opposing components. In Book I the various speakers, with the exception of the letter writer, are obsessed with a single, masterful scheme. Artists with an answer, they are authoritative in some threatening, sinister, or dictatorial way. But in Book III, the various speakers are obsessed with their inability to find any such ordering scheme. Artists without an answer, they cast about for some authority or leader to tell them what to do. The contrast between Books I and III is a somewhat rough and inelegant affair, but it nonetheless gave Auden what he needed in order to complete his poetic manifesto. Book I presented an opportunity for a series of parodies, Auden's acerbic versions of what *not* to do. Book III presented an opportunity for specific and satiric warnings.

We know from the reminiscences of Robert Medley that the "Address for a Prize Day," the first of the four parodies in Book I, had its origin in a sermon given by a new headmaster at Gresham's School when Auden was in the sixth form. This unfortunate gentleman was in the habit of underestimating his audiences and once, after beginning a sermon with "Jesus Christ cuts no ice in California," he proceeded to ask: "Who cuts no what, where?" A version of this fiasco, with which Auden entertained his schoolmates for weeks, supplies the well-known opening lines of the "Address": "Commemoration. Commemoration. What does it mean? What does it mean. Not what does it mean to them, there, then. What does it mean to us, here, now? It's a facer, isn't it boys?" But though the character and personality of the speaker for a Prize Day are taken from Auden's schoolboy reminiscences, the parodic target is T. S. Eliot. The parody has been obscured by the passage of more than forty years and the sober dust of reverence that settles upon the mighty. But the telltale signs are still there. The headmaster shares with Eliot a fondness for Dante, a genial tone of sniffing disdain, a bland assumption that he indeed has the answer to the problem of England, and most importantly, a weakness for sanctimonious moralizing. By the early thirties, Eliot had gained a quiet notoriety for a similar weakness.

Auden's fellow poets probably enjoyed his prank of turning the venerable Eliot into an addlepated headmaster, and Eliot probably enjoyed it too. But this criticism of the artist as naïve moralizer applied as well to Spender, Day-Lewis, Warner, and even to Auden himself. Though they wanted to contend with real and practical issues, the thirties poets, with their genteel Oxford literary backgrounds, were ill-equipped to do so. Consequently, they often did what the headmaster of the "Address" did, and what they accused Eliot of doing: they took refuge in fervent moralizing. Auden himself, with his early and infamously vague doctrine of "a change of heart" was sometimes as guilty as the rest. As the first of Auden's negative portraits of the artist in Book I, the "Address for a Prize Day" tells us much about the others. The humor is lively and the comic spirits are high. But Auden's parody contains a critique of the artist that is incisive and unsparing.

If the moralizing headmaster falls in "Address," then his plotting students are the victims of "Argument." Here Auden parodies the literary cultishness of the early Auden group. Stephen Spender noted in his *World Within World* that by the time he came up to Oxford, there was already a closely knit Auden cult. Initiation even then was difficult. The members of this cult were literary and ambitious, and like many literary and ambitious eighteen- and nineteen-year-olds, they felt a need for urgent social reform. But without a clear strategy, without even a clear notion of what needed to be reformed, the early Auden group had to sublimate its reformist zeal into the private myths of the Mortmere Saga. The Saga had been invented by Christopher Isherwood and Edward Upward while they were at Gresham's School. Auden was inducted into its mysteries in 1925, during a summer vacation on the Isle of Wight. In substance Mortmere was a literary boys' club, with surreal settings such as Cape Wrath and the Rat's Hotel, grotesque characters such as Laily and the Worm, and murderous action laced with utterly private jokes. But in function, the Mortmere Saga was somehow supposed to be therapeutic and socially redemptive. No member of the Auden group ever figured out how.

In "Argument," Auden makes the same point at the beginning of the thirties that Christopher Isherwood was to make at the end. The closed literary cult of Mortmere was no more than the private self-indulgence of defensive school-boys (*Lions and Shadows*). After the garrulous and familiar headmaster of "Address," there is a marked tonal shift to the surreptitious cultist of "Argument." This speaker's language, his beliefs, his rituals, and his intentions are all darkly portentous and suggestively significant in the approved Mortmere fashion. But they are portentous and significant only because they are so vague. Quoth the schoolboy: "Speak the name only with meaning only for us, meaning Him, a call to our clearing." Like the early members of the Auden group, this character genuinely believes that he is participating in some stirring social revival. He talks of a missing leader, of surreptitious warfare, of a coming revolution. But all that actually happens in "Argument," despite the portentous plotting, is an outing to the country and a channel crossing—typical activities for a schoolboy's long vacation. Auden's implied conclusion in this second parody is that the literary cultist cannot save society. At times, the parody grows a little ruthless. Frustrated at his inability to usher in the new life, the speaker in "Argument" must content himself by urinating "Resurgam" in a bank of snow.

The third section of Book I, "Statement," offers yet another voice, that of a shrill and uncompromising revolutionary: "To each an award, suitable to his sex, his class, and the power." Auden in this parody directs his attention to the artist as political ideologue. The beliefs of his artist-ideologue, for whom sex comes first and power last, are roughly those of D. H. Lawrence as he was interpreted by the early Auden group. (Lawrence was a frequent topic of discussion at Oxford, and Auden later cited him as one of the principal sources for *The Orators*.) Lawrence's appeal for the artist in the thirties lay in his direct gospel of passion and blood, strict authority, and blind obedience, a gospel especially attractive to Day Lewis and Rex Warner. In "Statement," however, Auden parodies these notions by seeing to it that his Lawrentian ideologue renders himself ridiculous. This speaker vigorously proclaims a new dispensation based on sex, vigor, and health. Yet his ideal society is riddled with perversion, anemia, and disease. Here, as in the Airman's Journal, illness serves as a reminder of human individuality and vulnerability. Such individuality is the point of all those endless catalogs of "One. . ." for which "Statement" is infamous. Analogues of human society, the catalogs insist that a group of individuals can never be reduced, as Lawrence at times seemed to hope, to a primordial and unthinking mass.

The negative portraits of the artist in Book I come to an end with a parody of the aesthete in "Letter to a Wound." Unlike moralist, cultist, and ideologue, the aesthete does not have some master plan of social Messianism. Instead, he locks himself in a hotel room where he proceeds to compose an intimate and even erotic letter to his own fatal illness, the wound. Thus the Letter does not deal with artistic temptations to play at redeemer, but with a reaction against this: to abandon the historical situation and retreat into aestheticism.

But the "Letter to a Wound," which might be expected to offer the easiest parodic target of all, turns out to be the most vexing and difficult section of *The Orators*. The letter writer is an outcast and a solipsist, self-indulgent, cowardly, dishonorable, and distinctly unhealthy. But at the same time, he is the most direct, honest, unillusioned, and likable speaker in Book I. It appears that in the ambivalence of the Letter, Auden's irony is momentarily out of control. Probably this is because Auden began his literary career as a late twenties aesthete, and only gradually came to accept a qualified notion of the poet's social responsibility. When Auden decided to address contemporary issues, about the time he wrote "1929," he had to reconcile this decision with his earlier allegiance to craftsmanship and artistic independence. In the ambivalence of the "Letter to a Wound," it is possible to see Auden struggling to reconcile two contradictory impulses within his own literary identity.

After the parodies in Book I, Auden shifts in Book III to the more serious mode of satire. The various speakers of these occasional odes are unable to find any scheme or plan for ordering their unruly worlds. Hence, in the words of the first ode, they seek "one with power." Originally there were six odes in all, but Auden dropped the second—an entertaining but adventitious description of a losing rugby team—from the 1966 edition. In the revised version, the first, third, and fifth odes chart stages in the search for some commanding leader: the Syrian rider of I, the infant savior of III, the implacable and inscrutable Father of V.

As writers responding to social crisis, the speakers in Book III inspire satire rather than parody because what they are doing is potentially more harmful. Auden knew that few people would pay serious attention to a poet posing as social Messiah. Herbert Read could hail Stephen Spender in the *Adelphi* (5 [1932]) as "another Shelley," and Read might even be right. But how large a following did Shelley ever have? When poets began, however, to promote not themselves but an independent political reality, it was an altogether different matter. A cause, a leader, or a campaign has a plausibility and an appeal that a poet does not. Should a writer recommend one of these, then serious propaganda had begun. The middle odes of Book III are each dedicated to people whom Auden knew—Edward Upward, Rex Warner through his infant son John, Auden's students at Larchfield Academy. When these dedications are taken as historical cues, as they ought to be in an occasional ode, they direct us to specific and satirical warnings against naïve political allegiances.

The third ode describes the voluntary exile, "forging from freedom," of the doomed middle class (cf. "Consider" and "Venus Will Now Say a Few Words"). It was a stock belief of English leftists, who hesitated to think very hard about such matters, that after the great revolution any surplus capitalists would simply be shipped away in the bright dawn of proletarian rule. But Auden's dedication to Edward Upward gives that exile a new meaning. The year before Auden published *The Orators*, Upward had returned from a vacation in Leningrad as the first full-fledged Communist of the Auden group. This would-be revolutionary, however, had returned to teach with Auden at Larchfield Academy, Helensburgh, which C. Day Lewis described as the "Wimbledon of the north" (*The Buried Day*). The third ode thus has a fellow traveler who is also a fellow teacher address Upward as the two of them ride a train north to Helensburgh in order to resume their academic duties. By turning this ride into a doomed exile, the poem reminds the politically zealous Upward that as a teacher at a stuffy English boys' school, he too must be numbered among the capitalist oppressors.

But the third ode goes well beyond this relatively mild satire to dismiss the whole basis of Upward's political activism—and by implication, that of his fellow leftists—as the impossible longings of naïve idealists. Upward was at the time working on a story that he was soon to publish in *New Country*, "Sunday," which tells of a vaguely dissatisfied young man's decision to join the Communist Party. The speaker in Auden's ode takes up this theme of discontent, but insists that far from being the basis for revolution, it is a human necessity:

> The slight despair
> At what we are,
> The Marginal grief
> Is the source of life.

Upward was one of the original inventors of Mortmere, and the second ode begins in that fantasy landscape, with Larchfield as a sinister hotel and the schoolboys as suspicious types. But the poem ends in the more sober industrial landscape preferred by Auden with a vision of "The flare of foundries at end of year." In this quiet shift in setting, the third ode moves away from schoolboy dreaming about noble causes, and the Communism with which it is associated, to an accepted realism.

Whereas Auden cautioned his fellow schoolmaster Upward against devotion to a cause, in the fourth ode he cautions his friend Rex Warner against devotion to a leader. A fine athlete and the captain of Wadham's rugby team during his Oxford days, Warner tended to think of social activism in terms of forceful leadership. The essence of his early political thinking, if anything so vague can be called political, may be found in his chorus from the *Dam*: "Where now is the designer? Has he died?/When will work start again on the dam, in the mine?." Auden satirizes his naïve faith in political leadership by having an enthusiastic but distinctly dim-witted speaker hail Warner's little boy John, to whom the ode is dedicated, as England's long-awaited secular Messiah. With his usual virtuosity, Auden capably mimics the glee of a spectator at a rugby match: "I cannot state it too clearly, I shall not refrain,/It is John, son of Warner, has pulled my chain." The likeliest candidate for the identity of this speaker is little John's adoring father, Rex. Auden derived several satiric benefits from this identification. In the course of praising John Warner, he was able to have his speaker disregard all the other political leaders who were then emerging: the proletariat, the upper class, MacDonald, Hoover, Baldwin, and Briand, as well as Pilsudski, Mussolini, and Hitler. And by ridiculously putting John Warner in their place, Auden could draw to his father's attention the dubiety of uncritical allegiance to a political savior.

Having cautioned against causes and leaders, Auden turned his attention in the fifth ode to the temptation of naïve political activism. He dedicated this ode to his pupils at Larchfield Academy, and the poem deals with the plight of youthful recruits conscripted to fight against some nefarious foe. But when one of the recruits asks for a better explanation, he is speedily shut up with a "Go to sleep, Sonny!" Toward the end of the ode, their adversary at last appears, and it turns out that the new recruits are merely fighting against a projected image of themselves, the seven deadly sins. The fifth ode, like its contemporary, "The Watchers," is thus a plea to the young for caution and restraint in action. Unfortunately, Auden's plea was to go unheeded. It is a sad irony of literary history that John Cornford took a line from this ode, "As Our Might Lessens," as the title of one of his own poems, which called for bold, armed conflict. A Cambridge graduate, gifted essayist, and promising young poet, Cornford was killed in December 1936 while fighting in the Spanish Civil War. It was a tragic and needless loss that confirmed what Auden had earlier guessed in the fifth ode. The artist who aligned himself with a political cause was destined to be used and discarded, as were Auden's youthful recruits.

As we look back on the thirties, Auden's accomplishment in *The Orators* is formidable. He had ended the era of *The Waste Land,* and he had opened the way for a new kind of poetry. Through his response to Eliot, Auden made the lyrical and personal voice available to poets writing about contemporary social issues. Unfortunately, Auden's poetics was to go largely unnoticed. As the thirties wore on, his fellow poets had to discover for themselves the ill-advised nature of their foray into political activism. For Auden, however, the decisions he made in *The Orators* enabled him to write about his historical era in a way powerful and memorable for its intimate humanity.

JOHN R. BOLY

The Romantic Tradition in
The Age of Anxiety

Perhaps this is where we shall yet discover the realm of our invention, that realm in which we also still can be original, say as parodists of world history and the clowns of God—perhaps, even if nothing else today has a future, our laughter may yet have a future.
　　　　　　　　　　　　　　—NIETZSCHE, Beyond Good and Evil

But he who wills in a religious sense must have a receptive attitude towards the terrible, he must open himself to it, and he has only to take care that it does not stop halfway, but that it leads him into the serenity of the infinite.
　　　　　　　　　　　　　　—KIERKEGAARD, Stages on Life's Way

Auden's vision of romantic origins is complex, but it is possible to get an overview of his position by using as our major texts three of his works, *The Prolific and the Devourer*, *The Enchafèd Flood*, and *The Dyer's Hand*. Essentially, Auden saw romanticism as embodying the main dilemma of Western culture. In the Renaissance, a new humanism, intent upon championing the heroic individual, discarded the impediments of medieval Catholicism's authoritarian church and absolutist metaphysics. It was to be the era of rational man, distrustful of what could not be seen and touched, secure in his newfound powers of empirical method and scientific invention.

From *Daedalus* (Journal of the American Academy of Arts and Sciences) 3, no. 3 of the Proceedings of the American Academy of Arts and Sciences (Summer 1982) *Representations and Realities*. Copyright © 1982 by the American Academy of Arts and Sciences. Originally entitled "Auden and the Romantic Tradition in *The Age of Anxiety*."

The official faith of the new humanism, Auden maintained, was the Protestant religion, which he tended to associate with a Calvinist expediency. Protestantism, in Auden's view, did not mean the nonexistence of metaphysical absolutes and spiritual reality, but it did mean their irrelevance. Accordingly, the Protestant compromise split the new humanist into an outer man governed by reason and the profit motive, and an inner man governed by sentiment and such glimpses of the divine light as grace and election vouchsafed. The outer man soon discovered that reason could justify anything, so he often became a hypocrite ruled by the genteel coercion of respectable appearances. The inner man, cast alone into the underworld of the subconscious, suffered the worse fate of perennial guilt. Without the symbols and liturgies of the discarded Catholicism— which during the post-Tridentine period was itself becoming emptily formalized— he had no mythic guide through the labyrinth of his own inwardness. Harrowing hell on his own, Protestant man discovered anew the depths of his depravity. He also discovered anew, well before Freud, the technique of ignoring that depravity through repression and its displacements.

Romanticism emerged as the new humanism's response to its own sense of discontent and failure. As would be expected in an empirical culture, romanticism began with an indisputable factual observation: the world created by a cold and calculating rationalism was a wasteland of dead mechanism and compulsive repetition, Blake's dark Satanic mills. In a double heresy, romanticism thus rejected both the Protestant split between outer and inner man and the rationalist faith in the sole privilege of reason to govern the external world. "The whole complex of ideas which we call romanticism," Auden wrote in *The Prolific and the Devourer*, "is the attempt of Protestantism to find its own brand of Catholic unity, as the evil effects of separating the private and public life become apparent." Henceforth, the real man of inwardly discovered passion and energy was to turn the fallen world into the New Jerusalem. But after its always brilliant beginnings, the romantic theocracy of inwardness soon ran into serious trouble. It in effect unleashed the Protestant nightmare of a guilt-ridden, hag-ridden subconscious into the daylit, conscious world. At first, this unleashing was symbolic, an aesthetic liberation of new and exciting energies. But eventually Caliban leapt off the stage and into the audience. Rightly or wrongly, Auden saw the English and European political arena of the thirties, together with its disastrous aftermath in the following decade, as the grim proving ground of romantic kerygma. In a famous passage from "Spain 1937," he pointedly rejected romanticism's naive faith that the god of unleashed desire could build a New Jerusalem:

> What's your proposal? To build the Just City? I will,
> I agree. Or is it the suicide pact, the romantic
> Death?

One could easily argue against this too simple view (as Auden himself did in *New Year Letter*), but that would be beside the point. With so radical a critic, the important thing is to find the threatening truth within his hyperboles.

Auden realized that both rationalism and romanticism were offshoots of the same Renaissance humanism, and as such, both attempted to found an absolute system on the capacities of a finite creature. But it is an ancient paradox that man, whether as mind or soul, is neither autonomous nor complete. When he tries to be, he becomes the victim either of a lifeless objectivity or an inchoate subjectivity. Romantic heretics were quick to see the limits of rational humanism, and every visionary since Blake has in one way or another resisted the "mind-forg'd" manacles that chain the imagination to a dead world of space and time. But as humanists themselves, they were slower to learn that the energies imprisoned in the subconscious, though as necessary as reason, were also incapable of delivering finite man from his plight of mortality. The romantic humanist, intent upon self-divinization, had to pretend that desire was creatively godlike and somehow eternal. Yet romantic demonologies, from Coleridge's Christabel to Eliot's Belladonna, proved the Protestant truth that desire was as readily destructive; and the notorious brevity of romantic inspiration, significantly the most obsessive theme of the new movement, proved that desire was tragically short-lived. Romantic humanism was consequently forced into a complex strategy of repression, in which its god was paradoxically denied through a truncated mythos, and its fears displaced into a compensatory poetics.

It took Auden most of the thirties to work out his objections to both rationalist and romantic versions of humanism, and as is well known, at the end of that decade he converted to Christianity. This may be seen, depending upon one's interpretive standpoint, either as a radical departure or a cowering retreat. Here I would suggest that Auden's conversion arose from his determination to regain contact with the strength of romantic origins, and that a decisive literary influence on his conversion was the mythmaking of William Blake. Auden discovered through Blake a visionary theism, closely related to the *philosophia perennis* of mystical religion, that formed within romanticism a counter-movement to its humanist origins. Such theism is not involved with the moralistic and dogmatic codes of orthodox religion, for which Auden had as little regard as did Blake for Deism, or Kierkegaard for Christendom. Still less is it to be confused with such pseudomysticisms as vitalism, pantheism, or occultism, which are simply displaced projections of subconscious energies. Rather, the center of this theism is to be found in an absolute and enabling love, whose creative power is best thought of as the realizing consciousness—infinite, because containing all places, and eternal, because containing all times—that is therefore the absolute ground of the individual consciousness. This is the "I" as pure subject rather than relative object, the final perceiver presupposed by any perception, who dwells in the eternal moment and is symbolized as God. To the visionary theist, the crisis is not in finding this absolute, but in withstanding its relentless presence. And for those few who can, the perception of the jumbled fragments of space and time gives way to the discovery of eternity, the archetypal symbols and mythic patterns of involution and evolution.

Blake portrays this act of discovery in his great monomyth of creation and fall, redemption and apocalypse. Although there has been a critical tendency to set Blake apart from the other romantics, his splendidly elaborated myth traces the same recurrent passage that Geoffrey Hartman has found most crucial to all romantic and postromantic poetry, leading "from self-consciousness to imagination." Within this passage, humanism as the despairing divinization of finite faculties gives way to the enabling presence discovered in visionary theism. To use Blake's virtual ideograph, natural Orc gives way to divinely empowered Los. And Blake is not alone. Shelley's Prometheus bound must give way to Prometheus unbound; Keats's Hyperion, to Apollo; Wordsworth's solitary, to the wanderer. Nor does romantic theory necessarily lag behind romantic practice. In Coleridge's brilliant deconstructive analysis of poetic inspiration in the *Biographia Literaria*, both rationally bound fancy and subconsciously bound Secondary Imagination must give way to the mystical presence dwelling in the Primary Imagination. To pursue Hartman's argument a bit further, romanticism in such apocalyptic passages betrays its humanist origins by recovering the sense of an absolute and enabling metaphysical ground, a ground beyond the subconscious psyche and its energies.

The interplay within romanticism of its theist and humanist elements is a fascinating process. But for our purposes, it suffices to note that Auden saw the tradition as gradually succumbing, in its later postromantic and modernist phases, to the humanist limitations inherent in its historical emergence. It tried to pretend that Orc or one of his relatives—Dionysus, Eros, Prometheus, or Priapus—was God. And since they were not, it was paradoxically forced to dismember and scatter the very gods it was supposed to liberate. Romantic humanism thus became a kerygma of repression, whose main liturgical acts were the inhibition and subsequent exaltation of desire, which was not deified but only displaced, and which became dangerously deformed in the process.

This is an extreme claim, but Auden's reading of the romantic tradition has been recently corroborated by one of the most adventurous of romanticism's critics. In his theoretical studies since *The Anxiety of Influence*, Harold Bloom has powerfully explored the romantic humanist's, or strong poet's, retrojection of anxiety from the mortal terminus that he cannot control, to the poetic origins that he can at least pretend to. Since absolute self-sufficiency would confer immortality, Bloom argues, the strong poet is hellishly bent on apotheosizing himself through some myth of self-derivation. But unfortunately, every poet knows that poems are made, not out of nothing, but out of other poems. Hence, the poet's path to the Eden of self-derivation is blocked by some Covering Cherub of a precursor. (Derived from Ezekiel, 28: 13–16, the Covering Cherub symbolizes the repressive fears and compensating delusions that prevent man from reaching the Tree of Life.) This ancestral figure enforces the confession of derivation, the mortality implicit in a coming into, and therefore a going out of, time, which the strong poet is doomed to deny. In the melancholy logic of romantic humanism, then, poetry lapses into a sadistic cycle in which the death-dealing precursor must be repressed, slain, and then guiltily imitated. The cycle is entropic as well, charting a general deterioration in the tradition, because the slain ancestor is ultimately another Orc, a figure of the poet's own lost energies. As Bloom sums up in *Poetry and Repression*: "Poetry, revisionism, and repression verge upon a melancholy identity, an identity that is broken afresh by every new strong poem, and mended afresh by the same poem." So inevitable is this logic, that Bloom, a painstaking and acute reader of texts, has convincingly shown its manifestation in a sixfold syntagm of modes and tropes that dominate post-Enlightenment poetry.

The difference between Auden's earlier deconstruction of romantic humanism and Bloom's later, more pessimistic version is the difference between the pure critic and the poet-critic. As an aspiring visionary, Auden had a personal stake in liberating poetry from the crippling consequences of romantic repression. To enable that liberation, he resorted to an adventurous misreading of Freud, a misreading he later supplanted with one of the few hopeful elements in Kierkegaard's anguished dynamic of faith. In an important article, "Psychology and Art To-Day," published in 1936, Auden acknowledged the subtle, but unvarying, disguises of displacement with which repression defends itself: conflation, inversion, reemphasis, and of course symbolization. But in noting the difference between fantasy and art, Auden insisted that art, because it emerges from a unified cultural system with a coherence of its own, is capable of forcing displacement to become self-revelatory. Analyzing the dream of a morphia addict, which impressed him as belonging more to art than fantasy, Auden wrote: "Not only has the censor transformed the latent content of the dream into symbols but the dream itself is no longer a simple wish fulfillment, it has become constructive, and, if you like, moral." The agent of repression, the defensive censor of the imperiled ego, frantically or cleverly displaces; but then the dream itself, the means of repression, subverts the censor by revealing the truth through those displacements. Auden ends by imputing to Freud the questionably Freudian notion that *repression is not cyclical but teleological and even self-limiting*: "Not only what we recognise as sin or crime, but all illness, is purposive. It is an attempt at cure." Freud at times saw the analyst, armed with the rationally explicative devices that Jung found so inadequate, as the hero, a restorer of the mature and adult ego. But Auden's metaphor of cure finds within the very process of displacement a revelatory and potentially evolutionary force.

This misreading of Freud brings us to the threshold of *The Age of Anxiety*, its intratextual dialogue with the romantic tradition, and its strategy of restoration. Nietzsche is the dark metaphysician of romantic repression, in that his doomed cycles offer to late humanism its main alternative to the void. In his prophecy of universal parody, Nietzsche gave the modern artist a dismal choice between explicitly accepting his mortal futility by remaining silent, or implicitly accepting that futility by mimicking exhausted forms. Yet what appears as a fate of compulsive parody to the humanist is to his theist counterpart an irrepressible process of literary evolution. The dream is waking the dreamer up. In his title, *The Age of Anxiety*, Auden establishes the concept of distinct and successive cultural periods. Not anxiety as pure, unchangeable fact, but as one of those phases that always seem permanent, yet never are. The justification for this evolutionary process is found in the Kierkegaardian metatexts, *Either/Or* and *The Concept of Dread*, which Auden invokes against the Nietzschean cycle of parody. For Kierkegaard, anxiety arises from a simultaneous awareness and refusal of the unrealized. Now, anxiety can be interrupted—in which case the result is some form of despair—but it cannot be indefinitely continued, because its tormented awareness eventually leads to the absolute ground realized in faith. It cannot end, as in Nietzsche, with a compulsive cycle driven by the desperate repression of a mortal emptiness. In terms of literary evolution, then, Auden's title invokes a force that must drive the romantic tradition's melancholy mimicries into the more terrifying realm of visionary discovery.

This is precisely what happens in Auden's long, subtle, and much neglected poem. Each of the four central sections implicitly acknowledges Nietzsche's dark prophecy, by committing itself to a parody of some clearly signaled aspect of romantic repression. As with all parody, these sections carry on an intratextual dialogue with a tradition so recognizable as to be assumed, for parody is a late product of canon formation. But Auden introduces into this dialogue a deftly analytical symbolism, through which the parody deconstructs the cycle of repression by revealing the very truth it attempts to conceal. *The Age of Anxiety* is, of course, splendid as a poem; but it is even more splendid as an ambitious deconstructive compendium that, through its status as literature, actually carries out the literary evolution made possible by its discovery of the latent power of displacement.

The action begins in a shabby bar on New York's Third Avenue, where Auden's four adventurers happen to meet while drowning their sorrows. These are Malin, a hypercritical scientist who is a medical intelligence officer; Quant, an elderly clerk with a casual, but wide-ranging, knowledge of mythologies; Rosetta, a successful department-store buyer who habitually daydreams about the idyllic childhood she never had; and Emble, a handsome young sailor who is terrified that he will not become an officially recognized success. It has been shown that a proximate source for Auden's characterization is Jung's fourfold division of the psyche. In this case, Malin would be intellect; Quant, intuition; Rosetta, feeling; and Emble, sensation.

But this fourfold scheme also establishes a profound connection with the romantic tradition, in that it recalls Blake's four Zoas, or giant forms, Urizen, Urthona, Luvah, and Tharmas. And to go beyond even Blake, the presence of this quaternary sets the fundamental problem that both forms of romanticism assume: man has fallen from a state of preconscious unity into one of self-conscious division. Symbolically, the fall is dramatized in the four rivers of Eden, which, though rising from a single fountain at the base of the Tree of Life, mysteriously flow into the perceptual passivity of Coleridge's sunless sea. In this way, the fall becomes the demonic creation that brings forth the "reality" in which most men dwell, a nightmare world where desire is repressed, distorted, and then projected into the tyrannizing delusions of objectivity. But Auden reveals his refusal to accept this fallen condition by having his four characters meet on the Eve of All Souls, traditionally a time of prayer, when those tormented in Purgatory might be released into Paradise. Or, to translate from the Roman Missal into the terms of romantic inwardness, All Souls contains the determination, not to unleash, but to transform and restore, the energies of the psyche that are imprisoned within the cycles of repression.

That transformation is a major, in fact, an apocalyptic task. Auden takes his epigraph from Thomas à Celano's *Dies Irae*, and this provides his poem with both a visionary context and a summary of its argument. The wrath in the Day of Wrath is not God's, but man's, and the judge in the Day of Judgment is God-in-man, the divinity of the spirit. As pretense and evasion burn away in the fires of a new visionary perspective, the *saeclum*, or epoch, created in the fall comes to an end. Auden's epigraph thus prefaces his absolute confrontation with romantic humanism. Since this humanism in some way involves every major poet from Wordsworth to Eliot, Auden can hardly be accused of timidity. Yet there is also a quietly analytical aspect to his deconstructive Day of Judgment, in that *Dies Irae* is also *dies illa*, that day, in the mythic sense of containing a continuously present truth. What Auden proposes to reveal about romantic humanism is only what has always been revealed in its own displacements.

The intratextual struggles effectively commence with "The Seven Ages," in which Malin, as a combination of airman, medical scientist, and social com-

mentator, leads the others through a modernized version of the triumph of
life. Auden begins, then, at his own beginning, since Malin recalls three of
Auden's early personae, and even sounds like them. He speaks in a combination
of what M. K. Spears has labeled Auden's clipped lyric and Nordic Mask, thereby
echoing the acerbic, yet fatalistic, choruses of *Paid on Both Sides* and some of
Poems 1930. Malin thus suggests Auden-as-modernist, and it is upon modernism
as a development of late humanist despair that the parodic analysis fastens.

    This lateness is a matter of symbolic self-perception, not literal chronology,
so it will vary in form according to the intensity of the poet's dissatisfaction
with his tradition. As noted, Harold Bloom has acutely traced the pattern in
which the later poet represses and then guiltily imitates the precursor who
stands between him and the illusion of self-derivation. But because Bloom so
closely follows Freud, who in matters of man's cyclical fate and parodic destiny
tended to be Nietzsche's disciple, he underestimates the transformative powers
of displacement, with the result that he neglects some of the most fascinating
developments within romantic humanism. At first, the precursor is indeed repressed. But eventually he rises from his vestigial presence as trope to a symbolic reappearance as the murderous father: Arnold's Rustum, Hardy's Doom-
sters, Yeats's Cuchulain. Again, this reappearance has nothing to do with literal
chronology, since it is possible to glimpse the evil precursor much earlier in
the Scottish King of Coleridge's epigraph to the Dejection Ode—significantly,
a reply to Wordsworth—who frivolously sends Sir Patrick Spence to his death.
In a subsequent development, the even more deeply enshadowed, but now
embittered, poetic heir begins to curse this doom-inflicting ancestor, as in the
old man of Coleridge's "Limbo," the Jupiter of Shelley's *Prometheus Unbound*,
or the implicit D. H. Lawrence of Auden's own "Prologue."

    Rationalistic Malin is happily unaware of the deeper evasions implicit in
his repression, but Quant, as occasional Los—or intuition—uses his eclectic
mythography to assess Malin's sense of abandonment. In his own parodic version
of the ancestor curse, Quant exposes the late humanist's bitterness and hostility
toward his tradition as a case of self-inflicted loss:

> His myths of Being
> Are there always. In that unchanging
> Lucid lake where he looks for ever
> Narcissus sees the sensitive face
> He's too intelligent to trust or like,
> Pleading his pardon. Polyphemus
> Curses his cave or, catching a nymph,
> Begs for brotherhood with a big stick,
> Hobbledehoy and helpless. Kind Orpheus lies

> Violently slain on the virid bank,
> That smooth sward where he sinned against kind,
> And, wild by the water, women stone
> The broken torso but the bloody head,
> In the far distance, floating away
> Down the steady stream, still opening
> Its charming mouth, goes chanting on in
> Fortissimo tones, a tenor lyre
> Dinning the doom into a deaf Nature
> Of her loose chaos. For Long-Ago has been
> Ever-After since Ur-Papa gave
> The Primal Yawn that expressed all things
> (In His Boredom their beings) and brought forth
> The wit of this world. One-Eye's mistake
> Is sorry He spoke.

The various fates of Narcissus, Polyphemus, and Orpheus suggest the poetic types of sensitive plant, buffoon, and sacrificial victim. A masterpiece of satirical concision, the passage suggests the peril of the too-facile assumption that Auden simply accepted modernism. Neglected Echo shows Narcissus's preference for vague and watery fantasies; mocking Galatea shows Cyclops's inattention to effective form—one of Auden's particular concerns. But it is Orpheus who is most interesting. He sings Blake's great visionary theme, that the chaos of passively perceived nature is destined to be transformed into a place of human significance. Yet his song is totally without power, a head without a body, because Orpheus has chosen powerlessness. In dismembering him, the Maenads of Quant's revision simply dramatize the sterility of Orpheus's own radical refusals, for they have discovered him, the mythic inventor of homoeroticism, sinning against kind on the banks of the eternal stream. Quant's revelation that the modernist has somehow chosen his fate of visionary powerlessness prepares the way for the more penetrating symbolic analysis of his conclusion.

Adapting Hesiod, Quant portrays the romantic ancestor supposedly responsible for the modernist's malaise as a combination of Cronus and Cyclops (Ur-Papa is also One-Eye). This cursed ancestor has the unlovable qualities of one of Hardy's deities, in that his maddening stupidity is enforced by irresistible power. His later offspring easily surpass him by replacing glottal yawn with articulate speech. But in doing so, they helplessly fall victim to an inwardness that brings with it not only the superiority of refinement and subtlety, but as well, an incapacitating sorrow, Auden's code word for guilt. The ancestor curse, then, revises in its own way the passage from powerful origins to the mysterious blessings of sterility and loss. This is exactly contrary to the apocalyptic passage from self-consciousness to imagination that Hartman describes; yet from Wordsworth's Immortality Ode onward, it has provided the normative mythos for romantic humanism.

Auden does not, however, intend to leave this regressive and truncated mythos unchallenged. Cronus and Cyclops, as Quant would surely know, are not the same figure, but father and son. By merging them into the confused identity of the romantic ancestor, Quant shows that the incapacitating filiation is really a projection. In other words, the ancestor is not a separate figure at all, but a justificatory symbol for the later poet's powerful denial of his own energies. The real anxiety, as Blake insisted in his symbolism of malevolent giants, is not of influence, but of having to realize one's own deep and perplexing inwardness.

Yet if we look even further into Quant's deconstructive symbolism, it becomes apparent that such anxiety must lead sooner or later beyond itself. The preposterous Ur-Papa is not merely a Hardyesque spinner of Maya, but also a vital and creative force. His glottal yawn recalls the Johannine Logos, visionary theism's symbol of the enabling presence through which eternity enters into time. Through this presence, Ur-Papa in fact accomplishes what his impotent offspring cannot. He gives, expresses all things, and brings forth life in a burst of creative generosity. The announced filiation thus contains a double descent, somewhat akin to a gnostic emanation, in which Ur-Papa emerges from the Logos, and then impotent heir, from Ur-Papa. At the risk of being obvious, Quant has shown that the energies explored by romanticism can create and then transform an entire world if those energies are sustained by a reality beyond humanism. But those same energies, if left purely to themselves, can bring forth only a repressed and enervated progeny, a progeny for whom the mythoi of self-justification are more congenial than the Battles of Eden. Thus the irony of the defeatism concealed behind an anxiety of influence becomes clear. Since empowered Ur-Papa is really a projection, he represents a possibility of poetic regeneration that, though doubly displaced from present to past and from self to other, has been unceasingly available.

At the end of "The Seven Ages," Auden is still a long way from his promised apocalypse. But we can begin to see how the revelations of this literary Last Judgment will emerge. The playful exaggerations and exuberance of his parody, which have persuaded some sober-minded critics to dismiss *The Age of Anxiety*, release the mythic and symbolic elements into an almost giddy literary freedom. But Auden's genius was to see that within such freedom, myth and symbol could not merely retain, but even more powerfully exercise, their formidably analytical capacities. Parody and mythopoesis thus work together in this text to carry out a thorough and frankly relentless deconstruction of humanist deceptions.

The other three characters have been growing increasingly suspicious of Malin's jaundiced self-pity, so at the end of this section they rebel, by having Rosetta as palingenetic Luvah, or feeling, lead them back to the strength of their origins. This produces "The Seven Stages," an at times surrealistic dream sequence that figures the katabasis, or descent, inward, to recover the source of unconscious energies. The surrealism is important, because it enables a juxtaposition of childishness and brutality, that in turn suggests the alternately naive and destructive quality of untransformed desire. It also locates the humanist quest for origins in the labyrinth of the Freudian subconscious, and predictably, it is a brooding monster, not regenerative innocence, that the four discover within themselves. Freud is virtually the nemesis of romantic humanism, because he exposed, with such bright candor, so many of its treacherous illusions. This is particularly true of his theory about the conservative nature of instinct. Since all desire (with the questionable exception of the sexual instinct) is regressive, an attempt to regain an earlier state, and since the earliest possible state is non-existence, Freud reasoned that desire must be ultimately thanatic, a death wish, or willing to end willing. Thus, in any system where the primordial force, however ingeniously displaced, is the soul's unconscious energies, a quest for origins must become a quest for some form of death. Auden accordingly has his parodic humanists set out for a Freudian idyll of soothing Thanatos, "The Quiet Kingdom" beyond the "Regressive road to Grandmother's House."

The Narrator provides an indispensable cue for interpreting the symbolism of "The Seven Stages," when he explains that the four search for "that state of prehistoric happiness which, by humans beings, can only be imagined in terms of a landscape bearing a symbolic resemblance to the human body." The mythologem of world as body is complex, but its apocalyptic quality as a figure of visionary potential is its central significance. Auden draws here on a tradition that includes the Adam Kadmon of the Kabbalah, the giant Ymir of the Elder Edda, the One Man of Emerson's *American Scholar*, and the Cosmic Man of Whitman. The world in human form symbolizes the dissolution of subject-object distinctions in the liberating realization that knowledge is a function of being, that all man ever has seen or ever will see is his own projected inwardness. A symbol of this realization must be gigantic, because it contains the strength to recreate the world through the transformation of that inwardness. The giants assume human form, because they show that one process of involution and evolution, the fall into time and the redemption into eternity, animates all reality. Typically, though, they are asleep, because the visionary finds human powers entranced within the illusions of time and space. It is of the greatest significance for Auden's deconstruction that in the postromantic tradition of late humanism, this visionary potential is seen, not as sleeping, but as dismembered or slain: the murdered landscape of Browning's "Childe Roland," the dead winterscape of Hardy's "The Darkling Thrush," the patient awaiting dissection that Eliot borrowed from Zola for "The Love Song of J. Alfred Prufrock," or the Adam's Grave that Auden ironically establishes as sentinel for the divided city of Western culture in "Vespers," from *Horae Canonicae*.

In "The Seven Stages," this tradition is parodically continued as Auden's four questers explore a literalized anatomy, whose energies are so dispersed, that there is no sign the sleeper will ever wake again. Sometimes the anatomy is a bit uncertain, but a reasonable reconstruction of the journey that gives rise to the seven stages would be: Mariner's Tavern (heart); Rival Ports (lungs); City (brain); Big House (womb); Graveyard (skeleton); Hermetic Gardens (sex organs); and Forest and Desert (intestines). This is a profound decline from the work's initial figuration of fallen man as composed of four imaginative faculties. The movement from imaginative to physical, as well as from quaternary to septenary, reveals in the ideographic language of symbolism the loss of energies within this thanatic quest. For the giant to be awakened, in at least one tradition, he must be touched by a ray of sunlight shining into his burial crypt—the slumber of visionary powers within the mundane skull—at dawn on the shortest day of the year. But even by All Souls, that day is still far off.

The poetry of "The Seven Stages" is as precise, yet subtle, as any Auden wrote. Though it is not possible here to examine all of it in depth, some sense can be given of its intratextual penetration. Rosetta at the end of the first stage aptly sees its goal as a mountainous landscape, symbol of the sacred locus of revelation from Wordsworth's Snowden to Stevens's hill in Tennessee. But Rosetta's coy diction, parenthetic syntax, and lingering description suggest a Keatsian or Swinburnian pastiche that is more suited to a child's savoring of forbidden delights:

> Now peaks oppose to the ploughman's march
>   Their twin confederate forms,
> In a warm weather, white with lilies,
>   Evergreen for grazing.
>
> Smooth the surfaces, sweeping the curves
>   Of these comely frolic clouds,
> Where the great go to forget themselves
>   The beautiful and boon to die.

Through their obvious association with breasts, Rosetta's mountains reveal as goal the petrifying maternity, cold, hard, and destroying, of untransformed nature. Certainly, the visionary must begin, as Wordsworth insisted, in nature's tutelary embrace. Yet in Christian mythography, this embrace is the swaddling clothes that entwine the infant Christ, a covering that later becomes the death shroud that must be torn off and left in the tomb. Expressly opposing the mountains, and here thwarted by them, is the figure of the ploughman as visionary. The ploughman's turning over the mundane shell of the natural world is a powerful metaphor that shows the mental activity that gives life to the symbolic seeds or archetypal bones buried within phenomena. On the mountain as stony breast of perceptual passivity, there is no such ploughing, only the grazing of the common herd.

Once this basic symbolism has been grasped, Auden's intratextual precision becomes clear. The juxtaposition of ploughman and mountains recalls the same symbolic pairing in Wordsworth's "Resolution and Independence," where he too mourned the death of vision in the fates of Chatterton and Burns. But Wordsworth's vexed response, his heroic assertion that "by our own spirits are we deified," contains the fundamental ambivalence between humanism and theism that is the whole subject of *The Age of Anxiety*. Are those spirits the soon-to-be-dissipated unconscious energies that are all too finite? Or, are they rather the eternal presence that is the absolute ground of consciousness itself? Wordsworth sublimely hesitates at this point, which Auden in an earlier poem, "The Watershed," figured as the essential division within romanticism. But in his own four adventurers, Auden shows the fate of those later humanists who were more desperately sure.

The exact center of this thanatic quest is the fourth stage, the Big House, which is symbolically a womb within a womb. Rosetta, as guide, happily explores this, the primordial scene, while the others eagerly await her revelation of the unconscious energies that dwell within. Yet in her report back to the faithful, "Opera glasses on the ormolu table. . . ," Rosetta concedes that the *genius loci* of romantic humanism is that ugliest of necessary angels, the Covering Cherub. In one form, it appears as a "Frock-coated father," fashioned after Henri Mannier's Monsieur Prudhomme, who shows the mind in complacent submission to conventional moral authority. Heterodox Auden, like that earlier visionary St. Paul, suspected external moral codes because they could accuse but not transform. The moralist is the inevitable companion of the humanist, because the repressions of the one distort desire, and so necessitate the ever more tyrannical rules of the other. But behind the frock-coated father there waits an even more baleful version of the Cherub in the form of the sadistic deity of Kebroth-Hattaavah (Numbers 11), whose more threatening mien betrays even more paralyzing fears. What is finally being repressed is the terror of mortality, the awful emptiness in the depths of finite man. As romanticism nears this center, its visions of the Covering Cherub must become more enraged and hideous. The reason for this symbolic intensification, which is really an inversion, is that romanticism dreads nothing more than the possibility of actually overcoming the Cherub, and as a result, having to venture beyond the cycles of compulsion that he enables. Auden thus locates this blocking figure, now exposed as a guardian deity, not at the edge, but at the center, of the romantic idyll. Were romanticism to go any further, it would have to go deeper, and leave behind its humanist origins by entering the void beneath even the profoundest reaches of the psyche.

Auden ends "The Seven Stages" with a powerful deconstruction that leaves no doubt about the confinement of the thanatic quest to the scene of repression. Separating into the psychic chaos of fallen man, the four adventurers wander alone through a dark and labyrinthine forest. This is the modern rediscovery of hell as the Freudian subconscious, into which a desperately self-divinizing ego casts the hateful energies that obsess it. At the edge of the forest, the four reunite before a vast desert. The desert as symbol is the companion of the forest, in that it shows the conscious displacements that emerge from the subconscious, both being offsprings of repression. As Auden noted in *The Enchafèd Flood*, the desert presents a place where the deformities are not hidden but horribly manifest. Here, inwardness is externalized in scenes of pure projection, as the realizing sun of intellect beats down in all its fury. But in a variation on the temptations of such visionaries as John or Anthony, Auden has his parodic adventurers fall in love with their demons:

> Boring and bare of shade,
> Devoid of souvenirs and voices,
> It takes will to cross this waste
>
> Which is really empty: the mirage
> Need not be tasty to tempt;
> For the senses arouse themselves,
>
> And an image of humpbacked girls
> Or plates of roasted rats
> Can make the mouth water.

The passage draws on the mythologem of the Messianic banquet, where angels wait on the visionary company as they consume those images of gross phenomena, Behemoth, Leviathan, and Ziz. But in Auden's post-Freudian parable of repression, Paradise is still the dry, sterile wasteland of untransformed phenomena, and the closest we get to vision is the mirages, the elusive displacements of the subconsciously obsessed mind. As is usual, Auden deploys his symbolism with the ideographic precision of Blake. The deformed maidens are variations of anima, or the psyche, but instead of being one, they are many, thereby showing divided, distorted, yet irresistible energies. The feast they offer, as alluring alternative to themselves, suggests the appeal of the displacements to which the repressed psyche gives birth. Thus the thanatic quest ends in a revelation of its nature as autophagy—which is apt, since the archetypal symbol for repression is the ouroboros, or snake consuming its tail. This, however, is not quite incisive enough for Auden, so he further stresses the sterile and self-indulgent nature of such grim psychodrama by adding a hint of autoeroticism: "the senses arouse themselves."

At this point, it would be safe to say, we are at the darkest place in Auden's katabasis into the nightmare of romantic humanism. But even here, it is possible to see the powers of displacement silently at work. Had the four not stopped at the edge, but actually crossed the desert, Malin notes, they would have found hidden streams that could restore life and an oasis where acrobats "make unbelievable leaps." In other words, had the four adventurers gone deeper into the symbol itself, they would have realized what its deconstructive ironies were trying to tell them. So Auden's dreadful pun on Kierkegaard's metaphor of faith is entirely to the point. Gradually, but inevitably, the disease is proposing its cure, the dream is waking the dreamer.

"The Dirge" and "The Masque" retrace the cycle of disillusionment and doomed quest, but now that cycle assumes a more radical and self-limiting character. Malin's bitterness, as has been seen, results from a refusal that brings an end to his heroic possibilities as poet. But whenever the mind cannot create, it must turn to destruction. This occurs as the romantic Prometheanism, in which the frustrated poet, unable to turn his benighted world into the New Jerusalem, begins to wish for the literalized apocalypse that will wreck it. But with the really desperate—because more powerless—Prometheans of modernism, these deformed energies are displaced into a worship of power, and then projected onto some suitable historical candidate. Auden explores this more recent version of Prometheanism in "The Dirge," which commemorates "some Gilgamesh or Napoleon, some Solon or Sherlock Holmes." The reference is purposely ambiguous. First generation modernists—Yeats, Pound, Eliot, and Wyndham Lewis—went to the Right; second generation modernists—Spender, Day Lewis, Rex Warner, and, some have mistakenly thought, Auden himself—went to the Left. But in "The Dirge," it makes little difference, since the colossal father retains an archetype's capacity to inform an indefinite range of intratextual possibilities.

As always, the poetry relies on the readers' ability to detect nuances within the symbolism. For a few lines, which perhaps recall that moment of naive political enthusiasm at the beginning of the thirties, it appears as if the new historical Prometheus will indeed become the hero of romanticism's adventure of inwardness. Riding the white horse of purified desire, he survives the tempests and droughts that represent the alternate fits and calms of subconscious energies. His journey of life is what Caliban called the disillusioned, yet still serviceable, metaphor for the continuous meditation that enables the hero to understand those energies (the shrine of gold), to transform their multiple vitalities into a sustaining strength (the waters of joy), and to direct that strength into a process of coherent growth (the tree of life). Perfect, one thinks, until the neatness becomes self-incriminating. The ultimate test for the romantic humanist is to harrow hell, to integrate the psyche. Yet this is impossible without the support of an absolute metaphysical ground that enables the quester to acknowledge all the energies that he has previously repressed. Without such support, the would-be hero can only ignore his nightmares and "put the clawing chimaeras in cold storage." He is, in other words, a fresh version of the tormented romantic whose repressed inwardness becomes a monstrous reality. But the chimera's union of lion, goat, and snake suggests desire not only deformed into domination, lust, and intrigue, but also equipped with flight—that is, executive force.

Auden had made the same point as early as 1932 in *The Orators*, an acute study of leadership as neurotic compensation. By 1947, when he wrote "The Dirge," poets had already retreated from their earlier enthusiasms about either the Left or the Right, and hardly needed further warnings. Yet this kind of retreat was not at all what Auden had in mind. His hope was that the disillusionment of the new Prometheanism would lead, not to a severance of art from life and another round of aestheticism, but to a rediscovery of poetry's true visionary task. "The Dirge" ends with the prophetic lines:

> For our lawgiver lies below his people,
> Bigger bones of a better kind,
> Unwarped by their weight, as white limestone
>> Under green grass
>> The grass that fades.

The movement from lawgiver to bones to limestone carries out the whole supercession intended by the poem. Mircea Eliade has pointed out that bones, far from being a death image, often represent the support of life. In as acutely intratextual a passage as this, which draws on an iconic tradition that includes Ezekiel, Luke, and Blake, that significance can be extended to bones as representative of symbols themselves, since they provide the basic support of meaning. Limestone is, of course, composed of vast numbers of shells and corals, though it may contain vertebrate remains, and it is this aggregate quality that makes it one of Auden's favorite figures for the poet's sustaining archetypes. Out of this ground springs, in a deliberately Whitmanian image, the fleeting growths of incessant displacement. With this in mind, we can see how the passage is trying to show that disillusionment with the new Prometheus may lead to the rediscovery of the true lawgivers, the mythoi and symbols that cannot be made to lie. It was Auden's hope that the failure of a misguided and somewhat vindictive prophetism would, as a self-limiting development of modernism, return poetry to its prophetic task, which grew out of the tradition of visionary theism. That tradition includes, as we see from the dense allusiveness of the above passage, both Testaments as well as Blake and Whitman.

Earlier, in "The Seven Stages," Auden had shown how the humanist quest for the liberation of desire must paradoxically lead to its repression. But what if the quester were to defy the Cherub's flaming sword, which is merely the image of his own fears? Perhaps he could then elude the demons of the subconscious and plunge directly into the pure depths of unconscious energy. That is the possibility, romantic humanism's last, most desperate gamble, explored in "The Masque." The main intratextual source for this section is D. H. Lawrence in his psychological writings and some of his later poetry. Like Auden, Lawrence deeply sensed that the romantic tradition had reached a crisis that could only be overcome through a restoration of its true origins. But unlike Auden, he located those origins, however fascinated with mysticism and comparative mythology he may have been, within humanism. In *Psychoanalysis and the Unconscious*, Lawrence based his dismissal of the Freudian nemesis on the distinction between the psychologist's subconscious and his own version of the unconscious. He unceremoniously dubbed the former a sack of horrors, the very antithesis of creativity. But the latter, the unconscious, was to be the unconceptualizable source of pure energy, the romantic fountain of eternal artistic youth. Lawrence's introduction to the American edition of *New Poems* is a paean to this unconscious source, disguised as a tribute to Whitman's free verse:

> Give me the still, white seething, the incandescence and the coldness
> of the incarnate moment: the moment, the quick of all change and
> haste and opposition: the moment, the immediate present, the Now.
> The immediate moment is not a drop of water running downstream.
> It is the source and issue, the bubbling up of the stream.

The passage is remarkable for its use of two visionary figures, the fountain and the eternal moment, to portray the quite unvisionary worship of a power whose entropic end Lawrence was already struggling to evade, "a drop of water running downstream."

Auden was deeply influenced by Lawrence at the outset of his own career, when he turned to Lawrence's theories in hope of recovering the vitality that Eliotic modernism implied had been irrevocably lost. But by the mid-thirties, Auden had determined that Lawrence's theory of the unconscious was simply not true. Desire, which Auden mythologized as Eros, was not the unfailing fountainhead, but a capricious and unpredictable creature who mysteriously came and went. He was not purely creative, but ambivalent, in that some of his moods were sadistically destructive. And one could even argue that Eros was not a god at all, since his blind impulses lacked either purpose or means, until further directed by that hateful spectre, the self-conscious ego with its powers of memory and reason. To worship so capricious and vulnerable a god was to wind up sooner or later in the sunless sea of Coleridge's "Kubla Khan." It is an interesting irony of literary history that Auden, the most original poet of his generation, spent the first years of his career implicitly working out the symbolism of Coleridge's River Alph, which figures the primordial energies of the psyche in their erratic, unapproachable, and ambivalent character.

As literary form, the masque is well suited to Auden's intratextual purposes, because it suppresses the intellectual aspects of the drama and focuses on a few iconic gestures. The four characters have by now left the bar and arrived at Luvah and Tharmas, feeling and sensation, the couple is to attain at last the *hieros gamos*, the sacred marriage, that in one form or another is the goal of every quest. In this parody of Lawrence, sensation is to become so intensified with unconscious energies, that it shatters the restraints of the ego and so enables an unmediated contact with pure being. Accordingly, Emble has been fortifying himself at the bar's fountainhead of aqua vitae all night. To equate the pursuit of unconscious energies with the effects of heavy drinking is somewhat closer to burlesque than parody, but the equation itself is neither inaccurate nor novel. Emble activates those energies in the same way as did some of the French symbolists and later the English decadents, and with much the same result. Rosetta returns to her apartment, after seeing the others off, to find the would-be prince passed out on her bed. The gesture itself is simple enough, but Auden uses it to conduct an incisive analysis. The descent into pure unconscious energy cannot transform human consciousness, only obliterate it. Thus, despite his vehement rejection of Freud, Lawrence characteristically falls victim to the Freudian nemesis after all, when he concedes that primordial desire is indeed regressive and ultimately thanatic. By figuring this concession as the inert Emble, Auden derives from Lawrence the final paradox of romantic humanism: a finite creature can divinize itself only through some form of self-destruction.

With the anticlimax of "The Masque," Auden brings his intratextual dialogue to a full stop. Yet it is the very strength of the Freudian nemesis that enables him to break Nietzsche's prophecy of doomed repetition. *Dies Irae* is the final day, not in some literally temporal sense, but in the symbolic sense of attaining, through its destructive insight, a final realization. Thus each section of *The Age of Anxiety* parodically deconstructs romantic humanism in a way that is both successive and self-limiting, until it necessarily reaches the promised apocalypse, which literally means pulling off the covers. The novelty of apocalypse is only a revelation of what has always been the case, and its mystery is only a measure of the mind's habitual entrancement. Beyond this point of absolute clarity, repetition is impossible. The choice is final, life or death, faith or despair. Auden's *Dies Irae* consequently leads to the division within romantic origins where a weary humanism and a visionary theism must part forever.

At this point, the enabling parody drops away, and *The Age of Anxiety* ends with one of the most remarkable passages of visionary poetry in the modern tradition. Rosetta casts her final meditation in the forms of Lurianic Kabbalism; Malin, in the forms of Christian mysticism; and together they enact the necessary restoration. This raises, willy-nilly, the issue of religion, which is unfortunately one of the most misunderstood aspects of Auden's mythography. So it would be best to permit the observation that for the text, at least, religion is not an issue at all. To Rosetta, orthodoxy is merely the spelling out of morals on monuments, a pious process of applying platitudes to someone else. Malin's views on what some of Auden's commentators mean by religion are even stronger:

> Yet the grossest of our dreams is
> No worse than our worship which for the most part
> Is so much galimatias to get out of
> Knowing our neighbor.

The visionary alternative is to restore religious symbols and mythoi by realizing that they refer, not to past historical events or to present moral restraints, but to the continuous adventures of human inwardness, or what Keats called the process of soul-making. In this sense, when Wordsworth alternately entitled *The Prelude* as *The Growth of a Poet's Mind*, he was designating himself a religious poet. Wordsworth's great innovation was the mythopoeically technical one of displacing the mind's inward transformations to a low-mimetic symbolism taken from nature. But Auden, arriving at a later and more reflective moment in the tradition, saw how easily such deceptively unrestraining displacements could go astray in so radically post-Protestant, hence individual, a movement as romanticism. He consequently restored the powerful lucidity of religious mythoi and symbols, with their prehumanist wisdom, in his adventure to regain romantic strengths. If this restoration is an act of intellectual cowardice, then Auden is the same kind of coward as Blake, who adopted his mythologies from the Bible and Jacob Boehme. In a similar eclecticism, which shows that he too saw religious symbols as visionary accomplices, Auden deliberately juxtaposes Jewish Rosetta and Christian Malin at the end of *The Age of Anxiety*. Critical attempts to differentiate the two miss the point, which is that both say the same thing.

The most puzzling aspect of Rosetta's meditation is the suddenness of its unexpected transformation. She returns, finds Emble asleep on her bed, and in less than Paul's "twinkling of an eye," the apocalyptic disclosures begin. The entire work has painstakingly prepared for this moment, with an ornateness of symbolism that Auden had warned in advance would be baroque. Yet the shift from humanism to theism, from a world dying to one continuously reborn, is itself no more than a shift in consciousness. Rosetta as key to translation (i.e., the Rosetta stone) looks at Emble as emblem of sense, and sees the mind trapped in the desperate world of mere phenomena, as caught in a sleep of death. Her reference to the exile, "and our words touched/On Babylon's banks," figures, in Kabbalistic symbolism, the fate of the soul in its separation from divinity, and its subsequent burial in the lower world of unilluminated matter, or *Malkuth*. Emble is thus the would-be bridegroom, the senses of man that could penetrate to a world of symbols, but in fact enslave him in the place of mortal frustration, until he becomes a murderous sleepwalker.

Yet, within Luria's theogonic concept of *Tsimtsum*, which provides the central form for Rosetta's meditation, limitation and contraction within the divinity precede flowing forth and expansion. Rosetta gives the form of *Tsimtsum* an anthropological and historical application, as Auden, with his limiting deconstructions leading to a restored mythography, may be seen as giving it a literary one. The process in which the *Shekinah*, or divine presence, escapes from its manifestations—in essence, overwhelms and shatters them through excess—is *Sheviroth Ha-Kalim*, or the breaking of the vessels, which is in turn involved with the perplexing origins of evil. In a radical discovery of *Sheviroth*, Rosetta casts it as that most appalling event, the holocaust:

> Nor His strong arm that stood no nonsense,
> Fly, let's face it, to defend us now
> When bruised or broiled our bodies are chucked
> Like cracked crocks onto kitchen middens
> In the time He takes.

Auden accepts a considerable risk here, but it is a risk inherent in visionary tradition. The supposedly external, objective, and determined world, to which political fatalists and judicious realists so earnestly preach conformity, is in fact no such thing. It is altogether the creation of the human mind, the projection of the fears, hatreds, and compensations of a culture's entranced sleepwalking through its own botched quests. Yet, despite this realization, the visionary remains an indomitable believer in mankind and perhaps the only true humanist. At a time when decent liberal optimism was as outmoded, in Malin's later phrase, as "peasant pottery," Rosetta's next words are the most surprising in the entire poem: "We'll trust." Somehow she has grasped the mysterious pattern in which *Sheviroth* enables *Tikkun*, or the restitution of the defect.

This restitution finds its enabling symbol in the Eye of God, which represents, through transposition, not God as aware of man, but God as aware *through* man—that is, the birth of divine consciousness. Rosetta is a more reticent visionary than Malin, in that she does not attempt to explain the nature of this birth and its mysterious emergence from catastrophe, but leaves no doubt as to its consequences. Many still associate visionary experience with an incommunicable ecstasy, in which individual identity and consciousness are blotted out. What Rosetta experiences, however, is neither incommunicable nor ecstatic. She accepts for the first time the human origins she has been repressing, and with the anxieties created by the hopeless task of self-divinization set aside, she can see the Covering Cherub for the infantile bogey it truly is: "My poor fat father." No longer confined within a demon-haunted idyll, Rosetta discovers the obligation of *Tikkun* as the time of desert wandering. The exile with which her meditation begins has thus given way, through the crisis of *Sheviroth*, to the once more searching community:

> Moses will scold if
> We're not all there for the next meeting
> At some brackish well or broken arch,
> Tired as we are.

The restitution is real, but so deliberately centered in the Eliotic wasteland, that it suggests a hesitant beginning rather than a serene conclusion. Humanism's Egypt, the fallen world of untransformed matter, is far behind. But just as distant is the New Jerusalem of an entirely visionary culture, and one suspects that the alternations of *Sheviroth* and *Tikkun* will have to occur many times before that destination is reached. Nonetheless, through the transformative power of Rosetta's meditation, the desert has become a place of realization leading to supercession. *Tikkun* occurs at the broken arch, a figure of the triumph that has collapsed into ruin, and from this scene spring the waters of life that restore because they are so bitter. As will become apparent, it is of the greatest significance that Rosetta takes Moses as guide rather than Joshua. The palingenetic Luvah of her creator, Rosetta as feeling can imagine for herself only more wandering in the deserts of supercession, not actual entry into the promised land.

Both Rosetta and Malin enact a restoration of romantic origins to visionary theism, but their iconography is different, even if their mythos is the same. Thus the paradoxical pattern of *Sheviroth* and *Tikkun* is replaced in Malin's meditation with figures of the cross and, not exactly resurrection, but something closer to Eckhart's continuously new birth. Emble as pure sensation had to give way to Rosetta as honest emotion; now Quant, as pure imagination, who weaves his Stevens-like fictions with a rapidity and silliness that betray their pathos, must give way to Malin's somber intellectual absolutes. After dismissing as pious evasions "Religion, Politics, Love," and after foreseeing as "horrid madness" the only future of mankind in which he can any longer believe, Malin abruptly launches into the possibility that such evasions and madness may contain their own resolution. He expresses this insight in a complex passage that joins Christian, Kierkegaardian, and mystical elements:

> Yet the noble despair of the poets
> Is nothing of the sort; it is silly
> To refuse the tasks of time
> And, overlooking our lives,
> Cry—'Miserable wicked me,
> How interesting I am.'
> We would rather be ruined than changed,
> We would rather die in our dread
> Than climb the cross of the moment
> And let our illusions die.

Despite its unusual juxtapositions, the best approach to Malin's meditation is through recollection of the deeper meaning of the cross. Essentially, that symbol uses an obsessive motif from the ancient fertility cults, the dying god hanged on the tree, to conduct an *Ecce Homo*, a final insight into the condition of natural man. Fastened to the wood, as *prima materia* of ordinary phenomena, by the wound of his five delusive senses, the god shows human vitality slain on the tree of life-become-death. The abstract form of the cross, with its regular divisions into contradictory opposites, suggests the perceptual consequences of this death, by showing a world of organized strife. Christianity's version of the hanged-god motif is actually quite restrained, compared to others, where the god is castrated and dismembered to display the impotence and dissipation of natural energies. But the distinctive element in the Christian adaptation of this ancient motif is its achievement of transformation through an essential intellectual insight. The cross as tree of death rises from the place of skulls, in some versions, from a skull itself, to show not only that it is wrought by the fallen mind, but that through the act of realizing what it has wrought, the mind can discover its true origins. This is the center of the *felix culpa*, in Auden's passage figured as Kierkegaard's death in dread: namely, that through a process of understanding, the very emptiness can lead to fullness. To be ruined is to be changed, if only—as Kierkegaard insisted—one is ruined fully enough: when the illusions of the natural man die, the visions of eternity can begin. The cross, then, is, together with the *Sheviroth*, an ultimately deconstructive device, in that both conduct an apocalyptic destruction or stripping away so absolute, that it enables a regeneration, which Malin figures as "the place of birth."

This is the point at which even the formidable powers of symbolism begin to falter, and in one last splendid and perplexing passage, Malin ventures still further. Between the ultimate deconstruction and necessary regeneration lies the elusive eternity, the moment in which the quest hero discovers an origin beyond space and time. Malin's justification for this discovery is the scholastic notion that the lower reveals the higher, just as the higher fulfills the lower: man could not desire the infinite unless he in some way already possessed it. But the passage is not really about rational proofs; it is about a metaphysical absolute contained in the human status as

> Temporals pleading for external life with
> The infinite impetus of anxious spirits,
> Finite in fact yet refusing to be real,
> Wanting our own way, unwilling to say Yes
> To the Self-So which is the same at all times,
> That Always-Opposite which is the whole subject
> Of our not-knowing.

Is this simply the "double talk" that Auden indirectly refers to a few lines earlier? Many will see it this way, for not even Blake tried to push poetry beyond symbolism into such pure, absolute definition. Yet within *The Age of Anxiety*, this definition is the other shore finally reached in the night sea-journey through parodic repetition. Auden is not generally regarded as a mystic, and perhaps he was not; but this passage is as frank an exposition of mysticism's central tenet as can be found anywhere, whether in Christian, Judaic, or Eastern sources. The Self-So is Auden's version of such linguistic surds as the *tat tvam asi*, which avow the unity of God and man in the ground of consciousness. This is the irreducible knower, the "I" as pure subject, the final beholder presupposed by every experience. This knower is not to be misidentified either with the objects or capacities of consciousness, for it is the mystery of consciousness itself, or what Western mysticism calls the spirit. Its power of realization directly participates, for the mystic, in the enabling power of love, the supreme consciousness that brings forth all existence. It is a "not-knowing," because the ground of consciousness cannot become an object of consciousness. It is "the same at all times," because, as the presupposition for space and time, it is not affected by their limits. It is "Always-Opposite," because the "I" as pure subject stands aloof from the "I" as dissociated object, which is the ordinary ego consciousness of fallen man, the dying god nailed to the tree of death. Auden concludes his deconstructive compendium, then, with a definition of the mystical absolute that he saw as discovering within the wasteland of late humanism the renewed possibility of a long lost strength and joy.

The Age of Anxiety is an undeniably adventurous work, though its adventure is elemental to the romantic tradition it assesses. The Keats of *Endymion* was responding to the Shelley of *Alastor*, who in turn was engaging the vulnerable optimisms of the early Wordsworth. Yet the extent and vigor of Auden's deconstructions, as well as his clear design of supercession, make him more similar to Blake. That angry visionary also intended to shake Albion from his stupor and call him to his proper heroic adventures, the Battles of Eden. But the comparison raises an important question, since it is Blake's anger, an emotive code for his irrepressible energy, that we miss at the end of Auden's poem. After deconstructing romantic humanism so thoroughly, Auden had certainly earned the right to prophetic utterance, more so in fact than most of the moderns who have attempted to claim it. Rosetta and Malin, however, only suggest the possibility of a new world, not the new world itself. As Malin's homeward-bound train crosses the East River, he catches a glimpse of the early morning sunlight. All the big, promissory symbols of epiphany are there: the return to origins, the bridge to a truly New Country, the dawn of another literary era, and most important, the glory in the dancing sunlight of the now revealed *Shekinah*. Yet the symbols are simply listed by the Narrator, not actually operative in the poetry. It is a long way from the apocalyptic splendors of Blake's "Night the Ninth."

I make the comparison with no intention of slighting Auden, but rather to raise a question about the perils of literary evolution. Auden emerges from *The Age of Anxiety* as essentially a Virgil figure, a guide who can lead the lost poet through the depths, but who cannot himself pass the threshold. The implication is that the tasks of deconstruction, especially within as formidable a tradition as romanticism, can become so obsessively demanding, that they exhaust the powers of vision and transformation. The cost of supercession thus becomes prohibitively, even self-defeatingly high as as tradition lengthens. After his own intratextual labors, Blake, in the Epilogue to *Milton*, had collapsed in his garden; but Blake then arose to write *Jerusalem*. For later Auden, the new poetic Jerusalem of realized vision must evidently be built by other hands since he, like Rosetta's guide Moses, takes us only to the vantage from which it is visible. This is an astonishing disclosure for so strong a poet to make at the height of his powers. What is even more astonishing is that Auden had apparently accepted his Virgilian role while still a student at Oxford. Some twenty years before, he had written what could almost serve as a secondary epigraph to *The Age of Anxiety*:

> Cocks crew, and sleeping men turned over.
> Rain fell for miles; ghosts went away.
> The jaw, long dropped, stopped at reply.

The curse of Nietzsche's *apophrades*, the return of the haunting images, is broken as the ghosts depart. But the cost is a silence born of both weariness and disappointment, as the sleeping men, those new and answering voices every visionary hopes for, ignore the summons to awake. Auden's last long poem of the forties, like his entire career, poses a challenge for future poetry, a challenge that may have become an indictment.

EDWARD CALLAN

Disenchantment with Yeats:
From Singing-Master to Ogre

D id those of Auden's friends who arranged for his memorial in the Poets'
Corner of Westminster Abbey think of him as the poet of only one poem,
"In Memory of W. B. Yeats," as one might think, for example, of Henley
as the poet of "Invictus," or of Gray as the poet of "Elegy in a Country Church-
yard"? At the Abbey ceremony in October 1974, John Gielgud read the third
movement of "In Memory of W. B. Yeats" (chosen for the occasion by Chester
Kallman), beginning with lines that seemed a little inappropriate for the unveiling
of Auden's stone:

> Earth, receive an honoured guest:
> William Yeats is laid to rest;

and ending with the lines permanently inscribed on the memorial:

> In the prison of his days
> Teach the free man how to praise.

Set in isolation these lines refer to poets in general, including Auden. But would
he want lines that brought Yeats to mind inscribed on his monument? I believe
he would not. In fact I feel certain that should his ghost visit the Poets' Corner
the inscription would vex it.

Of course Yeats had been one of Auden's first singing-masters (although
perhaps not always quite so fervently invoked as Yeats invoked his sages in
"Sailing to Byzantium": "O sages standing in God's holy fire/ . . . /Come from
the holy fire, perne in a gyre,/And be the singing-masters of my soul"). Auden's

---

earlier masters were Thomas Hardy and Robert Frost, for whom he says he developed a passion while still at school. Then T. S. Eliot, particularly as the poet of *The Waste Land*, attracted him during his Oxford years. So did Wilfred Owen, whose technique of slant-rhyme as we have seen helped to shape the best of his undergraduate poems. But W. B. Yeats, once Auden had discovered his later work, exerted a much more powerful fascination than any of these. This fascination grew in time into a kind of obsession. And when Auden's own changed attitudes caused him to turn so strongly against Romanticism, and to deplore the notion of the inspired "national Bard," the Irish singing-master became an Ogre.

Auden had edited *Oxford Poetry* in 1927 with Cecil Day Lewis. Forty years later in a Preface to *C. Day Lewis, the Poet Laureate*, he recalled that it was he who introduced Day Lewis to the poetry of Frost and Hardy, and that Day Lewis had introduced him to the later poems of Yeats. He remarked on Hardy's subsequent good influence on Day Lewis, and added: "I wish I could say the same about Yeats' influence on me. Alas, I think it was a bad influence, for which, most unjustly, I find it difficult to forgive him."

A number of Auden's undergraduate poems are quite evidently influenced by Yeats, in tone, rhythm, or rhetoric; but his early debt to Yeats goes much deeper. It was Yeats who invented a viable modern form for a particular kind of poem—the occasional poem in conversational style—at which Auden was eventually to become a master among poets writing in English. In 1918 Yeats wrote "In Memory of Major Robert Gregory," beginning with the lines:

> Now that we're almost settled in our house
> I'll name the friends that cannot sup with us
> Beside a fire of turf in th' ancient tower,
> And having talked to some late hour
> Climb up the narrow winding stairs to bed.

The opening lines of Poem XIII of the hand-printed volume, *Poems*, 1928 show that Auden as an undergraduate had tried to emulate this elegy:

> Tonight when a full storm surrounds the house
> And the fire creaks, the many come to mind,
> Sent forward in the thaw with anxious marrow;
> For such might now return with a bleak face,
> An image pause, half-lighted at the door . . . ;

And when, in "Yeats as an Example," Auden sought to identify Yeats's chief poetic legacy, he credited the Irish poet with transforming the occasional poem in English from an official performance of impersonal virtuosity, like Tennyson's

"Ode on the Death of the Duke of Wellington," into a serious reflective poem
having at once personal and public interest; and he identified Yeats's elegy for
Robert Gregory as the first successful instance of this transformation: "A poem
such as 'In Memory of Major Robert Gregory' is something new and important
in the history of English poetry. It never loses the personal note of a man
speaking about his personal friends in a particular setting—in *Adonais*, for
example, both Shelley and Keats disappear as people—and at the same time
the occasion and characters acquire a symbolic public significance."

As the thirties wore on, Auden's admiration for Yeats as an occasional
poet was tempered by his dislike for Yeats's fondness for the trappings of aristocracy and his flirtation with General O'Duffy's Irish fascist organization, the
Blueshirts. But this was mere distaste for Yeats's foibles. In the second half
of his life Auden developed an almost obsessive fear of the danger of Yeats's
kind of outlook, and much of the story of Auden's development as a poet
after 1940 is also the story of his struggle to exorcise the persistent spirit of
Yeats. The stages of his growing disenchantment with Yeats mark the hardening
of his conviction that the greatest threats to individual freedom in the modern
world—the Utopias of both left and right—were a direct legacy of the Romantic
outlook on which Yeats prided himself.

In a number of works—beginning with "Sonnets from China" (1938)—
Auden distinguishes two effects of Romanticism on the modern mind. The
first is the persistence into the twentieth century of the nineteenth-century
notion of a national Bard: a poet who regarded himself or who was regarded
by others as the embodiment of the soul of his nation. Wagner, Whitman,
and Tennyson represent this nineteenth-century notion in varying degrees.
Kipling is an obvious instance of the notion persisting into the twentieth century.
So also, with individual differences, are D. H. Lawrence, W. B. Yeats, and
of course Auden himself broadcasting on Spanish radio for the Republican
government in February 1937, for in an age of ideologies the notion of the
Bard persists in the official propagandist; and some of those who welcomed
Auden's revolutionary zeal in the thirties (not all of them lovers of poetry)
may have been merely on the lookout for an effective Bard—a Kipling for
the Popular Front. In time he became acutely conscious of a kinship between
the cult of the poet as national Bard and the cult of the "inspired" national
leader—Hitler, Mussolini, Stalin—that threatened the survival of European
democracy in the thirties. In the fifth volume of *Poets of the English Language*
(1950) he warned that to the would-be poet in whom the notion of the Bard
persists—since the Bard must be an apostle of something—"the thought of a
tyrant who will provide him with a myth of terror, of the prospect of total
war as a cult, are not unwelcome. . . ." It is in the light of this view of the

Bard as Bellman or court poet for the national leader who expects all to follow his dark intuitions that Auden eventually came to see Yeats as one of the Ogre's party.

Three things in particular mark the successive stages of Auden's disenchantment with Yeats: first, his revisions of "In Memory of W. B. Yeats," and second, his discarding of the highly popular poem, "September 1, 1939." The third and most direct repudiation of what Yeats stood for is the opera *Elegy for Young Lovers* (1961) in which the "great poet" Mittenhofer not only browbeats his devoted admirers but sacrifices the lives of the young lovers on the twin altars of his ego and his art.

II

Auden arrived in New York harbor in a near-blizzard on Thursday January 26, 1939. Yeats died in the south of France two days later, on Saturday, January 28. Auden, who probably read the obituary notice in New York newspapers on Monday, immediately commemorated Yeats's death in two ways. One, "The Public vs. the Late Mr. William Butler Yeats," was a prose exercise in the two voices of rhetorical dialectic in which "The Public Prosecutor" and "The Counsel for the Defence" present cases for denying or according to Yeats the title of "great" poet. The other was one of the most justly famous of his own occasional poems, "In Memory of W. B. Yeats." The law-court antagonists rely on formal argument, civilized and witty in the tradition of London's Old Bailey, to sway the jury, but the elegy emphasizes the healing power of the unconscious and the need for psychic wholeness attendant on the reconciliation of human intellect and feeling in a world on the brink of war:

> Intellectual disgrace
> Stares from every human face,
> And the seas of pity lie
> Locked and frozen in each eye.

Although its opening has the plangent quality of the poetry of Yeats's old age, this memorial to Yeats is not an overflow of powerful feeling. Speaking about his elegies on Freud and Yeats, Auden said: "These elegies of mine are not poems of grief. Freud I never met, and Yeats I only met casually and didn't particularly like him. Sometimes a man stands for certain things, which is quite different from what one feels in personal grief."

The first of the elegy's three movements draws on Auden's first experience of a New York winter to set Yeats's death in an allegorical landscape freezing into inactivity—

> He disappeared in the dead of winter:
> The brooks were frozen, the airports almost deserted,
> And snow disfigured the public statues;
> The mercury sank in the mouth of the dying day.

The word *disappeared* in the opening line is not an evasive substitute for *he died*; it is a measure of Auden's close reading of Yeats who uses this word in *A Vision* as a technical term for death. The initial imagery of airport and public statues—typical products of consciousness which in this winter landscape seem almost returned to natural tracts and shapes—gives way to a scene of natural permanence alien to—and even threatening to—the civility of the urbane "fashionable quays":

> Far from his illness
> The wolves ran on through the evergreen forests,
> The peasant river was untempted by the fashionable quays.

The wolves and forests evoke the instinctive natural world, beneath consciousness, of timeless Mother Earth; and the fashionable quays, like the airports and statues that are also man-made, suggest the distinctively human world of consciousness. The initial imagery of natural vitality and conscious fabrication is followed by an image of the city of the mind in dissolution. This image depicts the Irish poet's creative consciousness as ebbing, and its energy transferred to the living who read his poems:

> The provinces of his body revolted,
> The squares of his mind were empty,
> Silence invaded the suburbs,
> The current of his feeling failed; he became his admirers.

The imagery therefore emphasizes the role of the poet's consciousness rather than his unconscious (as the Bardic notion would have it) in the making of a poem.

The second movement of the elegy (added after first publication) addresses Yeats on shared human frailty:

> You were silly like us; your gift survived it all:
> The parish of rich women, physical decay,
> Yourself....

These lines pass over Yeats's personal shortcomings with just a flicker of recollection. The phrase "physical decay" may possibly glance at Yeats's decision to undergo the Steinach surgical procedure thought at that period to confer a measure of glandular rejuvenation and some stay against geriatric ills. More specifically, the phrase "the parish of rich women" casts Yeats in the role of the pastor of an admiring flock, and therefore in the role of Bardic apostle or priest of the imagination.

In the prose companion piece the Prosecutor also dwells on aspects of the parish of rich women. He points, for example, to the inconsistency of Yeats's extolling the life of the peasantry while preferring to live in "noble houses, of large drawing rooms inhabited by the rich and the decorative, most of them of the female sex." The Prosecutor also chides Yeats for his obsession with the occult and mocks his failure to outgrow his folly: "In 1900 he believed in fairies; that was bad enough; but in 1930 we are confronted with the pitiful, deplorable spectacle of a grown man occupied with the mumbo-jumbo of magic and the nonsense of India." Elsewhere, speaking in his own voice, and possibly with a malicious eye on Isherwood's Southern California mysticism, Auden again deplores Yeats's interest in the occult: "How on earth, we wonder, could a man of Yeats's gifts take such nonsense seriously? I have a further bewilderment, which may be due to my English upbringing, one of snobbery. How *could* Yeats, with his great aesthetic appreciation of aristocracy, ancestral houses, ceremonious tradition, take up something so essentially lower-middle class — or should I say Southern Californian. . .?" Yet neither in his own voice nor the voice of the Prosecutor does Auden name the several women close to Yeats, all of whom were in some degree devoted to occult practices or psychic studies. These included, for example, Yeats's wife, from whose mediumship he profited in *A Vision*; Lady Gregory, who shared his interest in psychical research; Annie Horniman, who helped finance the Abbey Theatre when her Tarot cards revealed the time was right; and both Maude Gonne and Florence Farr, who were fellow members of the Order of the Golden Dawn. But Auden was less reticent twenty years later in his comments on the origins of the opera *Elegy for Young Lovers* which satirizes Yeats and his entourage.

The second movement of the elegy also addresses Yeats on the limitations of art which, it implies, can no more moderate the madness of civil or international strife than it can change Irish weather:

> Mad Ireland hurt you into poetry.
> Now Ireland has her madness and her weather still,
> For poetry makes nothing happen: it survives
> In the valley of its making where executives
> Would never want to tamper, flows on south
> From ranches of isolation and the busy griefs, . . .

The phrase "poetry makes nothing happen" retains a faint echo of Wilfred Owen's "Preface": "All a poet can do today is warn" — an echo heard more distinctly in Auden's poem on the outbreak of war later that year, "September 1, 1939": "All I have is a voice. . . ." Such disclaiming of poetry's power to influence events may pain those who wish to cling to the notion of the Bard; yet Auden has bluntly said that no poem of his, or of another, saved even one Jewish victim of the death camps. The context invites the understanding that poetry is not a proper medium for Apostles, and is misused by Bards who think themselves called to an apostolate. In his unpublished 1939 Journal Auden said, referring to the Nazi propaganda minister: "If the criterion for art were its power to excite to action, Goebbels would be one of the greatest artists of all time." Significantly, in his final revision of this poem Auden changed the wording of his statement on poetry from "it survives/In the valley of its saying" to "it survives/In the valley of its making." The substitution of *making* diminishes the expectation of inspired Bardic utterance that *saying* may hint at. (Despite his fussiness on this point, his revision overlooks his unexamined assumptions in the phrases about "mad Ireland" and Ireland's "madness still." Books rather than life often supplied him with his impressions, and he assumes here wide recognition of G. K. Chesterton's rather condescending

> For the great Gaels of Ireland
> Are the men that God made mad,
> For all their wars are merry
> And all their songs are sad.)

To speak of the phrase "For poetry makes nothing happen" in isolation from the highly figurative elaboration that follows it may lead to misinterpretation. The "valleys," "ranches of isolation," and "busy griefs" speak of inner creativity in the language of Auden's allegorical landscapes; and the word "executives" has associations with the movers and shakers who get things done, including the scaling of mountains. (See the sonnets "Who's Who": "though giddy, climbed new mountains"; and "Two Climbs": "Fleeing the short-haired mad executives.") The key symbolic phrase in this elaboration is "flows on south," because in the general tradition of English poetry, and particularly in the Nordic myths that Auden knew from childhood, the north is represented as the abode of evil forces. In Jung's orientation of the psyche of the "thinking type" (personified by Malin in Auden's *The Age of Anxiety*), the north is associated with isolated, even malign, intellect, and the south with feeling submerged in unconsciousness. The achievement of a "whole" or "healed" personality requires that these opposing faculties move toward reconciliation. Therefore to say poetry "flows on south" is to represent it as an agent of emotional healing, capable of restoring harmony between intellect and feeling. This notion — central to theme of the final movement of the poem — is stated explicitly in the final stanza:

> In the deserts of the heart
> Let the healing fountain start, . . .

In this final movement the elegy for Yeats contrasts the ideal order the artist has power to command with the disordered European body politic—a disorder reflecting the dissociation of feeling and intellect in the consciousness of individual citizens. The artist, whose skill is limited to imposing order on his materials, cannot manipulate the political order; neither can he heal the disordered personality. Yet his "farming of a verse" can, by analogy, provide a glimpse of ideal, even paradisal, order; and so "make a vineyard of the curse." Also, his successful creativity within the bounds of formal necessity provides a model for the conscious exercise of human freedom within the constraints of natural necessity: "In the prison of his days/Teach the free man how to praise." Furthermore, although "the farming of a verse" cannot directly produce a wholesome psychic balance between intellect and feeling and therby bring emotional warmth to thaw "the seas of pity" frozen by national pride, the poetic process, and the constraints of poetic form may bring hidden emotions to con-sciousness—a process transcending the dialectic which, when re-created in the mind of the reader, can "In the deserts of the heart/Let the healing fountain start." Auden—who admired E. M. Forster's thought—may have in mind in these lines Forster's outlook on the colonial mentality summed up in a remark about Ronnie, the complacent young Anglo-Indian in *A Passage to India*: "One touch of regret—not the canny substitute but true regret from the heart—would have made him a different man, and the British Empire a different institution."

At least one image for poetry's intermediary role in establishing a dialogue between mind and heart—between isolated intellect and unconscious feelings—appropriately brings together William Blake's poem on the creation of opposites, "The Tyger," and the thought of psychologists who explore the "night side" of life. The appeal to poets:

> Follow, poet, follow right
> To the bottom of the night,

adapts a phrase of Blake's—"at the bottom of the graves"—to which Auden draws attention in his "Notes" to *New Year Letter* as "quoted by Yeats in *A Vision*"; and in the context of similar rhythm and syllable count, the reference to "the bottom of the night" may recall Blake's vision of the tension between good and evil:

> Tyger! Tyger! burning bright
> In the forests of the night,

> What immortal hand or eye
> Could frame thy fearful symmetry?

The third movement of the elegy originally contained three quatrains—
with Kipling and Paul Claudel as cautionary instances of Imperialist and Fascist
leanings—on how the passage of time erases the memory of an artist's personal
shortcomings. Revised versions omit these quatrains on time for good reasons.
One reason for the change was his recognition of the injustice done Claudel
by equating his Catholicism with Fascism—a facile equation commonly made
by English writers like George Orwell, for example, during the Spanish Civil
War. Reviewing *Voltaire* by Alfred Noyes in March 1939, Auden accepts and
elaborates on this equation in a passage beginning: "For if I know the good,
then it is my moral duty to persecute all who disagree with me. That is why
the Catholic church can never compromise with liberalism or democracy, and
why it must prefer even fascism to socialism." There is a mild modification
of this absolute stand in an unpublished passage he wrote three or four months
later: "Artists even when they hold religious or political dogmas, do not mean
the same things by them as the organizers of their church or party. There is
more in common between my view of life and that of Claudel than there is
between Claudel's and that of the Bishop of Boston." Some months later, while
reading Charles Williams's *The Descent of the Dove*, he would have encountered
a passage on Claudel's regard for Pastor Niemoller—imprisoned by the Nazis
for his opposition to their regime—likely to cause him to rethink his superficial
judgment on Claudel: "The separations. . . in Christendom remain. . . ," Williams
wrote. "But the vocal disputes are a little suspended, and courtesies between
the clamant bodies are easier; as when the Roman Catholic Paul Claudel wrote
in honour of the Lutheran Niemoller—'ce courageux confesseur de Christ.' It might
be possible now to praise the confessors of other obediences without supposing
that we compromised our own." An even weightier reason for eliminating these
stanzas might be that their theme: "Time. . . /Worships language and forgives/
Everyone by whom it lives," comes too close to echoing Shelley's Romantic
claim in his *Defense of Poetry* where, in a parody of Scripture, he says that the
faults of such illustrious poets of the past as Homer, Virgil, and Spenser "have
been weighed and found to have been dust in the balance; if their sins were
as scarlet they are now white as snow; they have been washed in the blood
of the mediator and redeemer Time."

Finally, in 1967, Auden changed the first of the repeated resonant lines:

> O all the instruments agree
> The day of his death was a dark cold day,

to the more matter of fact understatement, "What instruments we have agree," and it is this change that best indicates the arena in which Auden wrestled with the spirit of Yeats. The change may seem slight, but anyone familiar with his poetry will recognize the voice of Yeats in the line "O all the instruments agree" (compare the line "O sages standing in God's holy fire" quoted above), while those familiar with Auden's work will recognize the more matter of fact "What instruments we have agree" as authentically his own. (There is more to poetry than "*O Altitudo,*" Nevill Coghill had said in 1927.) The original line written in the voice of Yeats demands declamation. It generates an impulse to mount on a stage, or on a box, or on a boiler—and to intone like Bard or patriotic orator. One can imagine it spoken by the Delphic oracle, or by the god Apollo himself. The revised line, by contrast, shorn of its apostrophe and of its certainty, is spoken by a man banished from Eden: "What instruments we have agree." Earlier changes in "In Memory of W. B. Yeats" came from dissatisfaction with the poem; but this one, by muting the Yeatsian resonance and typical staginess that Auden referred to among friends as "walking in high heels," indicates disenchantment with the spirit of Yeats. The main battleground for this struggle was not the elegy for Yeats, but the even more popular poem of the same period "September 1, 1939."

III

In October 1939 *The New Republic* printed a poem of Auden's that took its title from the date on which Hitler's armies attacked Poland at the start of World War II. This poem, "September 1, 1939," was modeled quite closely on Yeats's "Easter 1916." It soon became a favorite anthology piece, at least in America where it was much in demand at poetry readings during the 1950's. At such times Auden would feel compelled to explain his revisions and deletions. His initial dissatisfaction was with the final line of stanza eight: "We must love one another or die," which accommodates both Christ's injunction and echoes of the love duet in *Tristan and Isolde*, which (taking Isolde's part) he used to sing as a child with his mother. He first altered this line to: "We must love one another and die." Still dissatisfied, he excised the stanza before including the poem in *Collected Poetry*, 1945; but, eventually, he discarded the entire poem. He told the whole story of his revisions and his rejection of the poem in his Foreword to B. C. Bloomfield's bibliography: "Rereading a poem of mine, '1st September, 1939,' after it had been published, I came to the line 'We must love one another or die,' and said to myself: 'That's a damned lie! We must die anyway.' So, in the next edition, I altered it to, 'We must love one another and die.' This didn't seem to do either, so I cut the stanza. Still no good. The whole poem, I realized, was infected with an incurable dishonesty and must be scrapped." He eventually found an appropriate place for the line "We must love one another and die" in his final work, *An Entertainment of the Senses*, where with the *and* italicized it caps the final chorus of the Senses in the presence of Death:

> When you get a little older
> You'll discover like Isolde:
> "We must love one another *and* die."

The simple explanation for Auden's dissatisfaction with "September 1, 1939" was his conviction that if his poems were to be *authentic*, the tone of voice must be unmistakably his own. He defined an authentic poem as one that convinces the reader that the poet has seen its vision of truth with his own eyes, and not through someone else's spectacles. Expanding on this idea, he said that every poet in reading other poets, "has to distinguish between their merits, which may be very great, and their influence upon himself which may be very pernicious. It was not the fault of Yeats or Rilke that I allowed myself to be seduced by them into writing poems which were false to my personal and poetic nature." Auden also says that he finds in much "serious" poetry an element of theater, "of exaggerated gesture and fuss, of indifference to the naked truth," that revolts him. Yeats was one of those whose too theatrical gestures he found himself imitating in "September 1, 1939."

But Auden's disenchantment with Yeats ultimately went deeper than his dislike for exaggerated fuss and staginess. It went deeper also than the political differences that divided them in the thirties. Auden's distrust of the imaginative Romantic genius who makes an infallible dogma of his own intuitions—a quality akin to the self-deification of intuitive Führers like Hitler—extended to what he called Yeats's "determinist and 'musical' view of history." For some of the same reasons he also came to distrust the theories of D. H. Lawrence who, like Yeats, had influenced his early works, particularly *The Orators*. At least in Auden's view, poets like Yeats and Lawrence, imbued with the notion of the Bard, made infallible dogma of their own intuitions quite as readily as Marx or Hitler. He says, "works like *A Fantasia of the Unconscious* or Yeats's *A Vision* are not humble attempts at private myths, but are designed as the new and only science." And reviewing Yeats's posthumous volume *Last Poems and Plays* in June 1940, he faulted Yeats most of all for "his utter lack of effort to relate his esthetic Weltanschauung with that of science, a hostile neglect which was due, in part at least, to the age in which he was born when science was avidly mechanistic." Both statements confirm that by 1940 Auden found Yeats's Gnostic outlook—his regard for truth self-derived from the God-within—more deplorable than his politics in the 1930's.

IV

In his later career Auden's preoccupation with Yeats tended to increase rather than diminish. In *Elegy for Young Lovers* (1961) he created the character Gregor Mittenhofer to embody, in caricature, the nineteenth-century notion of the Bard. It was Yeats who provided the chief model for Mittenhofer, as Lady Gregory provided the model for Mittenhofer's devoted admirer and unpaid secretary, the aristocratic Carolina, Gräfin von Kirchstetten. Other characters in the opera were given qualities in common with Mrs. Yeats and the Yeats's friend and physician, Dr. Oliver Gogarty.

Cyril Connolly reviewing *Dublin Portraits* by W. R. Rogers quotes a remark of Austin Clarke's (which he mistakenly attributes to Frank O'Connor): "As far as the younger generation of poets are concerned here in Ireland, Yeats was rather like an enormous oak-tree which, of course, kept us in the shade. We always hoped we would reach the sun, but the shadow of the great oak-tree is still there." Connolly suggests that this remark of Clarke's gave Auden the idea of creating Mittenhofer: "this, and some anecdotes of Yeats's life at Coole," says Connolly, "formed, I believe, the genesis of Auden's opera *Elegy for Young Lovers*."

Auden himself gives two accounts of the genesis of *Elegy for Young Lovers*. The first, "Genesis of a Libretto," which is signed by both Auden and his collaborator Kallman, tells us that the composer Henze wanted a chamber opera for a small cast and no chorus. To the librettists this seemed to call for "five or six persons, each of whom suffered from a different obsession." They first thought of a character obsessed with the past like Miss Havisham in Dickens's *Great Expectations* — an idea which survived in Hilda Mack, the old lady whose visions supply Mittenhofer with matter for his poems, as Mrs. Yeats's automatic writing supposedly supplied Yeats with matter for *A Vision*. For a variety of attitudes and operatic voices, they decided also on a boy, a girl, and a doctor. Their first idea for a central character with a suitably Romantic obsession was an actor whose supreme ambition was to play the lead in Byron's *Manfred*. But on asking themselves "What kind of person can dominate an opera both dramatically and vocally?" and "What kind of mature man can be intimately and simultaneously involved with a young girl and a mad old lady?" they decided the answer was "the artist-genius of the nineteenth and early twentieth century" — which is to say the poet as Bard. They go on to claim that this idea of the artist-genius is a genuine myth "because the lack of identity between Goodness and Beauty, between the character of a man and the character of his creations, is a permanent aspect of the human condition." And they add:

> The theme of *Elegy for Young Lovers* is summed up in two lines
> by Yeats:

> The intellect of man is forced to choose
> Perfection of the life or of the work.

Aesthetically speaking, the personal existence of the artist is acci-
dental; the essential thing is his production. The artist-genius as
the nineteenth century conceived him, made this aesthetic presupposition an ethical absolute, that is to say he claimed to represent
the highest, most authentic mode of existence.

The librettists say they chose Vienna as the setting because the myth of the
artist-genius was a European myth at the time when Paris and Vienna were
the centers of European culture; and having coyly warned us not to think of
Mittenhofer's outrageous behavior an Austrian characteristic, they say "As a
matter of fact, the only things about him which were suggested by historical
incidents were drawn from the life of a poet—no matter whom—who wrote
in English."

Yeats's life supplied most of this, but some identifiable material from Auden's
own experience as a poet is also used to flesh out Mittenhofer. For example,
Mittenhofer berates his aristocratic patron and devoted secretary, Carolina,
Gräffin von Kirchstetten, for mistyping the word *poets* in his draft of verses
as *ports*. Such a transposition had actually occurred in the case of Auden's
"Journey to Iceland," and Auden, unlike Mittenhofer, accepted the change as
unconscious wisdom. To some extent, at least, Auden in his earlier Byronic
phase is the butt of his own satire in *Elegy for Young Lovers*, as to some degree
Wagner and Ibsen are also; but Yeats seems to be the primary target.

"Genesis of a Libretto" does not directly name Yeats as the model of Mittenhofer, but Auden's T. S. Eliot Memorial Lecture, "The World of Opera," in
Secondary Worlds, comes very close to doing so. Speaking of the Miss Havisham
character, Frau Hilda Mack, Auden says: "Remembering that Yeats had a wife
from whose mediumistic gifts he profited, it seemed plausible that Mittenhofer
should have discovered Frau Mack and made it his habit to visit her from
time to time, bringing his entourage with him."

From so direct a revelation of "historical incidents drawn from the life
of a poet—no matter whom," it seems safe to conclude with Cyril Connolly
that anecdotes about Yeats's life at Coole Park supplied the character Carolina,
Gräfin von Kirchstetten, who corresponds to Lady Gregory (and in Auden's
own life to his American patroness, Carolyn Newton); and also to conclude
that a second character, Mittenhofer's personal physician, Dr. Wilhelm Reisch-
mann, who keeps Mittenhofer "in good health and youthful vigour with medi-
cines and hormone injections," corresponds to Dr. Oliver Gogarty, Yeats's
physician, who first suggested to him the Steinach procedure for rejuvenation.

To return briefly to the claim made by Auden in the quotation above, that *Elegy for Young Lovers* embodies a universal myth of the artist-genius, it is evident that the language in the quotation assumes wide acceptance of Kierkegaard's categories, the Aesthetic, Ethical, and Religious, as themselves universal. (This claim, fundamental to Auden's outlook, marks him as author-in-chief of "Genesis of a Libretto" and not Kallman, who found Kierkegaard's ideas uncongenial.) The immediate points made in the quotation are two. The first is that there is a dialectical tension between the Aesthetic and the Ethical modes as Yeats had recognized in his lines:

> The intellect of man is forced to choose
> Perfection of the life or of the work.

The second point—aptly illustrated above by the quotation on "the blood of the . . . redeemer" from Shelley's *Defence*—is that when the Aesthetic mode takes itself too seriously and refuses to be content to play, it mistakenly presumes not that its sphere is the Ethical, but that it is, in fact, the Religious in Kierkegaard's scheme; which is to say that where the notion of the Bard persists, the public, like the "list'ning crowd" in Dryden's "Alexander's Feast," shout "A present deity," and the artist preening himself like a deified Alexander, or Mussolini, as Dryden puts it:

> Assumes the god,
> Affects to nod,
> And seems to shake the spheres.

The relative proneness of Auden and Yeats to this temptation may possibly be gauged by their attitudes toward biographies of poets. Auden felt that, ideally, poets should be as anonymous as the builders of the pyramids. Yeats, on the other hand, declared: "A poet is by the very nature of things a man who lives with entire sincerity . . . his life is an experiment in living and those who come after him have the right to know it."

To Auden, the most dangerous legacy of Romanticism was the tendency to confuse the artist, the custodian of beauty, with the Apostle, the witness to truth. And it is no doubt his anxiety to proclaim this danger, not personal animosity toward Yeats, that led to the invention of Mittenhofer who so confuses the Aesthetic and Ethical—the spheres of beauty and truth—that he contrives the actual death of two young lovers to provide matter for his elegy.

Auden's quarrel with Yeats's aestheticism reflects his more fundamental quarrel with the Platonism that lay at the heart of the Romantic sensibility. One of his more ambitious undertakings—that has perhaps gone unrecognized among those he had hoped would find his views congenial—was an effort to formulate a Christian theory of art that would replace Greek aesthetics. His first podium for this was the weekly column he wrote for *Commonweal* during

November and December of 1942. He called this column "Lecture Notes" —
an allusion, no doubt, to that other famous reply to Plato: Aristotle's *Poetics* —
and he signed it "Didymus," possibly to represent the tension between faith
and reason in the Apostle Thomas who was called Didymus; and also to represent a Kierkegaardian double focus, or dialectic, running counter to the single-
minded Romantics whom he had dubbed "the either-ors, the mongrel halves/
Who find truth in a mirror" in "New Year Letter" the year before. (The first
title of that work, *The Double Man*, was intended to convey some of the same
significance as "Didymus.")

Auden began his second column in *Commonweal* (November 13, 1942):
"As a writer, who is also a would-be Christian, I cannot help feeling that a
satisfactory theory of Art from the standpoint of the Christian faith has yet
to be worked out. With the exception of Kierkegaard, most theologians . . . have
accepted Greek aesthetics too uncritically." Then, having distinguished three
religious standpoints, "Natural, Revealed, and Christian," he sought to color
the second of these Gnostic: "The second believes that the Unconditional is,
objectively, perpetually *absconditus*, but occasionally subjectively manifest to
exceptional groups or individuals . . . ." By contrast, the third "believes that
the Unconditional was objectively manifested upon one unique occasion (The
Word was made Flesh and dwelt among us) . . . ." Auden first developed these
ideas in *New Year Letter* (1940) and later in the long dramatic works, *The Sea
and the Mirror* and *For the Time Being: A Christmas Oratorio*. Simeon, in the
latter, puts the case for a Christian aesthetic: "Because in Him the Flesh is
united to the Word without magical transformation, Imagination is redeemed
from promiscuous fornication with her own images." In so refuting the Gnostic
way of the *illuminati* in all ages, Auden may have had in mind the imaginary
world of Yeats's *A Vision* — privately revealed through the instrumentality of
his wife's mediumship and his own fictional creations, Aherne and Robartes.

One of the last poems Auden composed before he died, "No, Plato, No,"
shows him still, in some degree, preoccupied with Yeats; for this poem is not
merely a general rejection of Plato as is "On Installing an American Kitchen
in Lower Austria," later retitled, "Grub First, Then Ethics." "No, Plato, No,"
is also a satirical response to "Sailing to Byzantium," in which Yeats, philo-
sophically following Plato and Plotinus, longs for his soul to be free from the
prison of the flesh:

> Once out of nature I shall never take
> My bodily form from any natural thing,
> But such a form as Grecian goldsmiths make . . .

Auden's "No, Plato, No" rejects such Platonic yearning to be "out of nature."
It offers instead a novel personification of bodily organs yearning to be free

from servitude to consciousness, to return to a quiescent mineral state, and to become, once more, irresponsible matter. (This is the "desire to be at peace"—the death-instinct of the early poems.) Ironically, because of the lines inscribed on his memorial in the Poets' Corner of Westminster Abbey—that national mausoleum for English Bards—Auden does not escape the shadow of the great Celtic oak-tree even in death. Furthermore, English reviewers of Auden's *Collected Poems* (1976) continued to deplore his revision of the line "O all the instruments agree." David Bromwich, in the *Times Literary Supplement*, found the change "painful" and wrote: "the poem has stopped singing."

Auden may have succeeded in exorcising the Bardic spirit—including the spirit of Yeats—in himself; but that spirit was still to bedevil him, unexorcised, in sundry friends and admirers—nostalgic for the thirties—who were reluctant to accept his revisions of his own poems. Among those contemporaries who survived him, few shared, or even approved of, his anti-Romanticism. One negative consequence has been the comparative neglect of his American achievement, particularly in the longer philosophical works, *The Sea and the Mirror*, *For the Time Being*, and *The Age of Anxiety*.

Chronology

1907   Wystan Hugh Auden born on February 21 at York, the third son of George Augustus Auden, a physician, and Constance Rosalie Bicknell Auden.

1915   Enters St. Edmund's School, Hindhead, Surrey. Here Auden first becomes acquainted with Christopher Isherwood.

1920   Enters Gresham's School, Holt.

1922   "One afternoon in March" Auden's friend Robert Medley suggests he write poetry. His first published poem appears, unsigned, in the school magazine in December.

1925   Enters Oxford, rooming in Christ Church College. Briefly studies natural science, then politics, philosophy, and economics, and finally English, with Nevill Coghill as his tutor. During his three years at Oxford Auden becomes familiar with Stephen Spender and C. Day Lewis.

1928   Stephen Spender privately prints an Auden collection, *Poems*, in an edition of about forty-five copies. In August Auden leaves for Germany, where he spends a year in Berlin.

1930   First edition of *Poems*, including *Paid on Both Sides* and a selection of shorter poems.

1932   *The Orators*. Auden begins three years as master at the Downs School, Colwall.

1933   *The Dance of Death* published, and first produced by the Group Theatre early the next year.

1934   First American edition of *Poems*, including *The Orators* and *The Dance of Death*.

1935   Publication and premiere of *The Dog Beneath the Skin*, written in collaboration with Christopher Isherwood. Auden marries Erika Mann, daughter of Thomas Mann, so that she can obtain a British passport. Later in the year, Auden works as a writer and assistant director for the progressive General Post Office Film Unit.

1936   Visits Iceland with Louis MacNeice. *The Ascent of F6* (with Christopher Isherwood) published; first produced 1937. *Look, Stranger!* (not Auden's title), a collection of lyrics, is published; the American edition (1937) is entitled *On This Island*.

1937   Visits Spain, working briefly for the Republican government. In May *Spain* is published. *Letters from Iceland* (with Louis MacNeice) appears in August.

1938   Auden visits China with Isherwood, returning via Japan and America. *On the Frontier* (with Isherwood) is published and premiered.

1939   On the eighteenth of January Auden emigrates to New York. *Journey to a War* (with Isherwood) is published in March. In the spring Auden first meets his lifetime friend and companion, Chester Kallman.

1940   *Another Time*. In October Auden returns to the Anglican Communion.

1941   *The Double Man* (English edition entitled *New Year Letter*). *Paul Bunyan*, an operetta by Benjamin Britten with libretto by Auden, is performed in May.

1944   Publication of *For the Time Being*, comprising both the title poem and *The Sea and the Mirror*.

1945   Publication of *The Collected Poetry*. For five months Auden serves as a civilian research chief in the Morale Division of the U.S. Strategic Bombing Survey, travelling in Germany and elsewhere in Europe.

1946   Auden receives American citizenship.

1947   First edition of *The Age of Anxiety*.

1948   First visit to Ischia, which becomes Auden and Kallman's summer home until 1957.

1950   *Collected Shorter Poems 1930–1944* published in Britain. First edition of a book of criticism, *The Enchafèd Flood*.

1951   *Nones.* Stravinsky's *The Rake's Progress*, with libretto by Auden and Kallman, premieres in Venice.

1955   *The Shield of Achilles.*

1958   First summer in Kirchstetten, Lower Austria, where Auden and Kallman spend summers for the rest of Auden's life.

1960   *Homage to Clio.*

1961   Hans Werner Henze's *Elegy for Young Lovers*, with libretto by Auden and Kallman, premieres in Stuttgart.

1962   Publication of *The Dyer's Hand*, a collection of essays.

1965   *About the House.*

1966   Henze's *The Bassarids*, libretto by Auden and Kallman, performed at Salzburg. *Collected Shorter Poems 1927–1957* is published.

1968   *Collected Longer Poems* is published; later in the year, *Secondary Worlds*, the first T. S. Eliot memorial lectures at the University of Kent.

1969   *City Without Walls.*

1970   *A Certain World.*

1971   *Academic Graffiti* published, a collection of clerihews with illustrations by Filippo Sanjust.

1972   *Epistle to a Godson.* In October Auden moves to Oxford, occupying a cottage in his old college, Christ Church.

1973   *Love's Labours Lost*, an opera by Nicholas Nabokov with libretto by Auden and Kallman, is performed in Brussels. In March, *Forewords and Afterwords*, a collection of essays and reviews, is published. On September 29, after giving a poetry reading in Vienna before returning from Austria to Oxford, Auden dies in his hotel room. He is buried in his summer home of Kirchstetten.

1974   *Thank You, Fog: Last Poems* published posthumously, edited by Edward Mendelson.

Contributors

HAROLD BLOOM, Sterling Professor of the Humanities at Yale University, is the author of *The Anxiety of Influence, Poetry and Repression*, and many other volumes of literary criticism. His forthcoming study, *Freud: Transference and Authority*, attempts a full-scale reading of all of Freud's major writings. A MacArthur Prize Fellow, he is the general editor of *The Chelsea House Library of Literary Criticism*.

CHRISTOPHER ISHERWOOD, novelist, playwright, translator, and writer on religion, was a lifelong friend of W. H. Auden and collaborated with him on plays several times during the thirties. His autobiographical novel, *Lions and Shadows* contains a fictionalized portrait of the young Auden under the name Hugh Weston.

JOHN HOLLANDER is Professor of English and Poet-in-Residence at Yale University. His numerous critical and poetic works include *The Figure of Echo* and *Powers of Thirteen*.

JUSTIN REPLOGLE, Professor of English at the University of Wisconsin, has published several articles on Auden in addition to the book *Auden's Poetry*.

FREDERICK BUELL teaches English at Queens College, New York, and has published works on Sylvia Plath and A. R. Ammons.

WENDELL STACY JOHNSON, an expert on Victorian literature, teaches at the City University of New York. He has published books on Gerard Manley Hopkins and Matthew Arnold.

JOHN BAYLEY is Warton Professor of English and a Fellow of St. Catherine's College at Oxford. His books of criticism include studies of Tolstoy and Hardy.

JOHN McDIARMID teaches English at Pennsylvania State University and writes on modern literature.

LUCY S. McDIARMID teaches English at Villanova University. She has published another article on Auden.

DAVID BROMWICH is Associate Professor of English at Princeton University. He is the author of *Hazlitt: The Mind of the Critic*.

WILLARD SPIEGELMAN teaches English at Southern Methodist University and edits *Southwest Review*. He has published on Romantic and Modern Poetry, Elizabeth Bishop, and James Merrill.

EDWARD MENDELSON, Professor of English and Comparative Literature at Columbia, is an executor of the Estate of W. H. Auden and editor of *Selected Poems of W. H. Auden*, *Collected Poems*, and *The English Auden*. His own works on Auden include the book length study, *Early Auden*.

JOHN R. BOLY teaches English at Dartmouth. He is soon publishing a book on Auden's aesthetics.

EDWARD CALLAN teaches at Western Michigan University. An expert on English and African literature, he has published works on W. B. Yeats and Alan Paton.

Bibliography

Bayley, John. *The Romantic Survival*. London: Constable and Company, Ltd., 1957.

Bahlke, George W. *The Later Auden: From "New Year Letter" to "About the House."* New Brunswick: Rutgers University Press, 1970.

Beach, Joseph Warren. *The Making of the Auden Canon*. Minneapolis: University of Minnesota Press, 1957.

Bergonzi, Bernard. "Auden and the Audenesque." *Encounter* 44 (1975): 65–75.

Blair, John G. *The Poetic Art of W. H. Auden*. Princeton, N.J.: Princeton University Press, 1965.

Bloomfield, B. C. and Edward Mendelson. *W. H. Auden: A Bibliography 1924–1969*. Charlottesville: University Press of Virginia, 1972.

Buell, Frederick. *W. H. Auden as a Social Poet*. Ithaca, N.Y.: Cornell University Press, 1973.

Callan, Edward. *Auden, A Carnival of Intellect*. New York: Oxford University Press, 1983.

Dûchéne, François. *The Case of the Helmeted Airman, A Study of Auden's Poetry*. London: Chatto and Windus, 1972.

Fuller, John. *A Reader's Guide to W. H. Auden*. London: Thames and Hudson; New York: Strauss and Giroux, 1970.

Gingerich, Martin E. *W. H. Auden: A Reference Guide*. Boston: G. K. Hall; London: Prior, 1977.

Green, Timothy. "The Comic Theory of W. H. Auden." *Renascence* 29 (Winter, 1977): 86–96.

Hoggart, Richard. *Auden, An Introductory Essay*. London: Chatto and Windus; New Haven: Yale University Press, 1951.

Hynes, Samuel. *The Auden Generation: Literature and Politics in the 1930's*. London: Bodley Head, 1976; reprinted London: Faber and Faber, 1979.

Jarrell, Randall. *Kipling, Auden & Co.: Essays and Reviews 1935–1964.* New York: Farrar, Strauss and Giroux, 1980; Manchester: Carcanet Press, 1981.

Johnson, Richard. *Man's Place: An Essay on Auden.* Ithaca, N.Y.: Cornell University Press, 1973.

Kauffman, S. Bruce. "'Orthodoxy' of Imagination: Auden's Later Poetic." *Thought* 52 (1977): 522–538.

McDiarmid, Lucy S. "W. H. Auden's 'In the Year of My Youth.'" *Review of English Studies*, New Series 29, no. 115 (August 1978): 279–312.

McDowell, Frederick P. W. "'The Situation of Our Time': Auden in His American Phase." In *Aspects of American Poetry*, edited by Richard M. Ludwig. Columbus, Ohio: Ohio State University Press, 1962.

Mendelson, Edward. "The Auden–Isherwood Collaboration." *Twentieth Century Literature* 22 (1976): 276–285.

———. *Early Auden.* London: Faber and Faber; New York: Random House, 1981.

Mitchell, Donald. *Britten and Auden in the Thirties: The Year 1936.* London: Faber and Faber, 1981.

Nelson, Gerald. *Changes of Heart: A Study of the Poetry of W. H. Auden.* Berkeley and Los Angeles: University of California Press, 1969.

Nemerov, Howard. "A Word From the Devil's Advocate." *Parnassus* 4, no. 1 (Fall/Winter 1975): 131–136.

New Verse 26–27 (November 1937). Special Auden Double Issue.

Ostroff, Anthony, ed. *The Contemporary Poet as Artist and Critic.* Boston: Little, Brown, 1964.

Porter, Peter. "The Achievement of Auden." *Sydney Studies in English* 4 (1978–79): 73–113.

Rees, Samuel. "'What Instruments We Have: An Appreciation of W. H. Auden." *Anglo-Welsh Review* 24, no. 52 (1974): 9–18.

Replogle, Justin. *Auden's Poetry.* Seattle: University of Washington Press, 1969.

Spears, Monroe K. *Auden: A Collection of Critical Essays* (Twentieth Century Views). Englewood Cliffs, N. J.: Prentice-Hall, 1964.

———. *The Poetry of W. H. Auden: The Disenchanted Island.* New York: Oxford University Press, 1963.

Spender, Stephen, ed. *W. H. Auden: A Tribute.* New York: Macmillan, 1974.

Waidson, H. M. "Auden and German Literature." *Modern Language Review* 70, no. 2 (April 1975): 347–365.

Warren, Austin. "The Quest for Auden." *Sewanee Review* 87, no. 2 (Spring 1979): 229–248.

———. "The Poetry of Auden." *Southern Review* 17, no. 3 (July 1981): 461–478.

Acknowledgments

"Introduction" (originally entitled "Poetic Misprision: Three Cases") by Harold Bloom from *The Ringers in the Tower* by Harold Bloom, copyright © 1971 by University of Chicago Press. Reprinted by permission.

"Some Notes on the Early Poetry" by Christopher Isherwood from *W. H. Auden: A Tribute* by Stephen Spender, ed., copyright © 1974, 1975 by George Weidenfeld and Nicolson, Ltd. Reprinted by permission.

"Auden at Sixty" by John Hollander from *Atlantic Monthly* 220, no. 1 (July 1967), copyright © 1967 by John Hollander. Reprinted by permission.

"The Pattern of Personae" by Justin Replogle from *Auden's Poetry* by Justin Replogle, copyright © 1969 by the University of Washington Press. Reprinted by permission.

"Auden After the Thirties" (originally entitled "After the Thirties") by Frederick Buell from *W. H. Auden as a Social Poet* by Frederick Buell, copyright © 1973 by Cornell University. Reprinted by permission of Cornell University Press.

"Auden, Hopkins, and the Poetry of Reticence" by Wendell Stacy Johnson from *Twentieth Century Literature* 20, no. 3 (July 1974), copyright © 1974 by Hofstra University Press. Reprinted by permission.

"Only Critics Can't Play" by John Bayley from *W. H. Auden: A Tribute*, edited by Stephen Spender, copyright © 1974, 1975 by George Weidenfeld and Nicolson, Ltd. Reprinted by permission.

"Artifice and Self-Consciousness in *The Sea and the Mirror*" (originally entitled "Artifice and Self-Consciousness in Auden's *The Sea and the Mirror*") by Lucy

185

S. McDiarmid and John McDiarmid from *Contemporary Literature* 16, no. 3 (Summer 1975), copyright © 1975 by the Board of Regents of the University of Wisconsin System. Reprinted by permission of the University of Wisconsin Press.

"An Oracle Turned Jester" by David Bromwich from *The Times Literary Supplement*, Sept. 17, 1976, copyright © 1976 by The Times Literary Supplement. Reprinted by permission of the Times Newspapers Ltd.

"*The Rake's Progress*: An Operatic Version of Pastoral" by Willard Spiegelman from *Southwest Review* 63, no. 1 (Winter 1978), copyright © 1978 by Willard Spiegelman. Reprinted by permission.

"Auden's Revision of Modernism" (originally entitled "Preface") by Edward Mendelson from *W. H. Auden, Selected Poems: New Edition* by Edward Mendelson, ed., copyright © 1979 by Edward Mendelson. Reprinted by permission of the author and Random House, Inc.

"*The Orators*: Portraits of the Artist in the Thirties" (originally entitled "W. H. Auden's *The Orators*: Portraits of the Artist in the Thirties") by John R. Boly from *Twentieth Century Literature* 27, no. 3 (Fall 1981), copyright © 1982, Hofstra University Press. Reprinted by permission.

"The Romantic Tradition in *The Age of Anxiety*" (originally entitled "Auden and the Romantic Tradition in *The Age of Anxiety*") by John R. Boly from *Daedalus* (Journal of the American Academy of Arts and Sciences) 3, no. 3 of the Proceedings of the American Academy of Arts and Sciences (Summer 1982) *Representations and Realities*, copyright © 1982 by the American Academy of Arts and Sciences. Reprinted by permission.

"Disenchantment with Yeats: *From Singing-Master to Ogre*" by Edward Callan from *Auden: A Carnival of Intellect* by Edward Callan, copyright © 1983 by Edward Callan. Reprinted by permission of the author and Oxford University Press.

Index